How to Get a Job in 90 Days or Less

How to Get a Job in 90 Days or Less

A Realistic Action Plan for Finding the Right Job Fast

Matthew J. DeLuca

McGraw-Hill, Inc.

New York   San Francisco   Washington, D.C.   Auckland   Bogotá
Caracas   Lisbon   London   Madrid   Mexico City   Milan
Montreal   New Delhi   San Juan   Singapore
Sydney   Tokyo   Toronto

Library of Congress Cataloging-in-Publication Data

DeLuca, Matthew J.
    How to get a job in 90 days or less : a realistic action plan for
finding the right job fast / Matthew J. DeLuca.
        p.   cm.
    Includes index.
    ISBN 0-07-016354-5
    1. Job hunting.   I. Title.
HF5382.7.D45   1994
650.14—dc20   94-32878
                                                                    CIP

1 2 3 4 5 6 7 8 9 0   DOC/DOC   9 0 9 8 7 6 5 4

ISBN 0-07-016354-5

*The sponsoring editor for this book was Betsy Brown, the editing supervisor
was Ruth W. Mannino, and the production supervisor was Don Schmidt. It
was set in Palatino by McGraw-Hill's Professional Book Group composition
unit.*

Printed and bound by R. R. Donnelley & Sons Company.

Contents

Acknowledgments

There are many individuals who were quite generous with their insights, comments, and other assistance throughout this project.

The first group are my professional colleagues who have always been most helpful and available: Gil Tucker, Irene Cohen, Maria Bruck, Vincent Lee, Lisa Wolf, Melva Diamante, Jeff Daum, Barbara Sadek, Adrian Mitchell, Leslie Prager, and Mary Ann Rice.

The second group to be recognized is the staff at McGraw-Hill. First among these is Philip Ruppel who brought us all together. Next is Betsy Brown who is a master at brevity and a real inspiration. Ruth Mannino steered the project to completion, and Peter Roberts provided a keen copy editor's touch.

I have saved the most important acknowledgment for last. Each time I have had the opportunity to write a book, my wife, fellow professional, and dear friend—Nanette—has played an increasingly active and collaborative role. I particularly appreciate her efforts because she could so easily decide to be "otherwise engaged" with all the other activities that demand so much of her time and attention.

Matthew J. DeLuca

Introduction

Help! I Need a Job Today!

Getting Organized and Off to a Good Start

Focus and Act!

You have picked this book up for one of the following reasons:

- You have lost your job.
- You hate your job and want to quit.
- You see the handwriting on the wall and want to look ahead for a new job.
- You are relocating to another geographic area and need a new job.
- You are looking for your first job.

Regardless of the reason, you have decided that you want a job and you want one *now!* Events, circumstances within and outside your control, and past experiences have brought you to this point in your professional life. Whether you are presently employed and are "shopping" for a better position, are facing being "downsized" in your organization, or are suddenly unemployed (by choice or chance), a job search involves many fears, frustrations, and anxieties. "What happened?" "What did I do wrong?" "What will I tell my family/ friends?" "Will I ever find a job?"

The first important step to take is a step forward...into the future. This may be the advantage you needed to take stock of yourself, your goals, and your expectations from your career, and look for a job that will satisfy your personal and professional needs. The time will come to examine the past in order to keep from repeating any errors, but that time is not now. This is the time to gather your thoughts and take action to change your present situation. In this book you will learn to take quick action during the early weeks, and to continue to revise and sharpen your skills until your goal has been reached. The more badly you need a job today, the more effective you should be in remaining focused on your goal. You want a job, and you want it now. The goal of this book is to help you get that job within 90 days—and if sooner, so much the better. To accomplish this goal, you must be action-oriented, and you must remain focused.

Legal Rights and Wrongs

Some loose ends may remain with regard to your prior position. Were you treated fairly? Did your employer discriminate in any of the terms and conditions of employment, on the basis of any of the following: age (if you are 40 years of age or older), race, religion/creed, sex/gender, national origin, color, Vietnam-era or disabled veteran, or disability. If you feel there has been an illegal action on the part of your employer, you have the right to file a complaint with the Human Rights Agency of your local government, or the Equal Employment Opportunity Commission of the federal government. Filing a charge of discrimination does not guarantee that you will win the suit; there's always a chance you'll lose, and that the time and effort involved in the suit will have taken you further away from your goal.

If you are still employed (but feel you may not remain so for long), look into all your rights to compensation (severance, health benefits, pension, lost vacation/sick/personal days). While employers do not have to give severance, most organizations have a policy of providing approximately two weeks salary for every year of service. Additionally, depending on the size of your employer, you may qualify for COBRA (Consolidated Omnibus Budget Reconciliation Act of 1985), whereby you may be eligible to continue to purchase healthcare benefits from your employer for 18 months after your employment was terminated.

If you are unemployed and have not done so yet, register for unemployment benefits. Check with your state's unemployment office for your area's rules as to accepting unemployment payments and severance simultaneously. You will need your Social Security card, pay stubs, and W-2 forms from all your employers for the past year, in addition to a second form of identification. Also, look into the requirements for reporting any freelance or temporary work you may find, as well as what information is required to substantiate your job-search efforts.

What Is a Job?

We all use the word *job*, but do we agree on its meaning? In our society we are often defined by our jobs. Meeting other people, we often inquire, "What do you do?" Human resource professionals are endlessly talking about jobs: job analyses, job descriptions, job evaluations. Labor law constantly refers to "jobs" throughout its text.

One common definition states that a job is *a combination of related activities, tasks, and responsibilities.* A dictionary definition terms a job to be "an activity performed regularly for payment; a specific piece of work to be done for a set fee." The concept is clearly one that involves gainful work, yet the actual nature of the work being done is seldom the reason people leave their jobs. A recently conducted survey by one of the leaders in the outplacement industry found that more than 80 percent of their clients (the terminated employees) said they had lost their jobs due to interpersonal relations. It appears that a job, any job, is more complex than the traditional definition allows.

A more relevant definition might be, "A job is not an entity, but a complex interrelationship of tasks, roles, responsibilities, interactions, incentives, and rewards." (Source: E. A. Locke, "The Nature and Causes of Job Satisfaction," in M. D. Dunnette, ed., *Handbook of Industrial and Organizational Psychology*, Rand McNally, Skokie, IL, 1976.)

Just as complex as the definition of a job, the search for the right job also comprises many elements. The initial source of information regarding job choices is *yourself and how you define yourself within a job.* When pondering that next job, consider this more complex definition, because you will need to determine all the aspects of a job in order to identify the most appropriate job for you. It is a combination of your skills, your preferences, and the work environment.

A book entitled *The Hundred Best Companies to Work for in America* (Robert Lovering, Milton Moskowitz, and Michael Katz, Addison-Wesley, Reading, MA, 1984) has been so successful that a second edition was released in 1993. This book is worth reading, for it provides you with an opportunity to consider what criteria the authors applied in their determination. It can be argued that there is no "perfect" company, and that no one person or group of persons can decide what is a good company for you to work for. The only person who can make that decision is you. Utilizing the more complex definition of a job, any job or any organization is a good one (or not), depending upon the specific needs and skills that each person possesses. Only when the organization and you have a "fit" in all or most of the categories mentioned in the definition of a job (tasks, roles, responsibilities, interactions, incentives, and rewards) is it likely that a hire will be a successful one.

Jump-start the Process: Spin Those Job-Seeking Wheels *Now!*

Now you're ready to leap out of the gate. From this moment forward, you need to constantly focus all of your energy on the objective of finding a job. Think about it. Set a tone. This is where you will concentrate your effort. The more your focus remains on getting a job, the more intense your desire for a job, the more effective your efforts will be.

Maintain a separate bulletin board, calendar, or tickler file for all your job-search information; don't divert your attention by posting unpaid bills here. Set up a "work space" devoted to your job-search efforts with all the materials you will need close at hand. A word processor or personal computer cannot be viewed as a luxury; they are requisites of your job-search campaign. If you have neither a computer nor the funds to purchase one, consider rental, or using various computer services (Kinko's, for example) or a secretarial service. You must be able to handle the basic chores of a job search: sending out letters and resumes in a timely and businesslike manner.

The basics, such as paper, pen, telephone, postage stamps, envelopes, and telephone directories, must be where you can easily locate and use them. Each item that isn't there when you need it can distract you from your search. Looking for the stapler may be easier than organizing a list of prospective new employers, but don't allow your energies to be diverted. The more organized you become, the less overwhelming the process will appear to be and the more creative you can be. Also, if you don't have a PC at home, consider getting a ream of personal stationery printed. Personal business cards for you to hand out while "networking" will prove a worthwhile investment. Remember, this is all part of packaging the product you are selling.

Communication is of paramount importance. If you're working out of your house, use either an answering machine or a service, and be certain you have recorded a professional message. You must maintain your good humor, but do not inflict it on others who telephone you. If you have others who answer your telephone when you are out (*adults,* please!), be certain they have message pads handy and know where they can reach you with an important message. Call in frequently to check for messages.

Your job campaign will consist of three phases:

1. *Self-assessment.* Personal review of experiences, skills, and achievements; exploration of career choices and objectives; work-environment considerations.

2. *Marketing tactics.* Preparation of resume and cover-letter prototypes; development of marketing strategy; identification of leads and networking situations; improvement of interview, selling, and communication skills; researching targeted organizations.

3. *Launching of job campaign.* Appointments scheduled; interview debriefing; progress review and strategy revision; salary negotiation; evaluation of offers; selecting the best position.

In the first week you will take those steps necessary to make presentations effective, while at the same time you will begin doing research on the job market and following up on leads.

Keys to Getting a Job in This Terrible Market

You have two choices: you can perceive yourself as the victim of a terrible economy, or you can capitalize on the growth and possibilities that are out there. If you sold buggy whips and the demand has fallen, sales skills are eminently transferable. You are not in the buggy whip business—you are in the sales business. What products or services are the "hot" items in the nineties? Which look to have long-term growth potential?

The key to success is being hungry—wanting that job! Remain focused on your goal, and take action daily. Reading classified ads will not count for a great deal; most jobs are found through networking and personal contacts, so you will concentrate most of your energies in those areas. In fact, 95 percent of your effort will be directed to soliciting contacts, leads, and referrals, from friends and even total strangers. Only 5 percent of your effort should be involved in answering ads; granted, some people do get their jobs through ads, but it's a long shot. You need to invest all of your time in those areas that have been proven to be the most effective.

In the first week you will complete Phases 1 and 2 to establish an effective plan of action (the job campaign/marketing plan), and then start right into Phase 3. You will continuously monitor results to enable you to revise and adjust your approaches in order to meet your objective.

Some Basic Job-Search Truths

There are more people than jobs. You must therefore optimize all of your contacts and turn possibilities into probabilities. Every person you know or meet is a potential job lead.

There is no one job market—there are countless job markets. You must determine which markets hold the greatest potential for you, and how to tap those sources that can gain you entry into the organizations that have the jobs.

These job markets are constantly changing. To stay on top of market shifts, you must remain focused and keep up contacts through networking.

He or she who is successful in obtaining a job offer is the skilled job seeker, not necessarily the best person for the job. By reading this book, you will become skilled in obtaining interviews, and will be able to convey to the recruiter your potential value to the organization.

Resumes are the junk mail of the nineties. Therefore, each resume must be geared to the specific job opening, and accompanied by a cover letter that tells the reader how you can solve his or her problems and add value to the organization.

You never know who your friends are. The key to successful referrals and leads is your memory bank of friends. I don't mean only those to whom you would lend money; I mean everyone you know and who knows you! You will also find, as you mail letters and make telephone calls, that you are repeatedly being surprised. "Friends" whom you thought would be the most helpful may turn out to be less so, while "mere acquaintances" may drop everything in their desire to help their "friend." Don't hold it against your friends when they don't come through for you—you can never tell what other pressures they are under, or whether they just don't have the contacts they always led you to believe they were favored with. But do keep in mind the names of everyone who has ever done any little thing for you—cheered you up, taken you out to lunch, invited you as a guest to a business affair, or even actually gotten you a job—and return the favor whenever you can.

Becoming a Salesperson

Are you a salesperson? If not, you will be. Looking for a job is a good opportunity to hone a skill that is essential to your personal and professional well-being: selling yourself. This skill will make you less dependent on others for assistance, and provide you with the confidence you'll need to perform well in any area of endeavor. Any salesperson will tell you that a primary key to success is knowing one's product—knowing what it can and cannot do, how to present it in the most favorable light, who the potential customers are, and most importantly, how to close the sale by convincing the prospective buyer of the essential value that the product will provide to him or her.

The product you are selling is yourself; how well do you know your product? Skills, experience, loyalty, interests, knowledge: all of these can be translated into *value added*. What value can you add to the organization that hires you? How can you "sell" that value to others? Your whole world can be broken down into those who feel you will be an excellent addition to their staff, and those who don't. Your task is to discover who among your fans is actually able to give you a job and be sure to spend your time with them. And remember that you want to find a job that fits you, not fit yourself to any old job.

The Post-World War II Job Market

Traditionally, if a person, in good times or bad, had a job, that job was always there. As long as the employer remained in business so did his/her employees. Nowadays, there is no job security. The only potential for security in the workplace is to continue to think of value added. If you are assisting the organization in reaching its goals, if you are continuing to add value to the organization, you will continue to be perceived as a solution and not a problem.

From World War II until the massive layoffs that started in the eighties, we Americans enjoyed a period of prosperity unequaled in the history of our country. Jobs were plentiful, and real income levels were rising. Workers enjoyed such job stability and security that they came to consider their job an entitlement. In such an environment, workers didn't worry if they would have a job next week or month, because there was a universal belief that if you held a position (particularly if it was with any of the large employers in the United States) you were set for life, not only in terms of current wages but retirement benefits as well.

The bubble burst in the eighties, and a vast number of major U.S. companies decided to either shut down or downsize their staff. This was a clear signal to the American worker that the implied contract between employer and worker that had been counted on in the past was no longer viable. Organizations were concerned with global competition, inflation, and their very survival. The American workers and their families had been lulled into a false sense of security. A new age of redefining work and the dynamics of employment had begun.

Two books heralded this change: *Pack Your Own Parachute* (Paul

Hirsch, Addison-Wesley, Reading, MA, 1987) and *The Age of Unreason* (Charles Handy, Harvard Business School Press, Boston, 1990). Both books stressed the fact that the old employer-employee relationship was no longer in existence, and that workers must think of themselves as free agents with skills and services to sell to any employer. This was the concept of *value added*. You have marketable skills and can "sell" them in the marketplace. But in order to sell your product, you must determine both what are the skills you wish to promote and what are the skills that the market needs now. When there is a match, then there is a probability of a job offer. This may be a radical concept to you if you have never thought this way before, and it may be unnerving to realize that there really is no job security in this market; but it can also be liberating, in that you need not feel that your destiny is tied to only one employer and that that employer's ups and downs will throw your professional life into a maelstrom.

Five Good Reasons Why They Should Hire You

It's time to consider the sales pitch, your pep talk to yourself (and others) before you go on the road with the product. Think of all the positive reasons why you would make an excellent employee. In addition to giving you a focal point when writing letters and interviewing, this list should bolster your self-confidence. When you concentrate on the skills you have to offer, you have greater faith and confidence in the product you are selling. In Phase 1, *self-assessment* will enable you to identify specific marketable skills that you possess that you will then be able to sell to the market.

Reason 1: You Are the Solution to an Employer's Problem. So you need a job; who really cares? It's your problem, and people don't want any of your problems because they have enough of their own. Keep any problems relating to your job search to yourself. Instead, present yourself as being the solution to another's problem. It's not so much that you need a job, but that you can fill an aching void in an organization. You are the answer to its needs. You will add value to the organization. This is both an optimistic mind-set and a valuable way of holding yourself out to prospective employers. Interviewing candidates is a time-consuming effort for an organization; its problem is to find the right person for the job. They want to solve this problem and to get on with their own jobs. If you can't be their solution and add value, you must go elsewhere.

Think economics. The organization must have the ability to pay your salary and benefits and provide the space and equipment you need to carry out your job. In addition to those costs, the organization also must generate a profit worthy of its efforts and the risks taken. How would you impact on the organization? How could you add value?

Reason 2: You Are Unique and Indispensable. By research into the prospective employer's organization and how and where it conducts its business, you can be specific and knowledgeable about how your skills and experiences can impact positively on the organization's operations. Relate your own past experiences to what is occurring in the organization or marketplace now.

Reason 3: You Have Your Potential Employer in Mind to Such an Extent That He/She Will Make a Mistake in Letting You Take a Job Elsewhere. The very fact that you can talk knowledgeably about the prospective organization's business and can "put yourself" into the picture, seeing exactly how you fit in, should impress them. Additionally, your ability to point out specifics as to how you can take action immediately if hired will convince them that the competition should not get you.

Reason 4: You Are Dedicated and Will Be Loyal. Depending on how many jobs your resume says you have had in the past (from none to numerous), some "spin" may be necessary to ensure future prospects as to the degree of dedication and loyalty you are capable of. If you're a recent graduate, point out accomplishments that called for tenacity and ability—research projects, summer internships, part-time jobs in related fields. Stress the positive points in being in the job market now: you have reassessed your goals and are getting a fresh start; you are eager to use your skills, and will be a valued employee. As you are aware of the fact that your value to the organization is the specific value you *add* to the organization, this businesslike assessment will be met with enthusiasm by prospective employers.

Reason 5: You Have a High Energy Level. Your sense of determination, organization, and self-confidence must come across to the interviewer, highlighted by those past achievements that you were only too happy to point out in your cover letter. You cannot just say "I am a high-energy person" and hope to be perceived as different from all the numerous other job hopefuls. Acting as if this is an exciting time in your life and demonstrating that you are in control and are well organized (and well informed, due to your research) will bring your energy, organizational skills, and enthusiasm across.

Job Hunting as a Numbers Game: Weighting the Odds in Your Favor

Currently, there is a real problem in finding a job. First of all, how do you find out where the jobs are? Any way you can! Be ever-vigilant: a picnic, a church gathering, a continuing-ed class. You never know when the opportunity will present itself to learn that a job is available. Reading the classifieds and sending the letters is simply not enough (and probably *never* was). You require ongoing *action* and continuing activities! You have to make things happen by getting around. Psychologically, being cooped up answering ads is a crash course in discouragement. Keep up with friends, the gym, the reading group, the professional organizations. Seeking out the services of a firm that promises in the local paper to "send your resume to thousands of employers" is *not* the answer. *You* must be relentless in your search for a job.

Our economy in the United States is so vibrant and dynamic that no one knows how many businesses are in existence at any one time anywhere in the nation. The U.S. Chamber of Commerce estimates the number of businesses at 11 million. While some are closing, new ones are opening; there is constant turnover. And within these 11 million businesses, there are many different job markets. For example, job markets could be broken down according to the following criteria:

government (federal, state, local)

not-for-profit

profit (private, public)

industry

geographical

The Focused Step Approach: A Key to the 90-Day-or-Less Campaign

This approach begins with the desired result—a job—and works back from there. What has to be done to get there as soon as possible? What steps are needed? Which steps can be taken one at a time, and which can be combined or taken jointly? There's no need to wait for Sunday's papers to look for a job, especially if today is Monday!

One way to remain focused on obtaining that job is to determine how many steps are needed to get there. The fewer the steps, the easier it will be for you to be focused and effective. Conversely, the more steps, the longer the process, and the greater the difficulty in staying focused and obtaining the most appropriate job.

For example, your present situation will dictate some of the steps open to you, as shown in Fig. I-1. In this example, if you are presently employed you have several directions that you can go in, both within and outside your current organization. You also have the choice of continuing in your current job field or obtaining employment in a new or related field.

If you are presently unemployed, you have similar alternatives, in that you may desire a new job or wish to continue in your old job but in a new organization. (That "new" organization could be a former employer.)

For those of you who are seeking your first employment, you must determine what types of jobs and what market to focus on in your job

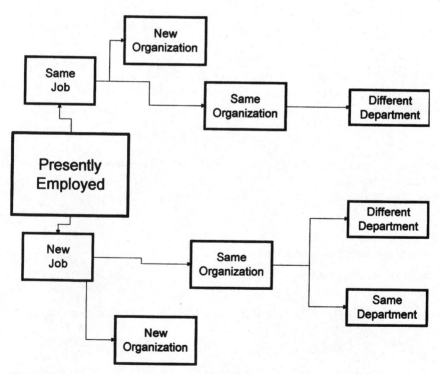

Figure I-1.

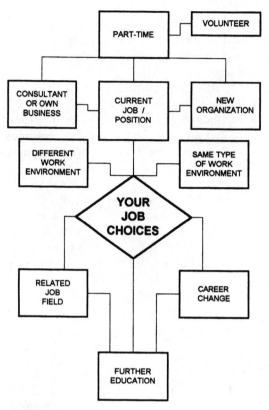

Figure I-2.

search. (See Fig. I-2.) Each of these situations—employed/unemployed, new job/old job—will entail different steps. These steps must be part of the plan formulated in your first days of Week 1.

Jump-start Checklist
Materials Needed

☐ Personal stationery (20-lb weight bond in ivory, cream, or buff) including envelopes

☐ Plain white envelopes, business size

☐ Postage stamps, $0.29 and mixed denominations for larger mailings

☐ Postage scale and postage requirements from U.S. Postal Service

☐ Business cards

☐ Notebook/three-ring binder (Job Search Log, Resume Log, debriefing notes after meetings/interviews—Meeting Journal)

☐ Telephone directories (local/personal/business-to-business)

☐ Appointment calendar (one page per day, with monthly overview and hourly log)

☐ Paper stock (20-lb weight bond in ivory, cream, or buff) for resumes

☐ Index cards and/or Rolodex (to staple business cards received, or notations for individuals/organizations contacted). Index cards useful for organizing thoughts for letters, resumes, "scripts" for telephone calls.

☐ File folders, marked as follows:

Research.   Magazine articles, newspaper stories, or trade journals on possible employers/key individuals, industry news, competition, associations, seminars

Expenses.   All job-search-related expenses, including supplies, telephone, travel (local and distance), publications, seminars, dues, business lunches, subscriptions, mileage, books, and postage, may be tax-deductible if your job search is in the same field as the old one. Total must exceed 2 percent of your adjusted gross income in the year you deduct them. Keep all receipts.

Resumes.   Copies of all versions of resumes in use.

Correspondence.   Your marketing letters with their responses attached.

Networking/contacts.   Organizations and people to contact, lists of all categories to approach or research—families, friends, neighbors, school alumni, former employers—and key people who may be approached.

Organizational prospects.   Keep a separate file folder by organization for each actual job lead (no matter how weak).

☐ Books, magazines, periodicals, newspapers to be read on a daily basis to keep up with outside news in general and your industry in particular, and related job-search texts.

Equipment Needed

☐ Work space (either outside home or separate inside home)

☐ Bulletin board

☐ Telephone; fax machine optional

☐ Answering machine, with businesslike greeting or outside answering service

☐ Personal computer or word processor, and letter-quality printer; not a dot-matrix printer or a typewriter. If none of these is available, obtain secretarial services.

☐ General office basics: scissors, tape, glue stick, stapler and staples, ribbon/ink for printer, pens, telephone message pad, clock/watch, disks for computer

Knowledge of...

☐ Local 24-hour copy shop
☐ Public library
☐ Research library
☐ Local/geographical job-search area—obtain a street map and/or guide to public transportation

Actions Taken

☐ Filed for unemployment benefits
☐ COBRA or other health insurance
☐ Committed myself to a focused, proactive job campaign

Week 1
Getting Your Act Together *Now*

Day 1, and Counting...

If this is Day 1, there are only 89 days left, and you haven't had one job interview yet. How to get those all-important interviews? The more interviews, the better the chances for job offers (and sadly, vice versa). Are you ready to "sell" your product? Do you know all of your product's best features? Have you targeted your market? Do you know how to reach your market? Have you any fears or frustrations nagging at the back of your mind? Since the key to your success is *total focus*, first be certain you have all the tools you will need to maintain that focus.

As shown in Figure 1-1, as part of "self-assessment" in Phase 1, you will first address your fears and frustrations so as to turn them around to work for you (a twist on the "visualization process" of a lot of motivation speakers). Second, you will doublecheck all the information needed about the product (yourself). This must tie in to your objective: finding a new job.

You must determine what job or jobs your skills and preferences are leading you to. For example, if you really want to be a fashion designer but have no talent for drawing, perhaps some computer courses and CAD (computer-assisted drawing) training can bridge that gap. If there are "holes" in your skills, you may look for entry-level positions where you can obtain "on-the-job training" or for organizations in your desired field that have a liberal tuition policy that may enable

The Job Campaign

Figure 1-1.

you to obtain the needed skills while still being active in your desired field.

Third, you will determine what markets you will approach and identify the ideal methods for approaching them. You will look at leads and take nothing for granted. You will learn what constitutes a lead, so that you will recognize one when you see it and know exactly how to maximize its potential. This all translates into a marketing strategy. And the one area you will concentrate on is developing lists of friends, otherwise known as *everyone you know!* You will go through all your personal telephone directories, holiday card lists, old high school and college alumni lists, names of everyone you ever worked for or worked with, in short everyone you know and who could possibly know you. Do not discard any names; you will decide at a later date which of them you feel have the greatest potential.

A brief look at the job market will ensure that you are in touch with reality. One key to a successful sales campaign is attractive, on-target product packaging. How are "you" packaged? How can your resume be made to stand out from multitudes of the others? Are there any keys to success in getting your resume read? How do you write a resume? Is one resume all that is needed for all job applications? What is networking? ("Direct sales by word of mouth" is one possible paraphrase for networking.) Is it useful in finding a job? What are the best avenues for you to follow in networking? Are there roadblocks ahead: people, places, and things to avoid if you are to hit your target and find a job within the next 89 days?

Since the business world is full of failures, organizations that had only one product on the shelf, you will consider alternative work arrangements so as to determine their usefulness to you in the interim, or as an alternative approach to work that is preferable to you in either the short or the long term. The last item on this week's agenda is to go over the Week 1 Checklist and evaluate progress to date.

How Did I Get into This Mess, and What Can I Do about It *Now*?

You didn't "lose" your job: you know exactly where it is, you just aren't in it anymore! Why? What might you have done differently? (Use the form in Fig. 1-2 to clarify your position.) What are the benefits of having gone through the experience? You will look at the situation, determine which factors were in your control and which were not, unpack any emotional baggage (*Why me? It's not fair! I don't want to be out looking for a job again*), and then get on with your current assignment—finding a job! This exercise is useful, for you will certainly be asked in an interview how you came to be looking for a job at this time. Being able to give an unemotional, businesslike analysis of why you are actively seeking a job (as well as a specific job in their organization) will certainly be impressive to a prospective employer. Write down the reasons you are currently in search of a job:

_____

_____

_____

What were the circumstances of your being "let go"? Were you caught up in a downsizing regimen, or an organizational realignment? Were you fired? If you still have the opportunity, leave the position as

LOOK-BACK ANALYSIS

Why I do not have the job I want now	What I could have done differently

Figure 1-2.

graciously as possible (or stay in it while you look—every paycheck counts).

Don't leave bitterness in your wake; instead, learn from the experience. Ask for an exit interview with a personnel representative and your former boss, and then listen. Address what part you may have played in being let go or fired. Weigh the explanation, and determine what you can do differently in the future. This is not simply a learning process—staying on good terms with a former employer has its crucial practical aspects. A job search is essentially a sales promotion, relying heavily on public relations. You may need a letter or telephone reference. If possible, come up with a joint "official reason" for your having left your former employer. If you provide one explanation and your former employer (if references are checked) provides another, it will prove embarrassing. Approach your former employer and say, "I understand that my employment here is finished, but I love doing _____ and I will look for similar work. When I'm asked why I left here, I want to give an answer that we are both comfortable with."

Of course, take with you whatever information resources (your Rolodex or computer disk with names and addresses of contacts, clients, customers, fellow employees; internal telephone directory; business card collection) are yours. Remain on excellent terms with any of your peers or support team; you never know when they may be in possession of an essential piece of information or may run into someone who asks for you. In the spirit of the theater, "leave them asking for more." Don't let the mere mention of your name to former employers or peers elicit their groans. Never express your negative feelings, no matter how annoyed you are at the role others may have played in your no longer being employed; you have everything to gain by being gracious and showing that you are putting the best possible spin on the situation.

Reality Check: Turning Your Fears and Frustrations into Motivators

Now is your chance to "vent": to identify and list the fears and frustrations that you are experiencing: that you may never get another job; that you aren't cut out to be effective working in a new organization; and that you will meet another group of miserable people in your new job, just as bad as (or worse than) the ones you just left. You don't know where your rent money will come from. You're embarrassed to tell your friends you're out of work.

Using the form shown in Fig. 1-3, list your greatest concerns. Brainstorm. What actions can you take immediately, and what plans can you make to counteract these negative influences? For example, if your biggest worry is meeting new coworkers, perhaps a course in public speaking or an activity such as a dance class could reinforce your "people" skills. Check your local YMCA/YWCA or colleges for low-cost courses.

If your most pressing concern is financial, make plans to review your financial situation in detail to determine exactly what your resources are, what expenses must be covered, and what other sources of cashflow are available to you. See Week 2 for a financial worksheet, if it's an emergency.

What job markets should you target? How do your skills, experiences, and job objectives translate into the optimal job markets to target? How do you get names, addresses, and telephone numbers of key people to contact in those organizations within the targeted job market(s)?

For example, you may have chosen to rule out privately owned or start-up organizations, in favor of larger organizations with a proven track record. In the service industry, you may prefer a large organization with many branches, in the hope of being able to travel. A lot

DON'T WORRY — GET MOTIVATED!
**List below those concerns that you are worried about.
Next to each, think of a solution or tactic that will counter the worry.
In the last column, think of at least one thing you can do to
improve your situation.**

CONCERNS	POSSIBLE SOLUTIONS	ACTIONS TAKEN
1		
2		
3		
4		
5		
6		
7		
8		
9		
10		

Figure 1-3.

depends on your priorities. As seen in Fig. 1-1, potential jobs may be found in several job markets. If you have some expertise in finance, potential jobs could be found in the fields of banking, brokerage, and insurance, and in both large- and small-sized corporations.

Think of the last five jobs you held (include voluntary activities if relevant). What did you like most about each one? List those qualities:

1. _____

2. _____

3. _____

4. _____

5. _____

What did you like the *least* about those jobs (why did you leave them)?

1. _____
2. _____
3. _____
4. _____
5. _____

What industry or profession would you most like to work in?

_____
_____
_____

Referring to the two lists you just made, how do your "likes" and "dislikes" relate to your targeted job market?

_____
_____
_____

List at least five career choices within that job market/industry that you can seriously consider. (For example, if you're interested in the publishing industry, and specifically in writing for publication, there are many different types of print media published on various subjects. But in addition, there are many large organizations that print newsletters and journals for their own staff. This could be a job market you have never considered before.)

1. _____
2. _____
3. _____
4. _____
5. _____

Learn All That You Can

If you know the industry in which you wish to concentrate your search, refer to the *Encyclopedia of Associations* at a research library, for associations and foundations to contact regarding membership, meetings, and seminars that you should attend. Look for publications that highlight trends and organizations in your field, such as *Modern Grocer, HR Magazine,* or *PC World.* Get accustomed to perusing copies of *The Wall Street Journal* or *Crain's* (the local version most relevant for you) for overall business outlook and profiles of specific companies.[1]

On a separate but more direct route, also consider scanning *The National Business Employment Weekly* and *The New York Times* (Sunday edition) for job notices wherever you are and wherever you want to be. *The National Business Employment Weekly* provides job advertisements, some of which are recopied from its sister publication *The Wall Street Journal* for organizations willing to pay the fee regardless of location. The Sunday *New York Times* has been able to attract employers throughout the country to advertise national and sometimes even international job opportunities in their business and/or "News of the Week in Review" sections, but the majority of ads are for employer locations in the Northeast and Middle Atlantic states. (Remember, only about 5 percent of your time should be spent answering ads, so be choosy about location when answering these advertisements. The higher the position in an organization you are targeting, the more likely it is that the source of the new job will be a personal contact or referral.)

List five different and specific resources (associations, publications) that can provide information about your field of employment and that you will contact to obtain information this week:

1. _____

2. _____

3. _____

4. _____

5. _____

---

[1]Additional sources are: *Gale Directory of Publications and Broadcast Media, NTPA (National Trade and Professional Associations of the United States), Standard Periodical Directory, Encyclopedia of Careers and Vocational Guidance,* and the *Job Hunters Sourcebook; A Gale Career Information Guide.* The last resource is particularly useful, in that it lists, by occupation/industry, sources for Help Wanted Ads, recruitment and job referral services, networking and contact sources, handbooks and manuals, and other leads specific to the area you are interested in. Most public and research libraries provide access to photocopy machines, so bring loose change with you so that you may leave with a dossier of information.

SKILLS INVENTORY CHECKLIST

Circle those attributes that apply to you. Add additional items to the lists.

Individual Characteristics		Things That I Can Do		Things That I Know	
Adaptable	Loyal	Administer	Help	Accounting	History
Aggressive	Methodical	Advise	Identify	Art	Language
Calm	Objective	Assign	Initiate	Bookkeeping	Literature
Cheerful	Optimistic	Check	Lead	Benefits	Music
Cooperative	Outgoing	Coach	Lecture	Computers	Photography
Creative	Patient	Compute	Negotiate	Economics	Politics
Dependable	Perceptive	Coordinate	Plan	Editing	Programming
Efficient	Polite	Dance	Problem-solve	Etiquette	Politics
Flexible	Positive	Delegate	Reason	Finance	Programming
Friendly	Practical	Design	Rationalize	Geography	Printing
Generous	Punctual	Draft	Summarize	Grammar	Repair
Hard working	Sensitive	Evaluate	Test	Graphics	Television
Honest	Tactful	File	Update	Health care	Writing

Figure 1-4.

Skills Inventory Checklist

Taking action is a great morale booster. One initial step to take right now is to get to know your product by completing the Skills Inventory Checklist (Fig. 1-4). Whether you have had one employer for the past 10 years or have held 10 different jobs, or this is your very first job search, it is crucial to assess your skills. Once you know all the things you *can* do, you can then proceed to determine those things that you *like* to do. And the best of all possible worlds is to be paid for doing what you like and for doing it well.

The Skills Inventory Checklist requires you to list those characteristics that pertain to you personally, those words that would be used to describe you as an individual. Choose among the examples, and also add any others that apply. Next assess your skills, those things that you can do. Don't limit yourself to the skills you now use professionally; look to your hobbies, interests, or "hidden" skills that you can offer

SKILL PREFERENCE WORKSHEET

A. List 10 skills below	B. Compare each set by circling your preference	D. Place your final rankings here
1	1 1 1 1 1 1 1 1 1 2 3 4 5 6 7 8 9 10	1st
2	2 2 2 2 2 2 2 3 4 5 6 7 8 9 10	2d
3	3 3 3 3 3 3 3 4 5 6 7 8 9 10	3d
4	4 4 4 4 4 4 5 6 7 8 9 10	4th
5	5 5 5 5 5 6 7 8 9 10	5th
6	6 6 6 6 7 8 9 10	6th
7	7 7 7 8 9 10	7th
8	8 8 9 10	8th
9	9 10	9th
10		10th

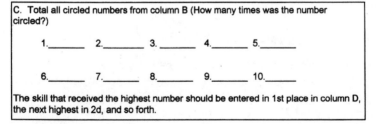

C. Total all circled numbers from column B (How many times was the number circled?)

  1._____   2._____   3._____   4._____   5._____

  6._____   7._____   8._____   9._____   10._____

The skill that received the highest number should be entered in 1st place in column D, the next highest in 2d, and so forth.

Figure 1-5.

a prospective employer. Lastly, list all that you "know"; again, do not limit yourself to on-the-job knowledge, but look both to "life experience" and academic credits. This isn't merely a workbook exercise. Information from this inventory will prove invaluable when you're writing your resume and cover letter. In fact, when you're stuck trying to come up with another winning letter, refer back to this inventory. It will provide you with adjectives and adverbs that can be used to help you sell your product.

The second step is to rank those skills whose utilization gives you pleasure versus those that do not. Using the Skill Preference Worksheet (Fig. 1-5), rank the skills you listed on your Skills Inventory Worksheet. Now you have a better understanding of what you truly like to do. How does this compare to the jobs you listed earlier? If there isn't a general agreement (you hate detail work and using a computer, yet you have your sights set on being an accountant), go back and review both your job-search goals and your Skill Preference Worksheet to determine where you have led yourself astray.

Just because you may have "drifted" into a particular segment of a job market is no reason to remain there if you're truly unhappy. Accept a "stopgap" position if one is offered, but put real thought into exactly what you want. Perhaps you really like being an accountant, but your last job was such a miserable experience that you're convinced all accounting positions are the same. Keep an open mind, and do research into the profession. Talk to other accountants in other firms; what are *their* workloads and responsibilities?

Achievement Worksheet

If you have been laid off or fired, or are just plain fed up with the job you have, you must look at all the good things that have happened to you and that you have caused to happen. Even the most miserable job situation has had some bright spots. You need to look at all the things that you have done right, if you are to know your product and be able to sell it.

To continue to be action-oriented, use the Achievement Worksheet (Fig. 1-6) to list at least 10 achievements that have been important to you. These could range from learning a second language to completing a difficult assignment ahead of schedule, or to taking and passing a course in public speaking. Look to goals that you have set for yourself and have met. Next to each achievement, identify the skills you used in meeting your goal (refer to the Skills Inventory Worksheet). In addition to forcing you to focus on positive actions taken in the past and to identify skills

ACHIEVEMENT WORKSHEET
List below 10 achievements that are important to you
and identify the skills that you utilized

ACHIEVEMENTS	SKILLS
1	
2	
3	
4	
5	
6	
7	
8	
9	
10	

Figure 1-6.

used, this list can be a great morale-booster on those days when you may feel that few of your goals are being achieved. You have been successful in the past; you will be even more successful in the future!

Post the Skills Inventory Checklist, the Skill Preference Worksheet, and the Achievement Worksheet on your bulletin board to reinforce your knowledge of the product you're selling. From time to time reread them, and pay particular attention to your preferences to see if they continue to be valid. As you continue to develop your "product" knowledge, you may discover that you have a skill heretofore unused or unrecognized. Update your list whenever necessary.

Selling to the Market

The recruitment and selection process hasn't changed in any substantial way since the dawn of civilization. What is this process? As I said before, a job search (the other side of recruitment and selection) is essentially a sales and public relations effort. You will spend an impressive amount of time impressing other people with your skills, abilities, common sense, and courtesy. To "close the deal" and get the job, you need to make the sale.

What type of organization will provide the best environment for your skills, interests, and values? You must explore just as many possibilities as you are able to. You must think "outside the box." (See Fig. 1-7.) Beyond "that's the way I heard it should be done," or "that's the only way I know how to do it," there may be untapped resources at hand—new ways to approach your future, your career choices, your job campaign.

Now is the ideal time to "break out of the mold" just a bit, to get the creative juices flowing. If you're accustomed to an hour's commute to work, get up at the same time but take a brisk walk, ride a bike, do some exercises, put on some music—do something for the right side of your brain. Is there any reason why you can't try something new? In addition to the mental relief this personal time can afford you, physically it can do you a world of good. In fact, schedule in your appointment book right now some time to do "something for myself," be it a concert, time to read a novel, go for a swim. Do this on a regular basis. When you were employed, you (hopefully) enjoyed some leisure time; if not, it is time you did! Just be certain you don't schedule these forays into fun at prime job-search hours. Keep regular "work" hours that

THINKING OUTSIDE THE BOX

Connect all nine dots using only four (4) straight lines, without lifting your pencil or retracing a line.

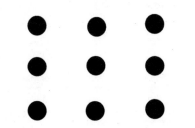

Figure 1-7. *(The answer is found on page 62.)*

mirror the hours kept in the industry or profession you are targeting.

A friend, finally let go from a job she held for 15 years when her department was eliminated, used running as a way of "pounding out" her frustrations. The side benefit was improved mental and physical health (she finally lost the weight she couldn't find the time to lose before, and her running improved considerably, thus bolstering her self-confidence), and an immediate benefit was the opportunity to network at road races with fellow runners. You never know who holds the key to that new job!

What Is Your Ideal Job Like?

You have moved on, either physically or mentally, by choice or not, from your old job. You've listed what you liked and didn't like about your prior employers. Now it's time to describe your dream organization.

To obtain information regarding your ideal employer, complete the Work Environment Survey (Fig. 1-8) to profile the type of people, work environment, and location that you prefer. These are preferences that you should keep in mind. When you're faced with a tempting job offer, it's easy to lose sight of the fact that you really prefer a creative working situation to one based on following a lot of rules.

For example, an individual who likes to work in an unstructured, people-oriented environment, where creative approaches are appreciated, would not be happy as a bank teller. A person in this job would work with the public, but in an environment where specific rules must be followed and creative alternatives are not actively sought out. Likewise, an individual who feels more comfortable being closely supervised, working with data, and having flexible work hours may do well in the operations department of an organization. Someone attending classes at night would not look favorably on flexible hours or frequent travel. The preferences noted today may change in the future, based on changes in your situation.

Look at the survey after you have completed it. List here those aspects that you must have in any new job situation (e.g., child care, flexible hours, salary rather than commission):

_____

_____

_____

_____

_____

WORK ENVIRONMENT SURVEY
Circle your preferences in each category

PEOPLE:

Individual Assignment
Alone   On a team   Combined alone/team

Supervision from Others
Close   Moderate   Little

Supervising Others
Great extent   Moderate extent   Very little   None

Customer/Client/Public Contact
Great extent   Moderate extent   Very little   None

TYPE OF ORGANIZATION:

Profit / nonprofit

Small / large

Products / services

Centralized / decentralized

Well-established / new

Self-employed / employed by others

Salary / commission

Stable work force / high turnover, good promotions

Private industry / government / association / academics / other_____

Clearly defined responsibilities / shifting responsibilities

Clear lines of authority / ambiguous authority or shifts with projects

BENEFITS DESIRED:

Medical   Dental   Tuition refund   Stock purchase

Matching gifts   Employee savings   Other:_____

Figure 1-8. Work environment survey.

Now, list those items that it would be great to find at your new employer (on-site health club, late-night door-to-door limousine service):

_____

_____

_____

WORK ENVIRONMENT SURVEY

LOCATION:

Within 1 mile of home	In urban center
In suburb	In rural area
Mostly outdoors	Mostly indoors
Both in and outdoors	Work at home
Work in office/shop/store	Work at desk or station
Highly mobile	Extensive travel
Some travel	No travel

WORK SCHEDULE:

40+ hours per week	5 days a week
30-40 hours per week	4 days a week
20-29 hours per week	3 days a week
10-19 hours per week	2 days a week
Less than 10 hours	1 day a week
Flexible	Standardized

CONTENT AND PACE OF WORK:

Deal mostly with   things   people   data

Combined   things/people   things/data   people/data

Same work as now   Different work as now   Similar work as now

Type of tasks: office   manual   service

Pace: slow   steady   busy/fast-paced

Figure 1-8. (*Continued*)

Leads: Find Them *and*
Turn Them into Prospects

Where to Start?

With your lists! Lists of friends, neighbors, former employers...anyone
you know or who knows you. I realize you may be saying, "I don't

know that many people," or "I can't ask my friends for help." Would you rather ask strangers? That's your only other option.

Turn to the Lead Organizer (Fig. 1-9) and, either using index cards, pages in your notebook, or a Rolodex, list everyone you know. Keep on going until your mind is a blank. Then put the lists aside and go for

LEAD ORGANIZER

Consider all the different roles that you play and the diverse circles you travel in to determine who might furnish a lead

YOUR FAMILY
- ☐ Aunts, uncles, cousins
- ☐ Spouse or significant other
- ☐ In-laws
- ☐ Exes and ex in-laws

FRIENDS
- ☐ Neighbors (old and new)
- ☐ Spouse's friends
- ☐ Parents of your children's friends
- ☐ Hobby groups

PERSONAL
- ☐ Religious, clergy
- ☐ PTA members
- ☐ Tradespeople (plumber, electrician, carpenter)
- ☐ Store owners (dry cleaner, barber/hairdresser)
- ☐ High school buddies
- ☐ Fraternity/sorority members
- ☐ Staff, editor of local newspaper
- ☐ Favorite staff at restaurant
- ☐ Students, former classmates, college professors
- ☐ Former guidance counselors
- ☐ Doorperson in residence
- ☐ Clubs, church groups

PROFESSIONAL
- ☐ Doctor, dentist, psychologist
- ☐ Accountant, financial planner
- ☐ Banker
- ☐ Real estate agent
- ☐ Insurance agent
- ☐ Attorney
- ☐ Librarians
- ☐ Consultants used

EVERYONE OUT OF STATE
- ☐ There is no one inaccessible or out of range

BUSINESS
- ☐ Secretaries
- ☐ Former clients, customers, buyers, sales reps.
- ☐ Recruiters
- ☐ Trainers
- ☐ Professional societies
- ☐ Current and former employers
- ☐ Chamber of Commerce members
- ☐ Security guards
- ☐ Your employed (and unemployed) peers

Figure 1-9.

a cup of tea or a breath of air outside (for 15 minutes or so). Come back and see who else you remember. Then, think of who each of these people might know. Lawyers, doctors, dentists, accountants know people in all types of professions; so do plumbers, electricians, your letter carrier. Get carried away...free-associate...let your mind wander. Look at your calendar or appointment book, going back as far as you can to remember meetings, social events, other appointments that you may have forgotten.

After you have (for now) exhausted your extensive circle of "friends" (you didn't know you knew so many, did you?), you must assess who can give you leads and who cannot.

A Lead Is...

What a lead *isn't* is an excuse to stop your job hunt, a sure thing, or an end to the search (although it certainly *could* be).

A lead is *the identification of a potential opportunity for personal effectiveness and/or success.* Frequently the term is used in a selling environment, when the salesperson is trying to identify prospects that may be interested in buying the product or service being presented. The crucial aspect of looking for leads is the ability of the seeker to separate the *viables* from the *possibles*, and the *possibles* from the *probables*. The probables are those who not only are interested (or may become interested), but who also have the ability to buy. A job lead is the identification of any potential job opportunity that directly or indirectly, sooner or later, may lead to a job opening.

Here again, it's crucial to the effort that when you seek the leads you be able to determine the probables. And don't forget the "indirectly" part. In the play *Six Degrees of Separation,* the point is made that there are only six people between you and anyone else in the entire world! You just have to determine the chain of communication. It is the "friend of a friend of a friend who knows a person who lives next door to another person who works for..." who may be the key to your wonderful new job. If you have any love for mystery novels or detective movies, now is your chance to go looking for clues. Clues that will lead you to leads that will lead you to prospects who can offer jobs! (If you don't like mysteries or detective movies, no excuse! Think "puzzle" instead.)

"Someone Said That Your Organization Is Hiring/Expanding/ Relocating..." The first step in winnowing the probables from the rest is to call the organization to see if what you have heard is true. If they are receptive and they are indeed hiring, then you can proceed with your research to determine if they are an organization for which you wish to work. Make another visit to the research library or reference room, to check with *Standard & Poor's* or other business directories for information and a profile of the organization in question.

The key to leads is that while they may pop up anywhere, they wear no tags or other identifying marks that say "Lead!" or "I know where a job is!" This raises two issues:

1. The more people you meet, the more opportunity you will have to identify and evaluate potential leads.

2. No one (and no place[2]) should be excluded from at least initial consideration.

Just because you have assembled a list of friends, don't think it ends there. You must constantly, daily add to those lists, index cards, Rolodex files. And you can't collect new "friends" just by sitting by the telephone waiting for it to ring, or reading want ads. You have to take *action*.

Another friend, an office services manager for a foreign banking facility located in New York City, was in his late fifties when let go from his employer of 10 years. He happened to mention (with much embarrassment and hesitation) to his next-door neighbor across a fence between their properties that he was looking for a new job. Guess what? The neighbor knew of a situation and followed up with an introduction. The job seeker got the job at a premium over his last salary, and a sign-on stock bonus. Another office worker in the manufacturing sector let her school acquaintances from a continuing-ed program know that she was about to lose her job. One of them spoke to a close friend of his, and she was promptly hired by the central headquarters of a religious organization. Leave no contact unmined for possible leads.

Give Others Some Breathing Room

Be mindful that, however desperate you may be feeling, life does go on, heedless of your job search. Not every moment or every event or

---

[2]In New York City, FAO Schwarz, Barnes & Noble Super Bookstore, and Bloomingdale's all have been identified as great places for singles to meet. You need to identify similar spots for your job search. Where do people in your field meet? Trade associations? Health clubs? Alumni reunions?

every person you come in contact with should immediately be prodded with questions regarding their assistance in your job search. This is simply good public relations. One key to success is follow-up. You don't have to corner everyone right then and there; find out where they can be reached and do it later on. ("Can I have your business card? I would really like to spend a few minutes talking with you, but I don't want to monopolize your time right now.") Be a good listener, filing facts away mentally for later use.

Do I Need a New Resume?

First, what *is* a resume? A resume is *a summary of professionally relevant information concerning yourself,* one that presents a complete overview of your experiences, skills, and abilities to date. Think of it as merely the key to getting you in the door, a marketing brochure, an ideal sales tool or "come-on." Remember that a resume will never actually get you the job—you alone can do that.

The resume also can be an opportunity for anyone with real or perceived power to screen you out—either because you don't have a resume or because your resume isn't "right" because it

Doesn't say what he/she wants it to

Doesn't look the way he/she thinks it ought to

Isn't flawless or attractive to the reader grammatically, technically, or typographically

A resume can be an excuse to bar you from consideration. The problem in this economy is that there is a proliferation of resumes (both good ones and amazingly poor ones). Therefore, even if you have the perfect resume for a particular position, you still may not be considered if it gets lost in the pile. Think of the possible opportunities for loss: the typical resume is reviewed initially for approximately 25 seconds by the gatekeeper. This first pass is given by the employment/human resource manager, an HR specialist, or even a clerk (I have personally been told that some HR managers have their untrained receptionist or personnel assistant make the initial review). I'm not saying this is the way it *should* be—quite to the contrary! But I want to be certain you are aware of the very poor reception even the best resume can receive. Other possible missteps your resume may be subjected to include: a malfunctioning fax (no paper, broken machine, problem with the phone line, unwillingness to admit they lost it); post office problems[3]; and staff changes.

I know a professional who was thought to be a shoo-in for a teaching job at a prestigious university, because a close friend from a high-powered executive recruiting firm asked if he had any interest in the position. When my friend showed enthusiasm and appreciation, the recruiter provided the details, including to whom he should send the resume. Two months later my friend got a form rejection letter. He was puzzled, but life went on. More than a year later he received a phone call out of the blue. The gist of the conversation went like this:

> "I've just been appointed director of the Management Institute. I was throwing out papers from the desk I inherited, and came across your resume. I don't know how it got here, but would you like to teach at this school?"
>
> "Absolutely!"
>
> "We must meet as soon as possible, because I'd like you to teach this semester."

Needless to say my friend got the job, and has been there for 11 years already—all thanks to a new staff member cleaning out a desk!

Regardless of the level or position you are interested in, if it's a job you're after, you'll need a resume. It won't get you the job, but without it you won't even be considered. (Unless you're *really* lucky and you meet one of the few people with the power to hire you on the spot. Or does that only happen in the movies?)

The first and most obvious question is, do you have a resumé?[4] If not, the next section will teach you how to write one. If you have one, do you need a new one? The questions in Fig. 1-10 will serve as a general guide to determine how much work your resume needs.

---

[3]Recently *The Wall Street Journal* conducted an unscientific survey, sending letters to various *WSJ* offices around the country. The result—only an 80% arrival rate after three days. That means that one out of every five mail pieces got there in four days or later—if ever. (Ever see one of those newspaper articles on a Christmas card that was sent during WWII and finally delivered?) Even "priority mail" (2 pounds, 2 days, $2.90) doesn't seem to work. First of all, there is no tracing mechanism. Second, in tests conducted by TV newscasters, they have found that there is no guarantee at all. On the TV news program sharing the results, there is the inevitable spokesperson (sometimes the Postmaster General himself) who agrees unashamedly that there are no guarantees. In fact, the postal service has changed its advertisements as a result.

[4]If you have a red-hot prospect, don't let lack of an up-to-date resume stop you from approaching this key person immediately. Either call, or send a marketing letter with highlights of your skills and experiences; then quickly work up a resume for a follow-up. See Fig. 3-2 for sample marketing letters. Don't delay until you have the "perfect" resume; that could be too late.

RESUME REVIEW

Does your resume

end three years ago?	_____yes	_____no
not have your most recent assignment?	_____yes	_____no
not reflect that you are considering a career change?	_____yes	_____no
have a typographical error?	_____yes	_____no
have more than two pages?	_____yes	_____no
seem to not be helping the process?	_____yes	_____no

If you answered "Yes" to one of the above questions, you need a new resume.

Does your resume

mention activities but no results?	_____yes	_____no
identify school activities and you've been out of school for more than three years?	_____yes	_____no
list positions that go back more than 10 years?	_____yes	_____no

Is it

a functional resume because of the advice of your neighbor (or friend, colleague, parent spouse, significant other, son/daughter or book)?	_____yes	_____no
one that you do not like?	_____yes	_____no
edited/written by an outplacement firm counselor?	_____yes	_____no
appropriate for only one of the two or three different jobs you are looking for at the same time?	_____yes	_____no

If you answered "yes" to any of the above questions, you probably need a new, updated resume.

Figure 1-10.

Building a Potent Resume

"How do I write a terrific resume?" There is no one right answer to that question. In fact there are three types of resume: the chronological, the functional, and a combination of the two. Figures 1-11 to 1-13

SAMPLE OF CHRONOLOGICAL RESUME

Mary Smithson   **(212)769-4081**
15 Battson Avenue
Sutton Place, New York 11228

OBJECTIVE: To obtain a career opportunity in a fast-paced payment environment where my PC skills will help the organization accomplish its tasks.

EXPERIENCE:

1989 to 1992   **Bank of the Spirit and Mind, New York City**
                             Senior Paying & Receiving Money Transfer Clerk
                             Paying & Receiving Department
                             Responsibilities included:

                             - Input of outgoing CHIPS, FED payments, money market, foreign exchange and loans in addition to paying and receiving FED desk;

                             - Verification of all ABA/UID numbers for input to CHIPS/FED fund;

                             - Manual input of credit payments received from the Clearing Bank;

                             - Handling of bilateral limit requests;

                             - Processing of customer credit advices;

                             - Daily interaction with money traders in the calculation and verification of money position;

                             - Advice to the Investigations Department of discrepancies and late payments;

                             - Back-up supervisor;

                             - Authorization to sell or buy funds if account is short or long from the Clearing Bank.

1987 to 1989   **Bank of Kobe Ltd., New York City**
                             Clerk, Paying & Receiving Department

                             - Input, Verification and Release of CHIPS and FED payments;

                             - Maintenance of various international accounts.

SKILLS: Micro Vax 3600 VT 320 Terminals, IBM AS/400 Terminals, Swift, Midas IBM Series II, Unisys B25, fluent in Spanish.

EDUCATION: **Grover Cleveland High School**
                             Academic Diploma

Figure 1-11.

show examples of each. There are as many different opinions as to what makes a great resume as there are people making screening and hiring decisions. There is a perception in the marketplace that a chronological resume is the resume of choice. However, if you have a

Sample Functional Resume

Louise Jackson
1432 Pennsylvania Avenue SW
Washington, D.C. 21708   (301)586-9124

Summary

A high-energy person with a history of accomplishments under diverse conditions and a broad array of people.

Project Management

* coordinated the purchase of a not for profit facility that included fund-raising efforts totaling $10,000,000

* created an advertising campaign by negotiating pro bono agreements with several local advertising agencies

Real Estate

* negotiated a real estate deal that included land purchase and a construction project that exceeded $1,000,000; required coordination with more than ten separate groups of contractors, subcontractors and local agencies — under budget and on time.

Team Building

* converted an unfocused group of individuals into a coordinated team that was able to raise more than $500,000 in just 14 weeks and create a program of activities that resulted in a student participation rate of more than 80%.

Presentations

* have made presentations in a variety of settings for groups as large as 40 and as small as 12 on subjects that included *The Economics of Unemployment,* *The Organizational Disorientation of our Youth,* and *The Clean Air Act and Its Impact on Our Neighborhoods.*

Education

Joliet University, B.A. and M.P.A.

Awards and Activities

District 12 PTA Woman of the Year, 1992

Figure 1-12.

Sample Combined
(Functional/Chronological)Resume

Frank Jordan
16 Fairbanks Road   Des Moines, Illinois 15690   (315)678-5509

SUMMARY

A professional manager with a variety of experiences and increasing
responsibilities in the public sector interested in applying those same skills in a
private environment.

Purchasing & Facilities

Coordinated operational budget for 300 staff in a defense facility.
$5 million

Provided leadership for automation of inventory control and accounts
payable systems

Project Management

Designed and implemented $12 million construction project of a year's
duration that required 14 subcontracts and an internal staff of more
that 200 employees. Project was completed on time and within budget.

Organizational Development

As Company Commander took a group of 150 individuals with low moral
and low productivity and developed them into a highly focused team with
a results-oriented approach to tasks and activities.

Employment History

United States Army 1970-1994, Lieutenant Colonel, Finance Corps

Education

University of Pennsylvania, 1970, Bachelor of Science, Industrial
Engineering

Special Skills

PC literate —— Windows Environment: Lotus 1-2-3, Fox Pro, Word for
Windows, Harvard Graphics

Figure 1-13.

work history with frequent changes or wide gaps in time, a functional resume may be more effective. Exceptional cases such as television writers, musicians, or theatrical personnel are more likely to present functional resumes, as they are more likely to have had numerous or diverse employers in a variety of settings.

There are two aspects of any resume that have to be considered very seriously: form and content.

How You Say It (Form)

Once you have come up with an initial resume, you can go to a printer and have at least 50 but no more than 100 copies made. This is an expensive option but will yield an attractive product. You need this minimum quantity to "test" the resume in the marketplace. Is it effective? Does it open doors for you? If not, you must revise and invest more money at the printer's.

A less expensive yet totally acceptable solution to resume preparation is to purchase a quantity of 20-lb bond stock with matching envelopes and print as you go from your PC. Resumes can easily be adjusted and revised as needed. These laser-printed copies may not be as impressive looking as those from the printers but may be the most effective way to target the job market. And the greatest advantage of this approach is that you can customize your resume for the unique needs and desires of each employer (more on this below).

There is no excuse for poor grammar, misspellings, and errors in a resume. Don't rely on the spell-check function on word processing software; it will accept typographical errors (*there* for *their; same* for *some*; and so on). You must go over every word carefully until you're certain the resume is 100 percent error-free. Even the most outstanding credentials and work history may be overlooked if they are presented poorly in written form. Don't get gimmicky or enthralled with all the fonts in your desktop software (unless, of course, that has a direct relation to the field in which you're looking for employment.) Outsized typefaces, unusual formats, or bouts of humor may get your resume noticed—even passed around the office—but will it be taken seriously?

What You Say (Content)

Given the PC there is no excuse not to make the resume *customer driven*. I'm certainly not telling you to lie (not even a little) on your resume. But at the same time, you should alter it so as to highlight those aspects of your background and experience that will be most convincing to the reader in terms of meeting the specific requirements of the position for which you are applying. If you didn't graduate from Harvard, don't say that you did. On the other hand, if you majored in cosmetology at some local technical training institute, and you're not applying for a beauty-related job, think twice before including it. The same certainly goes for your interest in fortune-telling. If you are applying to a not-for-profit organization, cite any volunteer groups you may belong to, or whose efforts you actively support. Refer back to your Skills Inventory and Achievement Worksheets. See everything from the point of view of your reader. What problems might she/he be facing, to which you can provide the solutions?

For example, if you have been active in your local Parent-Teacher Association and have chaired fund-raising committees, you should mention that fund-raising went up 10 percent (if it did)[5] while you were involved. When looking for a position that may involve lots of international travel, point out all the trips you have taken overseas and the foreign languages/cultures you are familiar with. But remember, the fact that you once ordered a pizza at Milan's airport on a layover doesn't make you an expert on Italy!

As Sergeant Joe Friday used to say every week on the old TV show *Dragnet*, "Just the facts, please." Your resume must provide accurate information. Use the Resume Worksheet (Fig. 1-14) to list your professional/job history in date order, starting with the most recent experience. This information will consolidate all the data regarding salary, dates of employment, possible references, and significant achievements. You can then refer to that data when actually writing the resume and the cover letter. This is also a handy review piece for you to consult before going on interviews or submitting names for references.

When Thinking Resume, Think "Purpose"

What is the purpose of a resume? Its initial purpose is to keep the prospective employer from dismissing your application for employment. Therefore my recommendation is that you hold on to your resume until it is required. Do of course send a resume and cover letter to answer blind[6] or other newspaper ads, and always bring a

---

[5]If the numbers are significant, include them. A 2 percent increase on a $5 million dollar sales volume is substantial, but a 3 percent change in personnel turnover may not be so impressive if the staff only numbers 40. This is a sales tool. Think marketing. Bigger, better, faster—you can do it! Don't be an elephant giving birth to a mouse.

[6]A "blind" ad is one that does not reveal the name of the organization seeking candidates.

RESUME WORKSHEET

Education:

School:

Address:

Dates attended:

Degrees:

School:

Address:

Dates attended:

Degrees:

Licenses/Certifications/Memberships/Appointments:

Special skills or achievements/Publications:

Hobbies/Other interests:

Figure 1-14.

resume with you on any personal visits. But the fact remains that the later your resume is asked for during the recruitment and selection process, the more likely it is you will get the job. When you are sending letters to targeted companies, or to follow up on leads, don't include a resume. Make your cover letter sufficiently tantalizing to get you the interview, and then you can deliver your resume in person.

RESUME WORKSHEET

Employer:

Name:

Address:

Phone #:

Supervisor (name & phone #):

Date started: Date left:

Your job title:

What you did:

Chief accomplishments/responsibility:

Ending salary: $

Employer:

Name:

Address:

Phone #:

Supervisor (name & phone #):

Date started: Date left:

Your job title:

What you did:

Chief accomplishments/responsibility:

Ending Salary: $

Figure 1-14.

Format

Using a chronological format, block out the information for your resume using the Resume Worksheet (Fig. 1-15) and the outline format (seen in Fig. 1-16). Use a clear, easy-to-read, conservative typeface, and proofread, proofread, proofread! Ask family and friends for their opinions as to how it looks and how it reads. No matter how strong

RESUME WORKSHEET
Chronological Order

Current/last employer:

Name:

Address:

Phone #:

Supervisor (name & phone #):

Date started: Date left:

Your job title:

What you did:

Chief accomplishments/responsibility:

Ending salary: $

Employer:

Name:

Address:

Phone #:

Supervisor (name & phone #):

Date started: Date left:

Your job title:

What you did:

Chief accomplishments/responsibility:

Ending salary: $

Figure 1-15.

the comments, consider them without rebuttal. Whether you incorporate suggestions is your decision. Remember it is *your* resume. And always remember to show your appreciation.

CHRONOLOGICAL RESUME FORMAT

Name	Telephone
Address	Fax #

OBJECTIVE/SUMMARY: Either describe position sought or describe your expertise.

WORK EXPERIENCE:

Date (years)   Organization name
City (state, if not obvious, e.g., Chicago, Miami, New York)

Corporate title
Functional title
Department
Bulleted list of accomplishments and achievements
•
•
•

Repeat for either 10 years or 3 jobs.

EDUCATION:

School, degree, date * (year) *optional; include if to your advantage

RECENT ACTIVITIES:

Professional memberships, associations, teaching assignments, speaking engagements, books or articles written, honors received

SPECIAL SKILLS AND/OR INTERESTS:

List those that you wish to highlight as job related such as language, travel, volunteer work

Figure 1-16.

More Product Presentation: The Marketing Letter

In many cases, the first information the person you are contacting will absorb will be that contained in your marketing letter. This is the prime selling tool. It is to be used in the following ways:

- To announce your job-search status to friends
- To ask friends to provide you with leads
- To ask friends to bring any contacts or job openings to your attention
- To write to all the leads, contacts, and referrals that you discover, either on your own or through your friends
- To answer blind ads or classified want ads, or to solicit information from strangers (cold calls)

Generally speaking, the later you send a resume the better. The marketing letter is the "tease"—telling them just enough to make them want to know more, to want to meet you in person. The entire—the only—reason for mailing any letter or resume, or making any telephone call, is to set up the one thing that can get you a job offer: the interview.

The most important item in your bag of sales tricks is not the resume itself. It is the "cover letter," written on your stationery, that is your prime marketing tool. Too often, these one-page marketing letters are written from the vantage point of the job seeker. Wrong! The recipient knows you want the job. The other hundred or so applicants all want the job. Turn things around by putting yourself in the place of the recipient of the letter. As was stressed in the introduction, remember that one of the five reasons you should be hired is that you are a *solution*. Think of the cover letter as your one opportunity to convince the gatekeeper that harrowing guilt, and perhaps even the loss of his/her own job, will result if he/she passes your application by! In other words, state in the cover letter why you are the *ideal* addition to their staff and how you will add *value* to the organization.

What's great about concentrating your primary marketing effort on the letter is that you may tailor it to that specific company position and person. Remember therefore that the following must always be done to absolute perfection:

Complete and accurate spelling of the organization's name and address.

Accurate name and title of the person to whom the letter is addressed. (It's easier to sell up than down; go as high in the organization as you can. If at all possible, avoid the human resources department, unless you have a good reason to go through them.) Never address a letter "Dear Sir or Madam," or "To Whom It May Concern." If the reader is important enough to you for you to be writing to them, it is important for you to do a little advance work and find out the correct person to contact.[7]

Accurate designation and title of the job or specific position for which you are applying. Be certain to state what job or position you are interested in.

Always include your signature on the bottom of the letter.

Avoid over-using the word "I"; think "you," to make the letter customer-driven.

Write in the same way that you talk. This is no time to get caught up in phrases such as "Enclosed herewith find my resume." Is that what you would normally say? Don't write a hot, bouncy letter if you are a button-down, conservative type. Say exactly enough, neither too little ("Please accept my resume as an application for the position of Senior Clerk") nor too much (a 30-line paragraph about yourself).

Make certain the letter is in every way complete. Don't abbreviate; spell out *Street* and *December*. Is there a date and a salutation? If you are including a resume, or an article, be sure it is in the envelope!

Be a bit creative in your closing. *Everyone* says "Sincerely" and "Yours truly." Imagine how boring that is for the reader, day in and day out, with the volume of mail he/she must get. Try an alternative: "With best wishes," "Kind regards," "With confidence," "Just to keep in touch with you," or "Warmest greetings."[8] Pay attention to how others close the letters you receive. Then come up with your own.

Consider using a blank envelope when you are mailing to a "cold" call or a referral that does not know you. Think back on all the junk mail that you discard immediately, upon seeing who it's from. Using a blank envelope may at least get you past the first hurdle. Avoid using labels—they scream "mass mailing." Neatly hand-address or type each envelope. Of course, if you're writing to someone who knows you, include your return address on the outside of the envelope.

---

[7]Be careful too to get the gender right. Names such as Adrian and Taylor may be male or female. Evaluate the accuracy of your source. A "temp" may be answering the phone when you call and she/he may give you the wrong spelling or an incorrect title. You will never know because your letter will wind up in the circular file.

[8]Instead of throwing out all the junk mail you receive, read it. Since most of it is sales pitches, take some clues from the marketers. Look for key phrases, closings, approaches. Never copy a letter, but be inspired by one.

Don't worry if you've written to a company before and gotten either a rejection or no reply. Pull out your copy of the old letter and try a different tack. Don't rule out sending it to a different person. And again, nothing will suffice except total grammatical and typographical accuracy. A recent *Wall Street Journal* article chuckled over the following typos: "I am a rabid typist," "Thank you for your consideration; hope to hear from you shorty," and "Here are my qualifications for you to overlook"! Be certain that your correspondence is no laughing matter. Sure, you want to be noticed, but for the right reasons!

The Last but Most Important Part of the Letter. This is a marketing letter. The ultimate goal is a sale. To get the sale, you need to get the reader to take the next step—wanting to see more of the product, to schedule an interview with you! You can either trust the person on the other end to do the right thing, or you can take the initiative and *help* them to do the right thing with a sentence near the end such as, "I will call you on [no more than seven to ten days after the letter has been sent] to arrange a mutually convenient meeting. I am sure it will be well worth your time." Very few cover letters take that initiative, from the most recent high school graduate to the more recently fired CEO of a *Fortune* 1000 company. Even sales and marketing people frequently omit it. Don't just *say* you will call—*make* the telephone call, exactly as you promised to do in the letter.

Sample cover letters are shown in Figs. 1-17 and 1-18. Again, remember that these important marketing tools should be customer-driven, and relate to the specific organization and job that is being targeted.

To Whom Should You Write?

If someone has referred a name to you, get as much information about the person as possible. If necessary, call the company directly to get the correct spelling and title (not to mention checking to see if the person is still employed in that capacity and at that location). Always confirm this information for every letter that you write. It may be time-consuming to make these telephone calls, but not as time-consuming as writing a letter that is wasted because it went to the wrong person or was returned to you.

There is no excuse for omitting the name and title of someone in every organization that you send a letter to (except for blind ads). The strategy is to aim high: write to the president, chief operating officer, chief executive officer, or the chairman of the board of the targeted organization. A fifth distant alternative is the department head of the

SAMPLE LETTER TO A FRIEND

Joseph A. Booth
6573 Main Street
Anytown, US 33445
123-456-7890

April 12, 1994

Brian Brothers
9870 Sullivan Road
Pittsburgh, PA 09947

Dear Brian,

Whenever I come across an alphabetical listing of names I never fail to think of you and all the years of school where we always sat next to each other in home room. At times, I was happy to go first to give a report, but there were those other moments I wished to change my last name to Zimmer!

Again, I am first...first to drop you a line and let you know how I am doing. I've heard that you recently had another addition to your family. Congratulations to you and Cathy. What's new with me is that, after five years, Smith Textiles and I have parted company. I am still interested in a career in finance, but I think this time I will look for a larger company with more sophisticated needs. I have really gotten involved in the capitalization aspects and attracting outside investors over the past year. While I was at Smith Textiles I was able to attract a substantial new investor to support the new equipment being installed. It was really exciting - I know, not as exciting as your English Literature classes are!

You have always known a million people. Can you look at my resume which I have enclosed? If you have any suggestions (you really have a way with words) or can pass a copy of it along to any of your business friends I would greatly appreciate it. I am willing to relocate and, who knows, we might end up in the same town again.

Best wishes to you and your growing family,

Joe

Figure 1-17.

unit in which you are seeking an opening, but don't open the letter with "Dear Marketing Manager"; be sure to include his/her name.

How do you get this information? Simple: telephone and ask the receptionist for the correct name, spelling, and title. In determining which individual to write to, check out a recent edition of *Who's Who* for the particular business or industry you're interested in. You may

Sample Letter to a Referral

(your name)
(street address)
(city, state, zip code)
(phone number or answering service number)

(today's date)

(name of your contact)
(accurate title)
(organization's name)
(street address)
(city , state, and zip)

Dear Mr., Mrs., or Ms._____

(First and last name of source, and organization if applicable) suggested that I contact you.

(Source) said that you were (Get the right wording here. Examples include: "a person who loves his/her work," "a dedicated business person who needed /or was looking for some help to address a major issue /or find a solution.")

I am presently exploring career opportunities and (source name) insisted that I call on you because he/she saw a link between (here provide a specific skill, interest, experience of yours) that is directly related to the situation you are facing. Let me tell you that I have (experience, skill, and/or interest) for more than _____ years and results of those efforts included ___, ___, and ___. What I am a looking for is (a job, a referral, advice.)

Let me suggest a brief, mutually convenient meeting. I will call you on ___. Of course, if you prefer please call me earlier.

Enthusiastically yours,

Your Signature

Figure 1-18.

learn that you and the targeted individual have similarities in background, education, or even gender. Write to the one who is most like yourself! Be subtle, and include the pertinent information in your letter.

What Should You Say?

In the first part of your letter, get the reader's attention by relating yourself to something specific about the person, organization, or job. For example: "In the June issue of *Fortune* I read that [name of organization] was listed as one of the 50 most innovative organizations in the United States. I was interested to learn that you will be coming out with several new products over the next year. As a manager of sales at [former employer] I was instrumental in launching a direct mail program that had an 8 percent response rate. This high rate of success was due to several innovations I introduced to our sales staff." If the recipient is interested in improving sales, you have already sparked his/her interest in how you can add value (increase sales) at their organization. Don't tell everything—make them want to see you.

Next, elaborate briefly on other achievements and skills you can bring to them, highlighting points covered in your resume and specifically citing the position or function that you feel qualified to fill. Put yourself in the reader's place and think of the value you can bring, the problem you can solve.

In your closing, be appreciative of their consideration, and specify a date and a time when you will call to arrange a convenient meeting.

An original copy of the cover letter (with or without a resume) is mailed to the prospective employer. A copy of the letter, together with the article or advertisement or notation as to who made the referral or what prompted the inquiry, is placed in your Correspondence folder.[9] Mark your appointment calendar with the name, telephone number, and date/time that you will call, as stated in your letter.

Some Letter-Writing Hints

Unless you're a writer by vocation, don't expect to dash off one of these letters in 15 minutes. First envision the reader: what problems might he/she have? How can you be the solution to them? Jot down various ideas. "I can save you money." "My experience will result in time-saving innovations." "The skills I bring in the area of management will build a stronger team." Use index cards or your notebook to write down action statements—all the things that you can do.

Look to establish rapport with the reader. People like people whom they believe to be like themselves. Show your excitement and enthusiasm. Let the reader know that you have done your homework, and know what their job and their organization is about.

Plan to spend some time writing and rewriting the letter. Do a draft; then take a brief break (maybe make some telephone calls?) and come back to it. Ask others to read it and give their opinions. When you have a version with a strong closing that reflects you and what the objective of the letter is, mail it. If it gets the response you want, then you've created a winner, and you can use it (or personalized versions

---

[9]Later when the prospect of a job develops through a favorable response to your letter, you will set up a separate organizational file.

of it) again. If you get no responses, then go back to the drawing board and try another version.

If you are targeting organizations and are planning a small mailing (avoid mass mailings) to key executives, try several versions and see which is most successful. Go with that one.

Networking: A Quick, Simple, Winning Way for Beginners and Experts

Networking is overused. Most people do it because they're told that's what you do, and assume that it works like magic. "If I spend x numbers of hours networking, I will be entitled to a job, regardless of the effectiveness of my networking efforts." It just doesn't work that way. In fact, it's getting ever more difficult to network, simply because the concept has been bandied about ad nauseam by job seekers and job counselors alike.

One HR professional told me recently of picking up the phone and hearing a voice on the other end saying, "My name is ————, and our mutual friend told me you would be a good person to network with. When can we get together?" That's an all-too-typical, self-centered approach to job seeking. Why should anyone agree to a meeting with that person, based on that arrogant performance?

Let us begin by defining what networking is, or *should be*. Networking is *a strategy for finding a job that recognizes relationships among those who may have access to leads, either directly or indirectly*. It has the key word "work" in it, because it's something that you should always be doing, not just when you find others to help you. After all, why should they go out of their way for you? To be truly effective in networking, start with those you already have ongoing relationships with. These are professional contacts, school contacts, businesses, customers, clients, suppliers—you name it. Finding bases of common interest lets others know that you are approachable, a source of information, and open to a mutually beneficial professional relationship.

List here the names, titles/functions, and telephone numbers of at least five people you can contact today (refer to your Networking Contacts file):

1. _____

2. _____

3. _____

4. _____

5. _____

Job-Search Roadblocks: How to Recognize and Avoid Them

To get that job within 90 days, it is essential right from the start that you recognize job-search roadblocks whenever they appear, and determine in advance how you are going to avoid them. It is also essential that some momentum and work habits be established immediately, to enable you to remain focused and *working* toward your goal. The following are some of those you should do your best to avoid.

1. *Your family.* This is the first group to avoid during your search. Keep them informed, but don't make yourself available for all family activities that crop up, lest these then force you to be more productive with the time that you have remaining. Your family may not be used to having you around during the day, and may view it either as a positive (an extra pair of hands to run an errand) or a negative ("Can I use the phone now?" "When are you going out?"). As far as possible, establish a normal "work" day for yourself. Get properly dressed, all ready to "go" to your job of finding a job. This is one reason I suggest a separate work area to function as your job-campaign command post.

2. *Neighbors.* It's amazing how quickly (sometimes within minutes on the first day) the word gets around that you are out of work, and therefore available to wait for the telephone repair people, the furniture delivery truck, and the Federal Express package. You could easily spend the next 90 days giving your time to one and all, and guess what you'll still be out of? That's a serious problem if you've lost your job involuntarily, and can be devastating even if you haven't.

Establish a coping strategy, a way of saying "no" without feeling guilty and without offering an explanation. "Sorry, but I won't be home"—and leave it at that. If questioned about it again, and you were home when you had said you wouldn't be (neighbors can be demanding people, and nosy too), again there is no need for an explanation. "My plans changed"—end of story. You need to concentrate all your efforts on finding a job. If you agree to even one errand, you are inadvertently setting up a scenario that implies you have the *time* to run errands. And once the word gets out, they will grow more and more time-consuming.

I once visited a friend who works out of his home, and in the half-hour I was there to discuss business we were interrupted no less than four times. One person was sick (medication was recommended and provided), another had lost her job, his eldest son was seeking advice in placing a sports bet, and there was a request to be available for a furniture delivery. I had thought it might just be coincidence, but my friend led me to believe it happens all the time.

3. *Your home.* This is *not* the time to take your mind off your troubles and order new drapes, plow the back forty, clean the gutters, or install a new shower. You do not want your mind *off* your problems, you want to focus *on* your job campaign. Of course if the water is up to your ankles from a leaky pipe, or the sweat caused by a broken air conditioner keeps making the keyboard slippery, by all means attend to these emergencies in the same way as you would if you were employed. But remember, you are *working* each day—on getting a job!

4. *Do-gooders who haven't got the jobs, the power, or the contacts.* There are a whole bunch of nice people out there who manage to fill their days with time-fillers. All too easily you can end up being a time-filler for them—instead of them helping you, you are helping them to fill up their day. You know the type: their most important activity is lunch. They start planning it as soon as they arrive, and start making the calls for the elaborate arrangements. While waiting for retirement or vacation (or both), they find people who are "networking" or performing some other aimless activity. They are not all as bad as I'm portraying them to be, but my point is that while these people are cheering you up, sharing job-search stories, commiserating because they are out of a job too, you still need a job!

Once you have determined that a person is unable to help you either directly or indirectly, be polite and firm and thank the person for his or her time and move on. Call back later to chat and give them their due (you don't want to get the reputation of being a mere "user"). Recognize this as recreation, best done after working hours.

5. *Incompetent executive recruiters.*[10] Remember who pays the executive recruiter—the employer! So remember for whom the recruiter is working. Try to determine the background and experience of the recruiter. Is he/she (the most exclusive firms are still male-dominated) an expert on the people side, or more of a salesperson? Does the recruiter have the jobs? If they are one of the best firms, when there is no specific job to fit your needs they may try to market you (and the best will). They can send you in without a job order, because they

---

[10]For a detailed discussion of recruiters, see Week 5.

know their clients so well. Their strong candidate could *create* an opening (there's that *value added* again).

Interview the recruiters as much as they interview you. Recruiters, especially in this economy and with these unemployment rates, could spend their whole day responding to the people who contact them, even when there's no news to report. Call only occasionally to remind the recruiter who you are (chances are they are not automated on the applicant side, and even if they are, the likelihood of his/her remembering you two, three, or four weeks down the line is remote). Use these calls as an opportunity to determine their professionalism. If he/she refuses to take your calls, find someone else. These are salespeople, and if they don't take or return calls, that may be a giant "avoid" signal.[11] Request that your resume not be forwarded without your specific approval; you want to know who is seeing it.

6. *Negative people, wherever you find them.* The world is divided into two sets of people: those with a positive outlook, and those with a negative. If you get the feeling you're not being highly regarded by the person you're dealing with, get out at the first opportunity. That encounter is only wasting your time and draining valuable energy that could be put to better use elsewhere. It could be a receptionist, a parking lot attendant, or a token-booth clerk (for those of us who live in major cities that still use tokens). But it is especially devastating if the negative person is the one you are involved with when applying for a position. I once saw a receptionist allow a job applicant to fall asleep in a chair. When the manager of the personnel department inquired, the receptionist said she didn't know why he had fallen asleep, omitting the salient fact that the applicant had been there for two hours. When the applicant was awakened, the manager discovered that he had fallen asleep out of boredom, because the receptionist had never told him what to do after he had filled out the application. The receptionist then said in front of both persons, "If he doesn't know what to do after he fills out an employment application, that's his problem!" She was fired that day, but the applicant wasn't hired either.

7. *People who don't understand their roles.* These can be the most deadly. It could be the security guard who refuses to let you get to your appointment on time, the receptionist who is distracted by his/her personal following, or a "temp" with too little to do. Or a personnel/

---

[11]Don't forget that it's difficult to determine when a phone call has not been returned. Thirty minutes? Two days? Somewhere in between or after? Don't take it personally, and if you *need* that individual, say so. Try calling at "off" times. In this profession, the good ones usually are available either early, late, or on weekends.

human resource "professional" without effective or ample training or professional maturity. Any or all of them could serve as effective and annoying roadblocks. Don't let them. Avoid them at all costs. As soon as you see it happening, retain control. Don't lose your temper. Stay good-natured. You win in two ways: good training and development for you, and a saved opportunity.

Fallback Options (Alternative Work Arrangements)

This early in your search, it's wise to consider fallback options. Depending on your financial resources, unemployment and severance may not carry you very far. You should first consider *freelance work* if appropriate. Utilize your typing, editing, writing skills by doing desktop publishing or term-paper typing in your home. If you are a financial wizard, perhaps the local college is looking for tutors in your field. Look back at your Skills Inventory Worksheet for ideas. A local business may need a bookkeeper to straighten out their records. A local store may need signage if you are a graphic artist. In addition to the cash brought in, these freelance jobs get you out and working while allowing time for you to search for a job. Also, these contacts can be a gold mine when it comes to networking.

You may also have to consider *part-time employment* as a stopgap solution. Also, there is no reason why you cannot combine two part-time jobs into one full-time career. Consider the position of legal aide or legal secretary. Cost-cutting may have hit like a firestorm in nearly every law firm that you approach. No one is hiring! Can you envision a lawyer burning the midnight oil, tired, getting stress from family and friends for the long hours—and the legal work is still not done? If you make a sales pitch to that type of customer, selling your part-time services on an as-needed basis, you may have more clients than you can handle. You can have flexibility of hours and will be able to sample many different law firms, while they may learn that you are indispensable to their operation. And it will all have come about because you got your foot in the door and then showed how you were going to add value.

If you're seriously planning a career change, consider doing some volunteer work in that area. You could contact some of the foundations and associations connected with your desired field; there may be some short-term research projects or other work that they would be delighted to have you do. Structure it right and, although you won't be paid, you will be working in your desired field. It could lead to further contacts, which in turn could lead to a paid position. Career changes are difficult and require a lot of effort, but skills, experience, and talents are transferable.

Should you feel pressured for financial reasons (no severance; just graduated from school; family to support), you should actively consider *temporary employment.* There are agencies that specialize in office help, health-care workers, professionals such as managers and accountants, and other fields. While it will reduce the hours you can job-search, you may find leads at the various places you work, and it will permit you to focus more fully on the job campaign if you aren't worrying about money.

Maybe it wasn't the *organization* that didn't fit you, maybe it was the *job!* Are you in the right career path? If not, by all means *change careers either completely or partially.* Granted, you may always have envisioned yourself as a superior bookkeeper, but all those papers and numbers have been getting to you. Do you really want to exchange the papers from your old job for papers to shuffle at a new job? What other options are open to you? Bookkeeping requires attention to detail, and math skills. What other careers have similar requirements? Maybe you need to learn electronic bookkeeping (Quicken, Quick Books, Peachtree Accounting, Managing Your Money, etc.) or upgrade yourself into the world of finance by taking a few courses while working as a financial assistant.

You also might decide that you wish to leave the field of "numbers" entirely and become an interior designer, using your attention-to-detail ability. Look into what is involved; is this a profession you can "apprentice" yourself to, or are classroom studies required? Get the information and decide.

Consider starting *your own business.* If you still want to use your present career skills, think about cutting out the "middle man" and selling your skills directly to the consumer. Many small businesses cannot afford a full-time position (accountant, human resource professional, inventory controller, secretary, lawyer), and you could sell your services directly to several of them.

List several of your skills that you could sell directly right now; this could be a source of freelance work, or the beginnings of your own business. It is important that you consider this in case an opportunity presents itself; you want to recognize every chance that comes your way.

1. _____

2. _____

3. _____

4. _____

5. _____

Staying Organized

You have an appointment book to get you to where you should be at the right time. But you're also making telephone calls, mailing letters, scheduling appointments, going on interviews—how to keep track of it all?

A job search log (Fig. 1-19) will help you to track all the contacts you have made, either through visits, by telephone, or by mail. For example, if you call Organization X and they tell you that there is a hiring freeze on now but to call back in six weeks, that should be noted in the log *and* written into your appointment book as a telephone follow-up to be made in six weeks. Enter all the names and data for people and organizations you have contacted this week (for contacts, information, leads). Refer to the lists you made in this chapter. Now is the time to rate your top priority contacts, the ones that you should reach first. List each of these "very possible" names in your job search log, and also schedule them into your appointment book. Reach a minimum of five people each day. As you do make the calls and write the letters, enter the appropriate information into the log. If you have additions, include them, and add the dates once you have made the contact. The "Remarks" column is to be used to track results and to follow up ("Send *Wall Street Journal* article of 3/15/94 on leasing").

For those instances where resumes are sent, a Resume Log (Fig. 1-20) will enable you to maintain records of exactly where your resumes are. One key to success is to watch the details. Call when you said you would call. Follow up the leads. Monitor the results, and make revisions in your tactics when necessary. Enter in the data for all the people/organizations/blind ads to whom you have sent resumes. If you have some that you are planning to get to, list them also, and insert the data once you've completed them.

You're Off and Running!

Now you're supplied with all the tools for your job search. You have a "customer" list to whose entries you will write or call, you have a product (you know your skills), and you have marketing tools (a marketing letter and a resume; presumably several versions of each). You

JOB SEARCH LOG

CONTACT METHOD & DATE	NAME & ADDRESS OF ORGANIZATION CONTACTED	NAME, TITLE, & PHONE # OF CONTACT	CONTACT SOURCE NAME, ADDRESS, TITLE, ORG.	POSITION SOUGHT	REMARKS & FOLLOW-UP NOTES

Figure 1-19.

RESUME LOG

DATE SENT	NAME & ADDRESS OF ORGANIZATION	NAME, TITLE, & PHONE # OF CONTACT	SOURCE OF CONTACT (NAME, ORG.)	POSITION SOUGHT	TELEPHONE FOLLOW-UP DATE	REMARKS & FOLLOW-UP NOTES

Figure 1-20.

will continue to monitor results, fine-tune, and explore a few more tricks until you reach your goal: a new job.

Week 1 Checklist

☐ Evaluated your job history, and determined what role you played in not having the job you want right now.

☐ Reviewed your current concerns and worries, and considered what actions can either be taken or planned to ease your fears.

☐ Considered job markets and careers to target.

☐ Contacted five resources to obtain information on desired field of employment.

☐ Completed Skills Inventory Checklist.

☐ Completed Skills Preference Worksheet.

☐ Completed Achievement Worksheet.

☐ Completed Work Environment Survey.

☐ Assembled a comprehensive list of possible leads.

☐ Completed Resume Worksheet.

☐ Wrote a chronological or other-style resume.

☐ Wrote a cover (marketing) letter.

☐ Networked with at least five people.

☐ Completed Job Search Log.

☐ Completed Resume Log.

☐ Entered all follow-up times and dates in an appointment book.

SOLUTION TO
"THINKING OUTSIDE THE BOX"

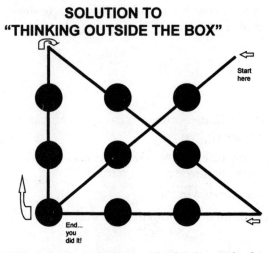

Figure 1-21. Solution to "thinking outside the box."

Week 2
How to Keep Moving to Create More Action

Day 8

Now we're into the second week of your search. The first step each week will be for you to review what you did last week and what items need further work. As of the end of last week (review the Week 1 checklist), you should have the following:

Working copy of your resume

Copies of several cover letters you have sent

Entries on your Job Search Log for contacts made during the past week

Names on your Resume Log who have received your resume

A long list of possible leads (or sources of leads)

Now confirm your objectives. Focus on exactly what you want. Write here what position you are seeking (brief description), what skills you can use in that position, and a profile of your ideal employer. Refer back to the Skills Inventory and Preference Worksheets, and the Work Environment Survey you completed in Week 1.

Position wanted: _____

_____

_____

Utilizing these skills: _____

_____

_____

Employer profile: _____

_____

_____

In keeping with your goal of obtaining this job within the 83 remaining days, you have identified leads and sources to contact and organizations to research, and have targeted the job market. Start this second week by reviewing the status of all of last week's activities. Some will require a follow-up telephone call. Check your appointment book and Job Search and Resume logs, and mark in your appointment book exactly what actions are required this week.[1]

What will you do today? _____

_____

_____

_____

_____

_____

In Week 2, real progress should begin to be seen, with the first meetings and interviews being scheduled and leads bringing you to further contacts and leads. Before moving on to more activities, it is extremely critical at this point that you make sure you have the follow-up and feedback system in place. Take time out to make sure you are logging all your activities to date on the Job Search and Resume Logs[2], and have targeted dates for the next call, indicating what has been accomplished so far and what further action is needed. [This system is as important for finding the job as it is to determining what (or who) is a time-waster for you.] The purpose of this tracking system is to provide

[1]Did you list at least five people from your "friends" list to contact, either by telephone or letter? Remember that you can only get leads, referrals, job openings, and interviews by actively seeking them.

[2]If you have regular access to a personal computer, this tracking system can be automated. Take this route only if you are already computer-literate and do not have to be trained in the software. Keep it simple—don't get distracted with shopping for computer software, etc. Use the paper system; it works fine.

information on your job campaign and an analysis of progress to date, and to lead you to your objective—a new job. There is no substitute for good work habits—keeping detailed notes, making regular entries in the logs and in your appointment calendar, and following through on all appropriate leads and contacts. As time goes on, you will analyze the information as to what you have done and what sources you have drawn upon to determine how hard and how smart you have been working.

Foolproof Methods for Turning Every Lead into a Real Prospect

Once you have qualified some prospects (that is, determined who is really able and willing to identify possible job opportunities for you), you then need to get results to turn these prospects into real job leads.

First, you need to brainstorm to consider all the possible additional places and/or activities that can be mined for leads. In Fig. 2-1, list at least 10 regular activities or places that you go where leads may be

CONTACT SUCCESS ANALYSIS

NAME & ORGANIZATION	SOURCE OF CONTACT	MEDIUM OF CONTACT

Figure 2-1.

garnered. Be creative, and don't overlook the obvious. Consider the church/synagogue you have been going to (or meaning to go to). If you have kids in school (or even better, if they are in more than one school), have you been meeting other parents at school functions, sports leagues, or even at the bus stop? Wherever you go, look to meet people who may or even may not be of assistance in your search. Maybe the neighbor down the street that you see at the corner deli can't offer you any leads, but she may be an ace of a writer who can review some of your letters and provide feedback. Or perhaps the woman in the garden shop, who worked in direct mail sales for many years before she retired, can give you some insights into sales techniques. Some spots are more obvious (a restaurant near a newspaper office, where all the reporters hang out), but others will attract a broader spectrum of people.

Evaluate the type of people in each setting (parents/professionals/ academics/nonworking/managers, and so on). Identify at least one individual in each place whom you will approach as soon as possible to inquire if he or she has any job leads (or a suggestion as to someone who might be of assistance). It doesn't even matter if you know their names. You can always use your charm and introduce yourself, using your common interest or predicament as an ice-breaker (e.g.,"Are the lines always this long at the bank at 11 A.M.?).

Now this calls for proper positioning. The real problem with networking (although the term has been used and abused, there is no other that so well describes what you are doing) is that the number of people who do it is in inverse proportion to the number of people who do it effectively. If you were ever approached by a "networker," how did you honestly feel? I am sure a basic question came to mind: "Why should I do anything for this person I don't know (or don't know well)?" If you as networker raise that question before you even make contact with the "networkee," then you both will be operating from a more realistic (and ethical) base.

There must be a real understanding as to what will prompt the other person to give you the time and suggest persons for you to see and even call, to open doors for you. All of this takes valuable time from the "networkee," and why should he or she consent to that? Only a few truly unusual people, or those who have reasons that you haven't fathomed (you helped them out once, or they are impressed by you, or they think you could help them if they are ever in a bind) will surprise you with their generosity.

There's a fellow in New York City who was looking for a job with his head between his tail, and in desperation he contacted a gentleman whom he had know casually when they had served on a nonprofit board together several years earlier. They had not kept in touch, but as this fellow was desperately trying to identify leads and job prospects, he turned to the other man. Well, he got a terrific reception, and several leads. The job seeker asked him why he was making such as fuss (and emphasized that he truly appreciated it), and the fellow making the arrangements said it wasn't a problem because he still remembered how this man had spoken up for a particular religious group when they were on the board together. He had appreciated that because he knew the other fellow wasn't a member but made his statements nonetheless. When the job seeker left the meeting, he thought back to an event that he didn't find so memorable and realized it had taken place at least 15 years earlier.

The point is, *go for it*, and don't be bothered if you can't figure out a reason why a person would go out of his/her way to be of assistance. The very fact that you realize you are asking for a real gift (time and leads) from this individual should at least put you in his/her good graces. Whether or not you're usually good at "small talk", these "out of left field" calls should at least be prefaced with the amenities. Remind the person of your current/former relationship or acquaintance; then state why you are calling and why you thought he/she might be of help. Be sincere in your thanks for any assistance he/she might render. If you can add to that basic message, so much the better ("I remember how successful your recent job change was..."). Meanwhile, make your lists, and keep them by your side so that you can add to them whenever another possible name comes to mind. In fact, keep it as a goal that whenever you return after any outside appointment (pleasure or business), you will add at least one name to your list.

Let as many people as you feel comfortable with know about your job campaign. Make a list of all possible contacts whom you know professionally, or even who might have heard of you. Stretch your credibility to the limit. Start with customers and other external contacts. Next turn to inside contacts, and then identify any other sources. Leave *no one* out. List these names on the Job Search Log and proceed to contact them this week.

Once the process has been set in motion, you can start to make the contacts. Should you visit, write, or call? Do the easiest first. If you see them, ask for a few minutes for a meeting, a face-to-face encounter. If you need to call because you haven't seen them, or you don't want to wait, go do it. As always, *action* is the key. Don't wait!

If there is any avoidance on the part of the person contacted, pursue so as to find out what the objection (hesitancy) is. Listen very carefully, and confirm what you think you are hearing. Ask, "Am I correct in hearing you say there is no reason to meet because...?" Don't take this reluctance personally, but do try to determine if there is an alternative that may be promising. If the person says he/she has no time to meet, then you might answer, "Perhaps that won't be necessary, but this is why I called...."

Rehearse, Rehearse, Rehearse

Before you go out and do any of this (in person, or over the telephone), find someone willing to go through some rehearsals with you so that you can begin to develop a script. Use those index cards again to design some introductory statements. The first statements that you wish to make should be well thought out, but also try to anticipate any questions that may be asked. Rehearsals "test" your delivery, let you listen to your statements, and allow you to be prepared without sounding like you're reading a script.

Do you know what the objective of your call is? Is it to get information? A contact? A job opening? If they say no, can you ask to speak to someone else, or for another time to call in the future? "I understand that you have no job openings at this time. Can you suggest any other organizations (departments, persons) that might be hiring?" "Yes, I see that this is a very busy time for you, with the new product about to be introduced. Could I call you back next month when the sales campaign is under way, and you might be able to share a few minutes with me?"

The person you're dealing with is giving you a limited amount of attention, and you don't want to use it up before the important opportunity presents itself for suggestions. Don't forget that the goal of the exchange is to determine if you should continue to develop your contact with this person because he/she is going to either directly or indirectly lead you to a job.

Sending Winning Letters

Letters are an essential element of the process, but their importance has been lost on the contemporary job seeker. First, there are "career counselors" out there (and I use the term loosely) who encourage those looking for a job to spend time, energy, and funds on mass mailings.

This approach is to blanket the universe with a pile of letters, and I guess statistics are used to justify the conclusion that there is a high probability that you will get from this mass mailing a few expressions of initial interest, and eventually a job offer. Personally, I have two problems with that approach.

First, it is extremely costly—not only in terms of the actual price you will have to pay for doing it yourself but even more so if you answer one of those ads that appear in the best of publications. If you do use such a service, beware, especially because they usually are not in your immediate area, so it's impossible to evaluate them except on an after-the-fact basis—either what they promised was true and you got the job, or you didn't.

When considering this approach, you also need to give attention to its *indirect* costs. If you send out a thousand letters, the logistics of keeping track of all the subsequent activity—not to mention actually doing it—is mind-boggling. Sending marketing letters without a telephone follow-up is simply a needle-in-a-haystack approach. The key to any mailing effort is not the mailing itself but the follow-up, which demands meticulous attention to detail. It's the follow-up that's going to get you the meetings—and ultimately the job offers—not the mere act of sending the letters in the first place.[3]

This approach also encourages an "all your eggs in one basket" approach, and "sit and wait" behavior. The way to find a job in any market at any time, let alone now in this most difficult one, is to get out there and make it happen. An *action* program, with lots of balls going through the air at once, is the key. Taking a mass mailing approach is too risky, for it hinders your ability to test the market to see what will (and won't) work for you. Also, while you are waiting for the letters to arrive, what are you to do? If you start to do other things and try other methods, it will be for too brief a period. Once those other steps have been taken, if they start to yield any results, you will increasingly be unable to follow up because of the demands on your time that the thousand-item mailing will require.

Let me add one last reason to discourage you from this approach. The ads that are used to advertise the benefits of this approach always include some success stories—and I mean *successes!* I recall statements

---

[3]Two of the hats I currently wear—one as a recruiter, and the other as a consultant on retainer for a major sports entertainment company—give me the opportunity on a daily basis to see the volume of letters and resumes generated by job seekers who are throwing their money and time away. Suffice it to say that "To Whom it May Concern" never seems appropriate for starters. A recruiter recently made the comment to me that "resumes are the junk mail of the nineties," so keep that in mind before you proceed to write any job-seeking letters.

of how this or that individual doubled his/her salary, or increased it even more. If you believe those ads, you also probably believe the "eat all you want and lose weight" and "wear this special hat and your hair will grow long and full" ads. I have personally met many job seekers who have come to me after they had gone through that mass mailing process, but were meeting with me after the fact because they had not a thing to show for it.[4]

Also, in this age of speed and utilization, oftentimes the traditional niceties of professional courtesy are unknown, forgotten, or ignored. Written communication is increasingly being avoided by the school system. Even graduate students in a variety of disciplines are given multiple-choice exams. This is particularly worrisome, because the workplace increasingly is demanding that workers at all levels be able to communicate effectively through the written word. The global marketplace, faxes, modems, e-mail—all of these dominant trends call for a capacity to write effectively. A well-written letter is not only an opportunity to demonstrate the fact that you are able to communicate effectively; it is also an instrument to display the fact that you understand what it means to be courteous. This is certainly something that will set you apart from so many others, and in this competitive marketplace anything that sets you apart from the herd in a positive way should not be taken lightly or ignored.

Remember that letters are a missed opportunity when not created from a marketing perspective. You can gear your sales pitch directly to your customer from the relative comfort of your home or office. You can agonize over each word and do it over until it is "right." If you send the same letter to several individuals, you can test-market your sales pitch and make adjustments when selling to others.[5]

---

[4]Let me also encourage you with a positive twist you can give to this process that is inexpensive in time and monetary terms. Consider an automated resume service. Computer technology has encouraged the growth of a new service that job seekers should consider, namely, keeping their resumes in an organization's computer databases. When you see an ad that is attractive to you, all you have to do is direct the service to forward your resume—they do the rest. Electronic as well as print ads are a low-return option for finding a job, for reasons that we will discuss later. That's no reason to ignore them entirely, and this is a good way to get attention with little cost to you. Just think: no stamps, no stationery, and only a small amount of time.

[5]If there are organizations that you do wish to approach but cannot find a contact to lead you in, make a list of them and the appropriate person (ideally by name, certainly by functional title) and send off five "generic" letters each week. These are somewhat of a long shot, but if you have done some research into these organizations and have geared your opening remarks to them, with a strong closing promising to telephone, they are certainly a step up from mass mailings. Consider these limited targeted mailings and do not devote a great deal of your time to them. Concentrate on networking and following leads.

Getting Meetings with Top Prospects

The toughest part about getting meetings with top prospects (either for further leads or for job openings) is to identify specifically who they are. Here I would like to reconsider a question raised earlier: Is it easier to sell *up* or *down*? The answer is simple: always sell "down" so when targeting prospects (those with the hiring authority to make job decisions or those with excellent contacts and referrals), choose those who are higher in the power structure. They, in turn, if they have "bought" your pitch, will then be in a position to "sell" you to the lower echelons (department heads, personnel). They will be in a position to be listened to.

But how will you get them to meet with you? This is the most important consideration. You must identify the best way to obtain the meeting: either directly or indirectly. The firmer the point of contact, the more likely the agreement to meet. As I mentioned earlier, *Six Degrees of Separation* makes the point that, as big as the world is, there are just six people (if not fewer) separating us from anyone in the world we would like (or need) to meet. What you need to do is to identify the links and then make the contacts. That could be anyone— friends, lovers (or former lovers), alumni, teachers, spouse or significant other, fellow joggers, relatives, politicians, neighbors, store contacts (cleaners, bookstore, bagel or coffee shop). It's a case of who knows whom.

As mentioned in Week 1, also consider part-time activities with not-for-profits on a voluntary basis. If you have the opportunity to join a particular not-for-profit organization, consider not only the mission of the organization but also the composition of its board and other volunteers. This may be helpful for three reasons.

First, it will provide variety. There is a certain amount of tedium that is associated with any job-search effort. The intensity level that I've asked you to develop warrants variety and a break from time to time. Joining a not-for-profit allows you to exercise your organizational and other professional skills while building your confidence and self-esteem. Also, by working within an organizational context, you may get insights that will add to your consideration of what to look for and avoid in your next position.

Second, it can provide contacts. By spending time at a not-for-profit, you will have the opportunity to meet other volunteers, clients, members of the board, and paid staff. Depending on your assignments, you may also have the opportunity to deal with vendors and other suppliers and constituencies—all opportunities to extend your network, and therefore worth your consideration. I do ask that you be sincere in your volunteer efforts: don't just "take," but give honestly of your time and talents. If you dislike dogs, now is not the time to join the ASPCA, regardless of what prominent member of your targeted job market "happens" to be on the board.

Third, you never know where a possible job opportunity may arise. Most not-for-profits have paying positions; consider the voluntary assignment an opportunity to get to know the organization better, and to give it a chance to get to know you. Once inside you can appraise the prospects for employment, and you may even recognize additional opportunities in other areas because of your activities.

Warning: When considering serving as a volunteer beware of the perception "you get what you pay for." If you are positioning yourself for paid employment, your prospective employer must recognize the cash value of your efforts. To emphasize the point, consider the fact that this is a variation of the "Why pay for the milk?" theme. The downside of making your services available for free is that you are conditioning the organization and its members to the availability of your services and the low price you place on them. To get them to reconsider by putting a price tag on what had been a free service will be a daunting (but not impossible) task.

One last suggestion on this topic: consider, if appropriate, the local group that provides executive volunteers for not-for-profit and public sector organizations. This is a not-for-profit itself, and, again, one more way for you to identify prospects. In fact, if your local community has no such organization and you have the inclination, you may have just created a paying (or nonpaying) job for yourself.

Turning Obstacles into Opportunities

One thing you should consider this early in the search is the need to shape perceptions. When making your contacts, be sure to take a positive approach to this process, particularly when dealing with obstacles. You need to identify obstacles when they arise, and determine what to do about them.

Consider this situation: You approach a prospect who tells you that his/her organization "can't possibly consider you for a job, because not only is there a hiring freeze but we're continuing to lay off staff." Frequently, organizations that downsize cut too deep, and even though they have let employees go, there may be opportunities on a contractual (temporary) basis. If you have specific skills that they feel they need, they may hire you on a part-time/temporary basis, thus achieving their cost-cutting goals while allowing line departments to function.

Frequently, it's a numbers game: "salary expense" must be cut, but no one is concerned about expenses for temporary help because they don't carry the costs of benefits the organization must also absorb when hiring. Find the line department person that may be hurting, and has the need, and see what he/she has to say. (In situations like this, always leave your business card in case the present scenario changes.)

Frequently the downsizing has included outsourcing; that is, it has moved activities to an outside organization that will be more cost-effective in meeting the organization's needs. For example, when a need is felt to cut salary expense, an entire department such as payroll might be cut, with Company X to henceforth provide the payroll service. Get the name of Company X, and the name of a contact person. Follow up to determine if there are opportunities with them, or if not them, others. Ask.

Lastly, listen to those who have been let go. Often the real reason why people lose their jobs is because of their interpersonal-relations skills, or lack of them. If the person who has left the organization has created an opening, that's something to consider, and an opportunity for an approach. Assess the situation and get the details, thus reducing the time you will need to conduct research.

Organizations in bankruptcy or having problems with management (recent examples include United Way, the Empire Blue Cross/Blue Shield network, Phar-mor [Ohio], and WQED in Pittsburgh) are often prime targets for specific skills. Sometimes these organizations have been in the news because of the problems they're having. If you identify yourself as skilled in areas especially useful to the organization in trouble (collections, inventory control, real estate evaluation, customer/public relations) through a marketing letter emphasizing the specific skills and experience that you would bring, this can be seen as helping the organization in general and the recipient of the letter in particular. Be as specific as possible. Be brief, and whet the reader's appetite to hear more and to see you in person.

Connecting with Others: The Pros and Cons

There is an up side as well as a down side to connecting with others. The up side is that interacting keeps you "sharp," which is always preferable to staying alone and getting dull. When you are alone a lot of bad things happen, even in your inactivity. You don't need to get dressed. Your perceptions are based on limited bits of information. Your mind plays tricks with you that lead to a raised level of insecurity. You spin your wheels rather than go forward. You get out of touch with what's happening in the real world. You become inner-focused, and sluggish.

The negative side of connecting with others includes

- Dealing with rejection and with the naysayers
- Being demoralized by hearing about their problems
- The follow-up work required
- The problem of being screened
- The debt you're building up to the contacts you're making

Now for the positives:

- You are making things happen.
- You are "in play"—the activity you are engaged in provides opportunity to test and hone your skills.
- You are taking a proactive approach that becomes more natural each time you get so engaged and that stimulates opportunity for more action.
- You become a person similar to others who see the benefit in connecting. People like people who are similar to themselves. Your interest in meeting others is shared by others who enjoy meeting others. Now even if nothing else about you is similar, this becomes a very important—and visible—similarity.
- It is personally rewarding. To get out and meet others opens a world that otherwise you never get to see, and people are interesting. By meeting them you grow.
- It is challenging. The whole process requires your creative, communications, and organizational skills. It takes energy to make these meetings happen. Consider your accomplishments when you actually successfully complete the effort.

Given the positive side, the negatives appear worth the effort to achieve your goal.

Ten Time-Wasters to Avoid at All Costs

1. Staying home.
2. Meeting people who don't really want to see you.
3. Agreeing to follow up with people, even after you've determined they won't be able to (or can't or don't want to) help.

4. Sending out a form letter and form resume directed to an organization rather than a specific person. (This is true both on a limited basis or a broad basis. For a small group, you are wasting a relatively small amount of time, but for a large mailing you are wasting a large amount of time.)

5. Promising to send things to others that will bring you no closer to your goals.[6]

6. Going to interviews/meetings unprepared.

7. Making time commitments during the work day that are not job-search-related.

8. Waiting for the phone to ring after any letter has been sent. *You* should call instead.

9. Waiting for return phone calls.

10. Waiting to improve your resume before responding to an ad or referral.

What about Money? Are Your Funds Sufficient?

You may have already cited financial concerns as one area of worry. The time has come to take a detailed look at your financial situation, now that you've entered the action phase of your job campaign. This is an optimal time for two reasons:

1. The earlier you understand what your needs are, the easier it is to plan accordingly.

2. You can use it as one more reason to be serious and persistent in your job search.

Complete the Monthly Income[7] and Expense Summary (Fig. 2-2). Once you have done so, determine what you will *need* on a periodic basis (daily, weekly, monthly, quarterly, or even annually) to survive.

---

[6]Promising to send someone a copy of an article relating to you, your job search, an activity you are involved with, is a creative way to follow up. It provides yet another reason to call ("Did you get it?") and forms another thread binding the two of you together—the beginnings of a relationship to benefit you both. It is amazing how often people do not remember the promise. Make the effort that will set you apart and label you a thoughtful and good listener.

[7]In terms of income, complete a summary sheet both including and excluding severance payments. Do the same for any unemployment benefits you may be receiving.

MONTHLY INCOME & EXPENSE SUMMARY

AS OF _____, 19____

INCOME		EXPENSES	
Salary	$	Rent/mortgage	$
		Utilities: Heat	
Bonuses/overtime		Electricity	
		Telephone	
Benefits:		Water	
Social Security		Other	
Pension		Entertainment	
Other		Charities/religious	
Cash/investments		Food	
Interest:		Loan/credit payments	
Savings		Dependent care	
CDs		Medical	
Bonds		Education	
		Home maintenance	
Dividends		Taxes	
		Transportation: fees	
Other sources:		Maintenance	
Business		Fuel	
Loan repayment		Other	
Loan proceeds		Personal: clothing	
Other		Hobbies	
		Gifts	
Alternative work:		Insurance: car	
Freelance		Home	
Commission		Life	
Part-time		Health/dental	
		Job search supplies	
		Travel	
Other		Other	
TOTAL INCOME	**$**	**TOTAL EXPENSES**	**$**

Figure 2-2.

Some economies may be required, and attention should be paid to expenses associated with the job search (travel, postage, stationery). Review the numbers, and consider this to be your "budget." Compare your actual expenses to the budget each month. You have no need for a financial crisis, to distract you from your job-search efforts.

"I Can't Make It Financially"

Do you have enough to make ends meet (outflow of funds compared with inflow)? This will impact on your job strategy. Frequently there are one or more community services that will help to provide financial advice, and sometimes even intercede with credit agencies and services.[8] The earlier you anticipate an inability to make a payment, the better it will be to discuss it with the lender and see if alternative arrangements can be made. The worst thing to do is to decide that the problem will go away. It never does, and each day the certainty of a huge problem looming over your head will serve to detract from your job campaign. The more serious the financial problem, the greater the distraction. There are choices to be made: either live less expensively (be ruthless in terms of what you need to survive; consolidate debt), get more cash into your life each month (freelance, part-time, or temporary work), or obtain legal relief from your creditors.

What is bankruptcy? It is nothing more than the absence of a sufficient amount of cash on a particular date. The law protects you from creditors exacerbating the situation. At some point in your professional life you may be associated with an organization that files for bankruptcy. Often it is allowed to do so, because only in that way can it be nurtured back to financial health. Think of taking the same approach personally, if need be[9], but don't let your financial situation distract you from the job search.

Financial considerations may encourage you to seek out a part-time position, or one that will allow for a quick turnaround. Local retail outlets, including fast-food restaurants, often represent opportunities for such employment, as do other retail establishments with seasonal needs. However, this employment should meet two criteria: it should be a true solution to your financial needs, and it should not derail your job campaign.

Although practical matters may induce you to accept an alternative work arrangement (temporarily, or on a part-time basis), there is no reason not to put the situation to your best advantage. Keep searching

---

[8]For example, BUCCS (Budget and Credit Counseling Service), 55 Fifth Ave., NY, NY 10011 (212-675-5070). If you are unable to find a similar organization in your area, check with your local bank or savings institution. Many banks will give debt consolidation loans; if you are still employed, consider doing this before terminating employment, to cut down interest expense and monthly debt service.

[9]In situations of financial hardship, refer to an accountant and/or an attorney for specific advice regarding your specific finances and whatever options you may have. If you don't *have* an accountant or attorney, seek referrals from family, friends, or peers; again, your local banking/savings institution may be of service. Even here keep in mind your job search. Evaluate the person not only in terms of competence but also as a network opportunity. You never know.

for contacts and leads, get all the experience from the situation that you can, and update your resume to reflect these assignments.

By keeping this financial element in mind, you will be helping yourself both personally and professionally. By managing your own finances (particularly taking notice of the expense side), you are sharpening your business acumen, and will be more likely to think in terms of "value added" when you approach prospects. Second, by staying interested and active in your own finances, you will be more realistic about what you can and cannot do. Foreknowledge of your financial situation will diffuse it as a "time bomb," and will enable you to take appropriate action rather than wait and be forced to react to others' tactics. This skill will help you to deal with the uncertainty of the job search, and you will project an air of confidence to others.

Week 2 Checklist

☐ Reviewed Job Search Log.

How many contacts have you reached? _____

What additional effort is needed (callbacks, visits)? _____

_____

☐ Reviewed Resume Log.

How many resumes have you mailed? _____
To "blind ads"? _____
To leads/contacts identified by you? _____

☐ Reviewed appointment calendar.

  ☐ Have you completed all this week's follow-ups? _____

  ☐ Did you schedule any follow-up activities for next week? _____

☐ Research

  ☐ Have you contacted any associations or publications, for additional information on your targeted job market? _____

  ☐ Which organizations have you targeted as possible employers?

_____

_____

_____

_____

☐ Prospects identified and followed up on:

_____

_____

_____

_____

_____

☐ Leads identified and followed up on:

_____

_____

_____

_____

_____

☐ Completed and reviewed Income and Expense Summary.

How long will your present income level cover your expenses?

_____

What income alternatives are you considering now?

_____

What income alternatives would you consider at a later date?

_____

When? _____

_____

Week 3
Places to Go, People to See

**Lining up
Those Meetings**

Day 15

This is a big week, because now you will start to reap all those "seeds" you have been planting. The lists, the calls, the letters, and the resumes will start to result in meetings, if they haven't already. If, by the way, you haven't been as rigorous in your search as you should have been, you also are seeing the results (or more accurately, the lack of results), because you have little to show for your limited efforts.

Now is the time for your first strategy assessment—time to determine what has worked and what hasn't, what needs adjustment or perhaps a whole new approach.

Look back at last week's (Week 2) checklist. How much time each day have you been spending "working" on looking for a new job? Have you gotten yourself organized and followed through on all the possible leads, trying to turn them into probable sources for a new job? No one will evaluate your effort; working for yourself may be the hardest job you will ever have. There are no set hours, no one to check to see if you've done it right and on time, and no one to fool with superficial results. As with any product being presented for sale to the market, the market will be the sole arbiter of your efforts. So the only way to do it right is to be successful.

How to Have Them Lining up to Meet *You*

How are the meetings going? Have there *been* any? How many have been set up? Are you meeting with the right people? It's time to reconsider the basic sales approach that is the starting point and the frame of reference within which you must work.

As I said in Week 1, a sales approach is the one to take during this entire job campaign. What are you selling? Yourself. How do you sell yourself? As a person that is going to directly add value to the organization that is lucky enough to recruit you. Solutions are what you have to offer, and you understand the dynamics of what is essential to success. Public relations is what you're all about these days.

Marketing: A Basic Ongoing Skill

Marketing is the tactic responsible for determining what to sell, and for identifying the markets to sell it to. Sales is the actual selling of the product. The better you understand the product and the markets, the more effectively you will link the product to the market that will most likely be a sales prospect. The less you understand these dynamics, the bigger your gamble and the more dicey your chances for success.

As I said, there are approximately 11 million businesses in the United States, according to the U.S. Chamber of Commerce and Industry. Additionally, there are thousands of not-for-profit and governmental organizations. In addition to taking a good look at the dynamics of our ever-changing economy, it's essential that you take a focused and limited market approach. This requires your ongoing research, and adjustments whenever you feel they are desirable.

Finding a job is difficult for the job seeker, because you must identify potential employers and, with 11 million businesses and thousands of not-for-profit and other entities, the exercise is akin to finding a needle in a haystack. But it is a fallacy to think that there's only one needle, or only one perfect employer. Out of all the possibles and probables, you only need to find *one* organization that has the optimal fit: your skills and needs with theirs.

Networking: A Contrarian View

There is a frequently touted view among out-placement counselors and other "career specialists" that has made quite popular a suggestion that goes something like this: "People looking for a job should spend their time and energy identifying people to network with. You call and tell them that you would like to meet with them for the purpose of [and here you are encouraged to be creative], and never, ever, disclose that you are looking for a job and, more importantly, that you are interested in having them give you a job."

I must ask you to consider the agendas of those who present this view. They need to generate "results," but to them results and activities get blurred, because they find the absence of action totally frightening. The maxim maintains that mere effort gets rewarded, for even if that effort and energy does not lead to a successful job, "at least you tried." I feel that over the long term such an approach is dangerous and, even in the short term, ineffective.

I have met numbers of frustrated people who put in the hours, days, weeks, and months of networking; they certainly got a lot of meetings, but they're still looking for a job. What could be the problem? Although each person needs to be considered individually, and there could be several problems for each person (lack of technical skills in targeted job area, poor interpersonal skills, ineffective communication), a common thread of people in this kind of situation is that they are great networkers but poor job seekers. Often they are totally frustrated because they feel they have followed to the letter the advice and direction given (most of their time was spent networking), but gotten no results. What went wrong? They concentrated on setting up network meetings instead of on getting jobs. Either they forgot the product they were selling, or they forgot they were selling at all. Mere effort will not guarantee results, but results can be achieved by directed and focused effort that includes networking as one of the marketing tools to identify prospective employers.

Reconsider *Your* Networking Approach

Is it an inwardly directed marketing approach? Are you suggesting that they meet with you to help you? Why should they? In fact, I have on several occasions (and I still do) engage in these sessions to try to identify their usefulness, but they continue to serve little purpose. Once in a while I'll meet someone whom I am genuinely interested in trying to market, but most of the time it seems to be a waste of time for the initiator of the meeting and for myself (although I am always interested in making new acquaintances).

As I have said before, an outwardly driven approach is more effective. It is more ethical to tell whomever that you are looking for a job, thus disclosing the true purpose of the meeting. To do otherwise is personally and professionally unethical. Networking isn't just about asking people to help you find a job, it's about building relationships. Recently I found a message on my home answering machine. A business acquaintance had given my *home* telephone number to one of her business acquaintances who was looking for a job; the acquaintance twice-removed left a message for me to call her to talk about people I might know that she could call for a job. Talk about a totally inwardly driven job seeker—she could give networking a bad name!

An inwardly driven approach makes the worst possible use of time. Consider the time and effort required to set up one of these sessions. Include *contact time, preparation time, meeting time,* and *follow-up time.*

Now consider whether a more direct approach would be preferable. Namely, identify those persons who have the jobs and are interested in meeting people who are genuinely interested in meeting with them (and who have done their research), to consider whether they would like a job there.

There is more opportunity for success in this approach, because there is no pretense or confusion about the purpose of the meeting. And if the other party agrees to meet, it's because he or she is genuinely interested in meeting with you, due to something that made you of interest to them in your preliminary discussions and/or correspondence.

In any case, it's essential that you qualify the prospect as quickly as possible, so that the time and energy expended is minimal. This outward-directed approach also enhances your confidence, because you are not ashamed or confused by the exchange. Consider the networking meeting where you are careful not to ask for a job. You might be cautious in your approach, and not be found out. Why waste time on the pretensions, and the picture you are trying to create? It is better to spend the time with those who need staff help or who know who else needs staffing help. The relationship is being built on the firm ground of honesty, and will more likely lead to successful results.

Who have you attempted to network with so far? Using Fig. 3-1, list the names you reached out to, what your objective was in making the contact (lead, information, job opening), and what was your result. Did you get what you wanted? Did you get something or nothing? Do you know why you were successful or not? Did you misidentify the person (really wasn't in any position to be of help), or were you unable to convince them of the mutual value of their assistance?

NETWORKING ANALYSIS

NAMES & ORGANIZATIONS	OBJECTIVE(S)	RESULTS

Figure 3-1.

Think Results!

By taking this honest and straightforward approach to networking, you will maximize your chances for success. You will get fewer meetings, but that will be time gained to locate more appropriate opportunities for more likely leads. The other way, you are getting all those meetings but also getting frustrated after a while, if nothing comes of them.

Referring to the list you just made using Fig. 3-1, list in Fig. 3-2 the sources of your successful contacts and the media (letter, telephone, visit) that led you to the objectives you had sought.

It is not enough to be competent in lining up leads and meetings, you must be *consciously* competent—you must know what you are doing that is right! How can you repeat the results, if you don't have a clue as to what works, and why?

ANALYSIS OF SUCCESSFUL
NETWORKING RESULTS

NAME & ORGANIZATION	SOURCE OF CONTACT	MEDIUM OF CONTACT

Figure 3-2.

So...How *Do* You Get Them to Line up to Meet with You?

Take a look at Fig. 3-3, and think of all the lists you've made since we started. You should have progressed from *everyone you know and everyone who knows you* to *names referred to you by all of the above.* You now want to progress to friends of friends.

As you dig deeper through the various layers of friends and acquaintances, you need to determine whom it will be best to meet, as well as the purpose of the meeting. Then determine what you can do for that person (organization). Next perform research to determine if they're hiring, for what positions, and who the contacts are. Then determine the best entry point—whom in the organization should you contact? Design a marketing letter/cover letter (be sure to close by setting a follow-up date). Then call and ask for the meeting. Figure 3-4 is another sample marketing letter.

Determine if this is a first contact, of if you have had dealings with this person before. If it's a first contact, then you need him/her, and don't be shy about saying so. If on the other hand you have dealt with the person before, and in fact did him or her a favor, it's fair to subtly drop a reminder: "Remember when I saved your life when we were in summer camp in 1965?" This is a great time to remind them in a "by

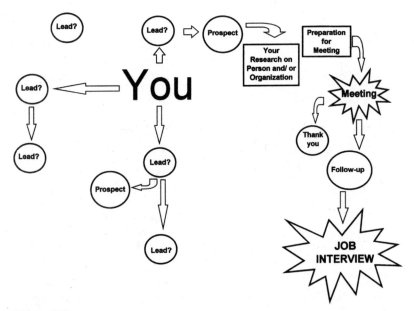

Figure 3-3.

SAMPLE MARKETING LETTER TO A REFERRAL

[ON YOUR LETTERHEAD]

March 1, 1994

Mr. Seymour Wiseman
Senior Vice President
S.W. Financial Services Corp.
78 East 67th Street
New York, New York 10028

Dear Mr. Wiseman,

My accountant, Danielle Shoreham of Woods, Shoreham and Nyman, suggested that I contact you in reference to my current job search because, in her words "...Sy really knows how to spot and develop talent."

Mr. Wiseman, in the seventeen years that I have been active in the field of middle market lending I have:

*increased loan yields on my portfolio of $208 million an average of 75 basis points over the past year;

*brought in new lending customers with loans totaling $43 million;

*decreased bad debt losses to less than .02% of my portfolio (compared with an average of .06% in the balance of the portfolio managed by others).

At this time in my professional life I seek to use the skills I acquired at several large corporations in a smaller, hands-on environment where both quantity and quality of loans are of paramount importance.

If you are in need of an aggressive, new-business-oriented account manager who knows the importance of the wise use of funds, a meeting would be to our mutual advantage. I will telephone you Thursday morning at 9:30 to determine a convenient time to meet.

Cordially,

Signature

Figure 3-4.

the way" fashion, and you now have a favor to request of them. Don't forget that it's a meeting you're requesting initially, not a job, even though you do let them know it's a job you're looking for. You want them to know up-front that even if they can't give you a job, they may be of assistance in providing further leads or contacts.

More Details, Details, Details

When you actually meet with this person or their referral, treat each session like gold. Keep in mind all the effort and energy it took to get the meeting and remember that you have only a few meetings scheduled (no matter how many, there's always room for more). You need to be thoroughly prepared, and conscious of the effort it took to get the meeting in the first place. Make the investment pay off by being prepared. If you are getting a referral, get as much advance information as you can about the person you will be contacting. Ideally, if your friend is recommending a close business associate or another friend, he/she will be a totally terrific friend and call in advance and presell you. "I've known Bill ever since summer camp, and he's a dynamic, energetic salesman. He's always been selling something— from lemonade stands to computer software. With your line of new video games, I thought he'd make an excellent addition to your sales force. I suggested that he give you a telephone call this Friday to see if you're interested in someone with his background." If the friend gets a strong negative reaction, or learns that the potential employer will be on a business trip to the Silicon Valley for the next 10 days, your friend can alert you and you can change your tactics.

Before the meeting, continue your research both about the person you are meeting and the organization. Usually, information about the organization is more available than about the individual you are meeting with. Don't be put off; find out about him/her. The more you know about the person you are going to meet, the more confident and prepared you will be, and the more impressed he/she will be with your preparation. Additionally, keep in mind that the friendliest sound for people in the United States (although I bet it's true anywhere in the world) is the sound of their own voices. The next best thing is recognition, and it's rare for people to know about most other people in a professional setting.

I know of a fellow who, upon reading about the president of one of the major fast-food organizations and their recent bold marketing strategy, decided to both compliment and congratulate him, as a fellow alum who hadn't seen him since they'd graduated together more than 20 years earlier. (Let me add that they had never been friends in college, but knew each other to say hello.) After he wrote this letter to the president, he was amazed that the president wrote back with a very warm message. That's certainly a "probable" for the letter writer to approach, if the opportunity ever presents itself.

Another example. Let's say a relative of yours has a neighbor who is a senior vice president at a local bank, and you're interested in obtaining a new position in banking, particularly in the corporate lending area. If you presume upon your relative to approach the neighbor and ask if you might telephone him/her regarding your immediate job search, and your relative is successful in providing you with a telephone number, you know that the banker is at least receptive to your telephone call (assuming that your relative heeded your request by being honest with the neighbor regarding your need for a new job).

Now, before you telephone, obtain some background information about the bank. Does it fit your parameters of a possible employer? Does it have positions for which you are qualified? Do you know if they're hiring? Have you ever sent that bank your resume, or been interviewed there before? If so, be ready with all the pertinent names and details. Do you know this banker's function? You will sound eminently more intelligent and sincere if you at least determine in advance whether you're interested in a job in his/her field, or in an area over which he/she has no influence. Obtain what information you can, and then make your telephone call.

When you telephone, identify yourself as the neighbor's relative, and thank the banker for being willing to take your telephone call. Now's your chance to impress the banker with some of your research: "I know that, although you are in the Operations Division, you have many day-to-day business dealings with account officers in the corporate lending area. I saw several notices in *The Wall Street Journal* that Bank _____ has been very successful in being the lead bank in loans to _____ Corporation. When I was with _____ Bank, I was the account officer for a similar corporation, and it was a great coup when the loan was refinanced and my bank was named lead bank due to my direct efforts. I have been attempting to reach _____ in your corporate lending area for the past few weeks, because I've heard there are several vacancies in that area. Might I meet with you for a short time at your convenience, to have you give me some advice on how I could get _____ 's attention, so that I would be able to highlight my past achievements and show how I could bring Bank _____ even more corporate loan business?"

The key elements in the above telephone call:

- *Appreciation* for the time taken
- *Research* done on the person you're speaking to, and the organization involved
- *Purpose* of requesting a meeting stated honestly
- *Possibility* of some *mutual benefit* (you = job, the lead = bringing a great employee to the attention of the bank)

Write out in advance an approach you plan to take. Try it out on your relative: the banker is his/her neighbor, after all, and hopefully your relative can give you some insight as to the banker's personality and interests, and an appropriate opening remark to break the ice.

The Meeting Itself: Seven Tips

1. On the day of the meeting, be well rested. No late-night celebrations the night before! This is a job *meeting*, not a job....

2. Be well fed, but not *too* well fed. Avoid strong spices and flavors that might interject themselves into your meeting unintentionally....

3. Be well groomed and appropriately dressed. This is not the time to parade your political leanings or espoused causes, with buttons and ribbons on your lapel.

4. Be well read. About the organization, about news in general, about the industry.

5. Be on time. End of story.

6. At the meeting, be a sponge and absorb! *Listen.* Communication is an art as well as a science. It's important that you listen to hear what is really being said, and give the right response.

7. Be courteous. Be confident.

Four Questions You'd Better Have Answers for

1. *What do you know about our organization?* Have you done any research? How interested are you?

2. *Why did you ask to meet with* me? Do you know who I am? What do I do in this organization? Do you know what my problems are?

3. *What can you do for us?* How can you help the organization? How can you solve my problem? How can you help me?

4. *What can I do for you?* Can we trade? Do I have something that you want? What good will it do either of us for me to help you?

Answers That Will Grab Their Attention

Regardless of the question, you need to demonstrate positive personal characteristics that will also indicate seriousness of purpose and intent on your part. Here, preparation is necessary. That means preparation first in doing your homework, to know the organization and the people you are dealing with. And second, preparation in the techniques of interviewing and conversational skills (including being ready to use effective listening techniques, which will be discussed in a moment).

When answering any question put to you, regardless of topic, be brief and informed. Determine the basis upon which the interviewer is asking the question. If asked at the beginning of the meeting "Would you like a cup of coffee?", give a simple "Yes, please" or "No thanks," without asking for half decaf and half espresso or "Do you have herbal tea?"

As the meeting progresses, keep an ear cocked to measure the length of your responses and thereby ensure you're not boring them with your preparation. Whatever the answer, be brief. If you wonder whether you should elaborate further, a simple "Would you like me to go on?" may be a good checkpoint question as part of your answer, to let the interviewer know you have his/her interests in mind.

How to Show Off Your Strengths, and Stand Out from the Other Candidates

What you need to get is *visibility*. You need to separate yourself from the herd. Look for opportunities to do so.[1] Personal strengths should include preparedness and professional courtesy. If these two elements are the underpinnings of your entire approach, and you use these as the basis for any action you take, you will be well on your way to demonstrating your strengths throughout the interview process.

Let me give you an example. You are going to follow up and confirm a meeting that was set up more than two weeks ago. You call the day before the meeting. When you call, the person at the other end may make the point of not identifying himself/herself when he/she first answers the phone. Regardless of whether he/she identifies himself/herself be careful, because this is a golden opportunity for you to shine: don't blow it. First, you are calling to show that you haven't forgotten the meeting, and to confirm that the other party hasn't forgotten either. (Your strengths are attention to detail and professional courtesy.) You may also be calling to confirm location and directions (more strengths—don't assume you know precisely where the meeting will take place; let them tell you). Second, the poise you reveal during the telephone call sets a tone that is so important, particularly as you have yet to identify the person with whom you are speaking—it may

---

[1]Take every opportunity to do self-promotion and publicity. If you are asked to give a speech or be on a panel discussion, accept graciously and take away a listing of who else was on the panel or who attended. Write articles, letters to the editor, and suggestions to magazines read by "the trade." You never know who may recognize your name.

be the person you will be meeting with, but it may also be his/her assistant or someone who just happened to be passing by and out of courtesy or curiosity took the call.

Before you leave the meeting, if there are any organizational publications, in-house newsletters, or annual reports there for the taking, by all means take one. You will become an inveterate list accumulator. If there are none, ask if you might have one if available.

The Follow-up

After the meeting, debrief yourself as quickly as possible. Use your notebook and the Meeting Log (Fig. 3-5) to keep records of these meetings. Ask yourself what it is you heard. Evaluate your performance. Record the other person's reactions. Write down any names or recommendations. Determine an action plan, and include the next step on your appointment calendar.

Get a thank-you letter out immediately. A sample letter of appreciation is shown in Fig. 3-6. In this letter, which should be brief, thank the reader for the time given on the stated date. Mention something specific from the meeting: information given, advice, contacts. Then state what you will do now as a result of this meeting: contact the name(s) given, attend a seminar recommended, revise your resume. (If appropriate, plan a second letter to tell the reader the results of the actions you took thanks to the meeting. Mark this down in both your appointment book and Job Search Log.) Then close with a final note of appreciation for the assistance. (See also Fig. 3-7, a sample letter of appreciation after a phone contact.)

Write thank-yous for every bit of assistance you receive. You want your name out there, on the tip of people's tongues, in the forefront of their memory with a positive connotation. Use handwritten notes only for very short and personal thank-yous. Use plain notecards; keep it businesslike. Don't deny the fact to yourself that these thank-yous are marketing tools in disguise. Put into them the time that they are due. Be prompt—send them within 24 hours! Good jobs come from good relationships; good relationships come from goodwill. Appreciation and attention to details build goodwill.

Write thank-yous for *job interviews, lunches, information shared, job-search help, meetings, referrals,* and *interesting articles, want ads, or any other pieces of information that have been sent to you.* Also remember to write a thank-you letter when you are politely declining a job lead that has been offered to you.

MEETING LOG

Date of Meeting:

With (Name & Title):

Organization:

For Position of:

How Contact/Prospect was developed:

What did you know about the organization/person before the meeting?

   Was this sufficient information?

   If no, could you have obtained the additional information before the meeting?

What information (leads, contacts, job openings) did you learn of?

   What actions will you take to follow-up?

   Have you marked these in your appointment book / Job Search Log?

How did you conduct yourself at the meeting?

   What could you have done better?

Date Thank You letter sent_____

Figure 3-5.

SAMPLE THANK YOU LETTER AFTER A MEETING

[ON YOUR LETTERHEAD]

May 23, 1994

Ms. R.T. Wilson
Assistant Vice President
Express Export Company
65 Thruway Lane
Boston, MA   97595

Dear Ms. Wilson,

Thank you so much for your time and courtesy when meeting with me on _____.
The information you gave regarding jobs in the _____ industry was very
helpful.

Taking your suggestion, I contacted the _____Association and asked that I
be put on their mailing list. I also plan to attend their luncheon next month. Jim Jones
was extremely cordial to me over the telephone.

Although I do understand that _____ Organization does not have any job
openings in my field at this time, I was very interested in the organization's operations,
particularly after you showed me the recently remodeled shipping and receiving area.
It was easy to see why you were so proud of that department. Of course, if the hiring
situation does change at any time in the future, I would appreciate your contacting me.

Again I wish to thank you for all your assistance. I will look forward to seeing you at
next month's Association luncheon.

With best regards,

Figure 3-6.

_____

Week 3 Checklist

☐ Reviewed Job Search Log.

How many contacts have you reached this week? _____
What additional effort is needed (callbacks, visits)? _____

_____

How many new names have you identified to add to your
list? _____
How many of the contacts that you made this week achieved your
objective? _____

SAMPLE THANK YOU LETTER AFTER A REFERRAL

[ON YOUR LETTERHEAD]

May 23, 1994

Mr. Rashad Sonalli
The Import-Export Institute
5 Fuller Ave
San Francisco, CA 00988

Dear Mr. Sonalli,

It was such a pleasure speaking with you on the telephone yesterday. In such a short time you provided me with a great deal of useful information. I was not aware of the classes you held for busness people who wish to learn more about the intricacies of importing merchandise into the United States.

This morning I followed up on your suggestion to get in touch with Miss Gregori at Tesoro Shipping. She did in fact confirm that a job in my field had just opened up and she graciously agreed to meet with me next Monday.

I look forward to my interview with Miss Gregori and to receiving the current schedule of classes from you. Thank you so much for your help.

With best regards,

Figure 3-7.

☐ Reviewed Resume Log.

How many resumes have you mailed this week to "blind ads"? _____

How many resumes have you mailed this week to leads/contacts identified by you? _____

How many responses were received? _____

☐ Reviewed appointment calendar.

Have you completed all this week's follow-ups? _____

Did you schedule any follow-up activities for next week? _____

☐ Research

Have you requested/received any additional information on your targeted job market, or on possible leads or employers? _____

List: _____

_____

_____

Of the organizations that you targeted last week as possible employers, what additional information or contacts do you now have? _____

_____

_____

_____

_____

☐ Reviewed networking approach.

List new names to contact on Job Search Log: _____

_____

_____

☐ Reviewed meetings that took place this past week.

Completed the Meeting Log in notebook, with details of meeting(s).

List at least three things that you could do better at your next meeting, based on the results of the meetings that you have already participated in:

1. _____

2. _____

3. _____

☐ Sent thank-you letters to all the persons you met with, or who provided you with assistance.

☐ Planned follow-up meetings (additional information, contacts, interviews) marked in appointment book.

Remember: Keep all receipts for job-search expenses and keep them together in one place.

Week 4
The Interview

Day 22

Last week you concentrated on pursuing all the leads and contacts you had available; doing the follow-up telephone calls; arranging and going to meetings; making entries in your Job Search and Resume Logs; doing the follow-up on meetings, including making notes, analyzing the interactions at the meetings, and writing thank-you letters; and, lastly, taking heed of all the advice garnered and names recommended, in order to bring you to the point of having an actual job interview. And not just to an actual job interview, but to the real goal, a job offer and a new job within the next 68 days.

What organizations have you targeted? What skills and values have you identified on your part that you can bring to these organizations, so that they couldn't possibly spurn the opportunity to add you to their employee roster? What have you learned about these organizations that leads you to believe (1) you want to work there, and (2) they need your particular talents and skills? In other words, have you now come to know both your product and your market?[1]

The Best Applicants Don't Get the Jobs

The best *interviewers* do! In our society, and perhaps even in earlier ones (did stone-age man or woman interview his/her neighbors

---

[1]Do you have any uncertainties as to this key issue, your job objective? If you still aren't sure what your product is and who and where your markets are, go back and review Chap. 1. You *must* have a clear idea of what you want, whether full-time or part-time or one of a number of positions with similar (or different!) job descriptions and responsibilities.

when they wanted to get paintings on cave walls or the wheel fabricated?), the interview has been used as a basic recruitment and selection instrument. No viable substitute has emerged for the eye-to-eye, one-on-one sizing-up of each other, prospective employer to employee. Unfortunately, the basic skills of interviewing have been always taken for granted, and assumed to be something we are all innately capable of doing.

Can you get a job without being a good "interviewee"? The answer is yes, but the odds are low. If you're seeking a position in the federal or other levels of government, written tests are frequently the rule, but I can't think of anywhere else where you can avoid the interview as part of the process. Just as resumes seem to have become one essential job-searching requirement of the nineties, so has the interview—even if the job the applicant is pursuing doesn't require oral-presentation or communication skills. It all comes down to, "He/she looks good on paper, let's see what he/she is really like." Don't forget that curiosity is a two-way street—you should have as much interest in meeting your prospective employer and forming your opinion as they have with regard to you—but if you want the job, you must become a terrific interviewee—there's no other way.

What Is an Interview?

Think for a moment of a situation (personal or professional) you were in recently for which an interview was required. What was the purpose of the interview? Describe it in Fig. 4-1. What worked and what didn't?

If you can't think of a prior interview, turn on the TV for this brief assignment. Look at any of the talk shows. Notice the host(ess). What is he or she doing? Yes, the star is conducting interviews. If you are a devotee of these prolific talk shows, ask yourself what makes a good host(ess)? Aside from the sensationalism of some of the subject matter, consider whether the interviewer is on top of the situation. Does he/she seem to have done his/her homework on the people/subject at hand? And most importantly, is he/she an active listener?[2] What about body language? Gestures? Facial expressions? Turn down the volume, and see if you can follow the "interview" without words.

There is a story told by President Eisenhower, when he was trying to make a point about how to get people to do things your way. Put a

---

[2]An active listener maintains eye contact with (but doesn't stare at!) the speaker, makes comments showing that he/she is listening ("Yes, I see." "I understand."), and paraphrases key points back to the speaker ("I see that you feel that...." "Although you seem to..., I find that the opposite is true. For example,...").

INTERVIEW DESCRIPTION

Name an interview you participated in:

Where was this interview?

Who conducted the interview (name/title/organization)?

What was the purpose of this interview?

Was the purpose achieved?

Why or why not?

Any specifics that either positively or negatively influenced the outcome of the interview?

What was your impression of the person who interviewed you?

Figure 4-1.

piece of string on a smooth table. Try to push it to the other side of the table. You can't control the direction, can you? Now try *pulling* the string. Effective, eh? It's the same with an interview. You can't push in a direction too successfully, but you can pull—draw an interviewer in the direction you prefer—through your answers, active listening, and body language.

Try to gain a more focused idea of what an interview is, and an appreciation for its prevalence in every area of our lives (even during our moments when we wish to be entertained). Let me say by way of definition that an interview is a *conversation with a purpose.* David Letterman, Oprah Winfrey, and all the others conduct interviews so as to entertain viewers. Personnel and human resource professionals do them so as to evaluate who will be a successful and effective employee, and for a host of other job-related reasons in various other circumstances as well.

An Innate Skill?

The problem with the interview is essentially the same as with the definition of a job (as discussed in the Introduction). In fact, the problem is true with anything that is taken for granted. The interview is so common, and so much a part of our lives, that it's something we never think about. To compound the issue, it is related to a skill that is regarded as innate and that is *communication.*

The more we consider the interview and its communication aspects, the more its dynamics and complexities will be appreciated as well. First let's consider a basic communication model (Fig. 4-2). Simply put, it contains the following elements:

Sender	Environment
Receiver	Filters
Message	Noise
Medium	Feedback loop

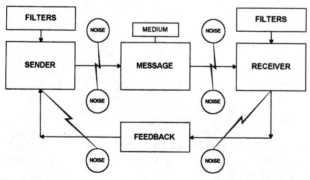

Figure 4-2.

In everyday activities, you (the sender) may be trying to tell (medium) the dry cleaner (the receiver) that the stains did not come out of your shirt as promised (the message). You may be trying to say this over the din of ringing telephones (noise) and a crowded store, with others being annoyed that you are taking so long (environment). Furthermore, the dry cleaner does not remember promising any such thing (filter), while you are getting more angry and concerned that you will be late for an important interview (filter). You do not want to hear excuses (feedback)—you want the stain out! The dry cleaner wants you to calm down and let the shirt go through the cleaning cycle again (feedback). These messages can fly back and forth with each taking turns (or not!) being the sender and receiver, until the feedback is mutually satisfactory and there is either nothing more to say or there is a perception that it's no use continuing the communication.

The Interview as Communication

In a job interview, determine who is playing the following communication roles:

The sender. Who is it, the interviewer or interviewee?

The receiver. Again, who's who?

The message. Who's trying to say what to whom?

The environment. Who controls it?

Let's say you're sitting in an office, across from a desk (the environment), being interviewed by a representative of Organization X. You, through body language, the way you are dressed, written communications (your resume and cover letter), and your speech patterns, are trying to send a message of confidence, ability, value, and sincerity in talking about a job with this organization. At the same time you are hoping that this will be it, and wanting to be liked, you wonder if the people at this organization are like the ones in your old place. The interviewer, on the other hand, may have several agendas: sincerely wants to find the best candidate for the position; wants to cut this short for a lunch appointment; knows the job is already filled, and that this is just to satisfy the person who recommended you (a courtesy interview); is interested in impressing you with his/her importance; or is a poor interviewer, and this is a fishing expedition. However, the message being sent and/or received by you may be none of these! There is a maelstrom of

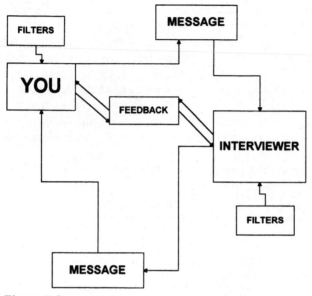

Figure 4-3.

messages being sent (overtly and subconsciously) and received, some simultaneously and some at cross-purposes. And any and all of these messages may not be correctly interpreted!

The other elements are easily understandable. (See Fig. 4-3 to gain a better understanding of the relationships among the various elements.) The *environment* is the location of the interview. *Noise* includes any distractions (sound or visual) that make it difficult to comprehend the message. *Filters* are the compendium of factors that influence the messages we are sending and receiving (prior experiences, stereotypes and prejudices, hidden agendas), and the *feedback loop* is the opportunity to make sure that the message is being understood as it is being sent (active listening[3]). Is it any wonder there's a lost art to listening? It's a lot of work.

---

[3]Another tip to help you impress others with your listening skills: become an expert at remembering names. When you are first introduced, are you listening to be certain your name is pronounced correctly, or are you intent on learning the other person's name? An easy trick, when you are introduced, is to repeat the other's name immediately: "A pleasure to meet you, Mr. Richards." Get business cards, or write the name down as soon as possible. In the course of the conversation, repeat the other person's name several times. Second, get them to talk about themselves. Third, what people like best is hearing other people say their name (correctly, of course). If you are terrible at remembering names (a distinct disadvantage), pick up a book on building memory skills and use it. Don't forget this valuable skill!

Interviews: Some Questions and Answers to Increase Your Chances for Success

There are several questions that arise with regard to interviews, and here we will ask and answer a few of them (see also Fig. 4-4), so as to help us appreciate the difficulties one may have being successful with the process.

First, *whose interview is it?* This is a key question. Let me answer it simply. Always remember to ask, even though you may have initiated and he/she agreed to the meeting, who is the buyer and who the seller? The buyer has the choice of all the applicants, the buyer has the power, and it's the buyer's interview.

If you stay focused about who has the position and the power (to at least recommend, if not outright be able to hire), while remembering that you are the one who wants the job, then you will be establishing the right perspective on this dynamic process. If you fail to keep this perspective clear, the more likely it is that the effort will fail. And the less qualified the interviewer(s) that you have to deal with, your chances for success plummet even lower.

At the same time, be careful to ensure that the interview accomplishes what you want. Make sure the objective is well defined. This is why "networking" gets such a bad reputation, because oftentimes the job seeker is encouraged to couch the real reason for the meeting (a job) in vague explanations and false pretenses.

Second, *what's more important to you, that the person who owns the interview sends the message, or receives one?* That he/she receives your message ("Hire me!") is the key. At its most basic level, the most

Figure 4-4.

important question the person conducting the interview needs to get answered is, "Do I feel confident and comfortable with the person I am interviewing?" The questions about working for this organization will be raised only if and when this gate has been passed.

Third, *is interviewing an innate skill?* One of the problems professionals who use interviews as the basic foundation of their profession sometimes face is the skepticism of people outside their profession in terms of the time and energy they give to the interview process. This perception is compounded in the workplace. "You get to *talk* all day, and you call *that* work?"

Finally, *who usually has the ultimate authority for hiring the job candidate?* The line manager. *How much training has that person had, to achieve competence in a skill (interviewing) that he/she is using to make a hiring decision?* It depends on the organization. Take a look at the human resource or personnel professional. What training did he/she get in interviewing techniques (and more to the point—in recruitment and selection interviewing techniques)? These are two separate processes, although many times the separate steps are combined for expediency or some other motive (such as that they just don't know).[4]

I Know You *Hear* Me, but Are You *Listening?*

The question of interviewing as an innate skill involves the issue of communication and the scant attention communication skills are given. There is a book[5] out that says we spend by far the greater portion of our professional lives speaking and listening, and yet the skills we spend most of our time improving in school are reading and writing (and with the proliferation of multiple-choice tests at ever-higher levels of education, for various reasons, even those skills are being deemphasized).

The confusion really comes from a general lack of appreciation of the difference between *hearing* (an innate ability, for all but those born with a hearing impairment) and *listening*—a skill that must be developed. Once hearing has been confused with listening, and the dynam-

---

[4]*Recruitment* is the personnel human resource function with the mission of finding and attracting a suitable pool of qualified candidates from which a hiring decision may be made. *Selection* is the process of identifying and hiring the most appropriate candidate from those recruited. If an organization starts to select too early, it may choose the wrong candidate, or if the offer is made and declined, then the organization may have no other candidates from which to select and therefore be faced with the prospect of starting the process all over again.

[5]*Listening: The Forgotten Skill,* by Madelyn Burley-Allen; New York: John Wiley and Sons, 1982.

ics of the interview missed as well, little wonder that interviews, even though frequently relied upon as the sole source for hiring applicants, are so often ineffective.

When engaged in any conversation, each person is involved in two processes: speaking and listening. Listening goes beyond hearing (a motor skill) and takes into consideration a process known in technical communications jargon as *decoding a message*. Even though it's technical, I can think of no better term to describe the process. Listening is a process that is multisensual. Think of the listener as a sponge who soaks in all the messages, verbal and nonverbal, that the sender is offering. The words, voice tone, body position, use of other body gestures and movements—even the choice of lighting, pictures in the view of the listener, organization of work area, position of the listener's chair (unless he/she insists upon standing)—all are elements that make up the message that the speaker wishes to convey.

To make the process all the more complex, the very choice of words, concepts, and style of speaking contributes to the current interview through the speaker. Lastly, all the life experiences that have happened to the speaker, from her earliest memories right down and through the traffic accident she was in this morning just before arrival at work, are all included in the current conversation and the presentation that she makes.

The same is true for you when it's your turn to become the speaker, but as we already saw, the process starts much earlier. So, prepare for this meeting and its complexities. Rehearse answers to questions you're anticipating. Even ponder your choice of clothes, and small-talk topics that might enhance the meeting and your image in the interviewer's mind.

We have just been discussing the listening aspects of the interview. Don't forget the speaking aspects. Make sure that when you speak you're an effective "turn taker." Speak briefly. (*Never* too long!) Don't interrupt. Look for conversational linkage; that is, each time you speak, make sure that what you say is relevant to the discussion and tied in some way to the immediately preceding comments. If the topic is new, make sure that the listener understands that you are moving on. Watch the listener's verbal and nonverbal cues to ensure that he/she has moved on.

An important question you should ask is, *what is the relationship of the interview to the job?* When reviewing and preparing for the interview, identify the relevance of the interview for the job. Will the meeting center around determining whether the skills you have are relevant or appropriate? If that is the approach, be prepared with brief but detailed answers to show your technical proficiency. If on the other hand you think you're going to be considered on the basis of your potential, then direct the interview in that direction. A major-money-center bank recruiter once mentioned to a human resource class—to stimulate a discussion—that human resource professionals tend to focus on skills and past experiences, whereas line managers tend more toward potential. She got no takers, because they all agreed. This isn't to say that her opinion may be universally applied, but be ready for both and *listen* for the cues that will make you head more in one direction rather than another. If you miss the signposts (and they sometimes are rather opaque, because the interviewer didn't read this book and isn't aware of the complexities of the interview process), you may find yourself missing the message entirely.

The complexities of the interview often are not fully appreciated by either party, and frequently are missed altogether. To begin with, let's go back to the communication model shown in Fig. 4-2. During an interview, who is the sender and who is the receiver? In the ideal situation (and if the interview is being conducted competently), the answer should be that each of the participants is engaged in both roles. The key is to know who is doing what (are you sending a message, or receiving one?), at what time, *and* to understand when the roles have changed (you're switching from one to the other). Make a total switch, and act appropriately. Hopefully this makes sense. Communication sometimes is difficult to understand in the abstract, specifically because of its conceptual side. Let me illustrate, though, what switching roles is all about.

Think about a situation where you have been invited to meet with the director of human resources for a first and "strictly exploratory" meeting. The first step to having an effective interview is for both parties to understand the purpose (objective) of the meeting. Notice that I described the meeting about to take place, but I didn't identify the person who referred to the meeting as "strictly exploratory." (Consider the source.) Nor did I mention the date when it was so described (don't forget that situations change). So at this meeting, after small talk[6] has been dispensed with, the interview should move on to more serious matters. At this point the purpose of the meeting should be agreed to. If the host of the meeting (the person who either has access to jobs directly or is considered by the person who wanted the meeting to be at least an indirect source) doesn't clarify the meeting's purpose, the guest who wanted the meeting should do so. It never hurts to communicate too much, and that's certainly true here.

---

[6]The term unfortunately is a misnomer. So-called small talk is an important element in any interpersonal interaction. It is the grease that addresses the human side of the person with whom we are dealing. You need it personally and professionally. This is discussed in greater depth in Week 7.

Consider for a moment the risk of leaving the meeting's purpose undisclosed. The problem? Each party may have different reasons for the meeting, and neither will know what the other is looking for. Let's say the host of the meeting was asked by a colleague, as a favor, to meet with you. That's a different scenario from the person who has agreed to a meeting based on the strength of the letter you sent, and the follow-up phone call that you made. In the second instance there is more likelihood that there is initial interest, or little likelihood of the host agreeing to a meeting in the first place.

Don't forget to consider "the clone factor"—an essential part of listening is trying to determine the similarities you bring to the interview with the person you are facing. It's a psychological fact that in social as well as business situations, we look for similarities whenever we interact with another individual. It could be the school, the neighborhood (where you grew up or are now living), your vehicle (conventional car, truck, van, recreational vehicle), country of origin, religion, political affiliation, outside interests, or technical expertise. And there are a bunch of others: height, weight, baldness, fashion designer, or vacation choices. The fact is that people tend to like people who are similar to them. Not only do they like them but, in study after study, the results show that in evaluating others, people always evaluate those similar to themselves with a higher rating than those who are different. The reason for mentioning those conclusions here is that you must remember that recruitment and selection interviews are subjective evaluation processes.

Four Mandatory
PreInterview Activities

1. *Determine the reason for the meeting.* Be clear in your own mind, as preparation for the meeting, that you know its objective. Even though all these interviews are to get a job, don't jump-start, but rather go one step at a time. Determine whether the meeting is to get *another interview,* to obtain a *referral or lead,* to *find out some information or get advice,* or even to *practice interviewing skills.*

If you have gotten your foot in the door and are now going to have a first meeting in the organization you were trying so desperately to gain entry to, you may only be told beforetime that the reason for the meeting will be "strictly exploratory," or worse, that the meeting will be a courtesy because no hiring is being done and you came highly referred. Well, if that's true, remind yourself before the meeting to ask, just in case the situation has changed since the meeting was arranged.

Unless there's a major change of thinking at the organization, the meeting will not (in all probability, although it's not unheard of) conclude with a job offer. Set your sights simply on getting another interview in the organization at a later date, or getting a referral. To get another interview is a valid goal of any meeting, if you subscribe to the theory behind networking.

2. *Be prepared, and on time.* Be up on the organization, the individual, and the day's news; go for a "dry run" to the location if the meeting is of prime importance, and/or if you have any doubts as to location or route. Don't be too early, and certainly *never* late. Don't forget the amenities: shake hands, greet the other by name, thank him/her for seeing you. And look and *feel* great!

3. *Rehearse.* Before the meeting, have a final study session/dress rehearsal that will prepare you for the meeting ahead. Write out portions of a script: why you have sought a meeting with this organization, what you can trade (give and get), and alternate plans if prime objective is not met. (No job—try another time? referrals? advice/comments on your letter or resume?)

4. *Build up your confidence in any and every way you can.* Look forward to the meeting. Be there with time to spare, and with all the materials you had planned to bring.

Interview Checklist

Always be sure you have with you before you leave, in written form,

The name and title of the person you are meeting (correct spelling and pronunciation)

The name of the organization, its address and location (cross streets, freeway exits, floor)

Research notes, to refer to en route or in the waiting room, particularly if you're making more than one call that day (the ideal goal— clusters of meetings—but avoid scheduling them too close together)

Salient points about what the organization does, how business has been lately, and how the department or position you are interested in fits into the organization's mission

Remember what an interview is. An interview is *a conversation with a purpose. Whose* purpose, you might ask? *Both of yours* is the best answer. You have your agenda, and the interviewer has his/hers. Both are valid and legitimate. In order to have an effective meeting, you need to meet the needs of the person conducting the interview, but as interviewee, you have certain rights as well.

How to Control the Interview

Did you happen to see David Letterman's mother interviewing Hillary Clinton at the Winter Olympics in Norway? The point is that Mrs. Letterman performed a task for which she didn't seem prepared. Interviewing is a tough enough skill to learn, without having to learn it before an international mass audience. Additionally, she seemed overwhelmed by the First Lady. That was made very apparent, for just prior to that she had been interviewed by her son (who is an astute interviewer), and she certainly took no lip from "Da-vid," which is what she calls him!

When the time came for her first interview with Mrs. Clinton, Mrs. Letterman obviously was in awe of the First Lady and didn't know what to say. Disaster was imminent, but Mrs. Clinton saved the day. As one who has certainly played the roles both of interviewer and interviewee at many times in her life, she had to be careful not to overwhelm Mrs. Letterman. Yet she was so entirely smooth and gracious while taking control of the interview that even Erma Bombeck (a national columnist) didn't seem to notice, because a few days later the columnist praised Mrs. Letterman's interviewing skills. This was a classic opportunity to see how skillfully an interviewee can gain control of an interview—frequently it's not too hard to do; what takes real skill is to do it "seamlessly," as Hillary Clinton did. But taking control is what you should do, if you determine that's what must be done. When does the interviewee have to take control of the interview? The answer is, when the situation warrants it, but generally that's *when the person facing you doesn't seem comfortable with the procedure.*

In such a situation, the more you make the interviewer feel comfortable, the more effective you will be. If the person is shy, you need to ask brief, open-ended questions, to attempt to stimulate the discussion. Perhaps he/she has just had a bad day. Remember not to take it personally. On the other hand try to listen very attentively to determine what it is that is making them feel uncomfortable—even though it may not be, it *may* be you.

There are always considerations that should be given to the different types of thinkers: the *reasoners* (sometimes call *analyticals*) and the *creatives*. Frequently they respond very positively to a person who thinks alike, and may be very negative toward those who take an opposite approach. Most of us combine both approaches to a greater or lesser degree, leaning more one way without excluding the other. Of course there are the extremists at each end. The more compatible the style of interviewer and interviewee, the easier the "fit" of the interview. The more diverse, the more difficult it is to maintain conversational symmetry. Throughout the interview, try to assess the interviewer's thinking style and to respond accordingly.

The Unprepared Interviewer.   The interviewer may be obviously unprepared, or more subtly so. Be on the lookout for either of these signs:

- The interviewer comes right out and says "I'm terribly sorry, but I forgot we were meeting today."

- He/she pretends to be prepared, but raises questions with you that are obvious signs he/she has not reviewed your resume before the meeting (another reason to try to avoid giving out resumes too early).[7] You may recognize this situation, because the interviewer is spending more time reading than what one might call "a glance." Or he/she is surprised by an answer to a question regarding your experience that is clearly mentioned on the resume.

Other Problems...

There are all types of people in this world—a book could be filled with all the unusual and surprising things that happen at interviews. Some interviewers subject you to what can only be termed a *stress interview.* They put themselves in a confrontational mode, with you as the adversary. They can project a gruff exterior and try to intimidate you, to "test your mettle." Or they can press you for an answer before you've had a chance to think. "We've got a lot of people who want this job. Take it or leave it—now! Go down to personnel to fill out the papers, and you can start tomorrow." It could be nirvana—the job offer—but why the rush? The worst thing is to take the wrong job, particularly if it's not the only one available.

Situational interviews include either a work sample or a job preview. "Let's just put you in the driver's seat and see how you handle this baby." "Why don't you answer the telephone for a while; it isn't too busy now. We can see how you like it." You may be asked to return on another day to make a presentation (these are like auditions)

---

[7]The other day I witnessed just the opposite. The interviewer was raising questions about a language ability that wasn't on the resume in front of him. Although puzzled, he asked the applicant if she had this ability. She beamed and disclosed that she had given him an earlier version of her resume but had omitted the language proficiency because she wondered about its relevance. This is an example of what happens in a positive give and take. Both individuals grow in confidence (unless of course the interviewer begins to suspect dark motives for the applicant's omission from the resume presented to him, or interprets it as a very conscientious person trying to put together the exact resume appropriate for the particular job for which they were meeting here).

to key people who will be involved in the hiring decision. Sometimes these "auditions" are disguised as lunches with the firm's partners, a dinner with a few of the department heads, or an informal event ("Join us for the game tonight. We'd like to get to know you better.") These aren't altruistic offers whose purpose is to feed and entertain you. Make no mistake: they have their microscopes out and want to examine you in detail.

...and What You Can Do about Them

These tactics, or ineptitudes, do happen. But you are not at the mercy of the meeting. Part of your preparation is to expect these wrinkles from time to time, and to hope that if it's ever one of your "off" days, the interviewer will be courteous and professional. Some tips:

- Don't get annoyed. To do so is to blow the meeting. You leave with a victory of sorts, but you don't accomplish your objective.

- Look for opportunities to subtly and gradually move the interviewer from "don't know" to "fully informed." Look for opportunities to link what the interviewer just said to items in your own background. Keep it short. As a turn-taking opportunity, try to switch from speaker to listener. When your listener's attention wanes, be quick to close your mouth.

- Test the interviewer with questions like, "Is this a good time to meet?" or "How much time do we have left?" If the interviewer asks, "Is everything okay?", be prepared to answer, "What makes you think it isn't?"

The "Tell Me about Yourself" Interviewer

This person may be astute, unprepared, or merely an incompetent who just heard somewhere that this is a great interview question. Don't take the easy route and go into a personal and lengthy version of *This is Your Life*. (Even a half-hour, the length of the old show, may seem briefer than what your life truly deserves, but save it for the day when the show is brought back....) Regardless of your conviction that this person "really wants to know," suppress it and don't give in—not now, not in any situation. If you are still unconvinced, read on.

Let me tell you what's wrong with this picture. Go back to our communication model (Fig. 4-2). If you're telling your life story, *you* are speaking. Who knows your life story? You do. But what are you there for? Not to talk about you, but rather about how to get a job in the organization the interviewer represents. How are you ever going to get that job (or any job) if all you do is talk? Remember what the process is all about and *listen*.

I heard recently about a forty-five-year-old fellow who was told to list all his accomplishments, beginning in high school. He thought he was a sharp interviewee, and asked carefully how much time he had (a half-hour). He then proceeded to ask if the interviewer was well rested, because this was going to be a boring journey. So far so good (is he trying to dissuade the interviewer from proceeding?), but what does he do next? For some strange reason, he proceeds anyway! After it's all done he thanks the interviewer for a terrific meeting; he had never before had a chance to tell someone else about his accomplishments in life starting with high school (I bet he wished he'd been able to go back even earlier). But guess what he didn't get—an invite to go back for a second meeting. What else would he have said, anyway?

How to Respond.   Refuse to bite. Get the person to elaborate. What does he/she want to identify about your past: work experiences, skills, education? You need the interviewer to disclose what he/she is concerned about, so that you won't waste his/her time.

Ask questions frequently. "Is this what you were looking for?" "Is there anything I have mentioned just now that you would like to learn more about?" If you get a strong no for an answer, watch out. Try another question that hopefully will elicit interest from the interviewer. "Before I proceed to the next area, is there anything you'd like me to emphasize that was mentioned in the resume?"

There are some more typical interviewing situations that you may run into out there. See Fig. 4-5 for some suggested ways of neutralizing the problem.

The Goal of Any Effective Interview: Sharing Control

If an interview is to be effective, control must be shared between interviewer and interviewee. No matter how bad the job market, the best interviewer is the one who makes you feel that he/she is genuinely interested in meeting with you, and that any relationship you and the organization have, beginning with this meeting, will be mutually beneficial. An effective interview is one in which there is give and take, so that both parties feel they achieve their personal objectives and are glad that the other party was conversationally competent.

INTERVIEW PROBLEM	YOUR TACTIC
Talks in concepts	Briefly demonstrate your ability to portray your thoughts abstractly as well (What is the mission of your organization?)
Rambles on	Listen carefully to identify the point - if you feel you don't have it, say so but gently
Asks yes-no (close-ended) questions	Elaborate BRIEFLY whenever you feel it important to do so. (The great thing about yes-no questions is that they frequently suggest the answer if you listen carefully. "Do you mind working overtime? ")
Interviewer constantly allows interruptions (takes telephone calls incessantly)	Suggest that perhaps this is not the best time for an interview (he/she seems so busy): "Shall we reschedule?"

Figure 4-5.

Pitfalls to Avoid

Dealing with Silence.   The Japanese have the reputation of being great negotiators. A major reason for that legendary status is that the Japanese, when they have nothing to say (or don't know what to say), remain silent. But Americans are seen as weak negotiators, because when we don't have anything to say or don't know what to say, we blow the situation by blurting out something simply to avoid the silence. Then when we lose the negotiation, we don't admit blowing by saying something foolish instead of remaining silent. To make it seem that we Americans were bested by a better negotiator, we enhance the Japanese legend by saying how great *they* were!

The same scenario applies to interviews. Remember that you can control the interview with silence. Always consider the other party when silence occurs. Is the person reading your resume and looking for the next question to ask, or does he/she want to challenge your attitudes about silence in interviews, or something else? Silence doesn't mean that something is wrong, so if you don't have something to say that relates to what preceded and adds value to the discussion, *don't say it.*

Questions and Requests You Must Be Ready For

The first questions you must be ready for are the ones asked on the employment application.[8] There is no reason to be unprepared. A copy of a typical employment application may be seen in Fig. 4-6. Use it to prepare for those questions you should always be ready to be asked, and take the time to prepare answers in advance. Review your answers to ensure that they sound right and are consistent with any replies you will provide during the interview process. The following are questions or requests for information that you always must be prepared to deal with *before* any interview.

---

[8]Will you always be asked to complete an application? The answer is no, but the more astute organizations will ask you to complete one at any time before the offer is made. The lower the position you are applying for, the more likely it is you will be asked to complete the application before they even agree to meet with you. Suggestion: When scheduling an appointment, ask to receive a copy of the application prior to the meeting, so that you can answer the questions at your convenience and think about each before responding. Some organizations insist that you complete the application in their presence. It never hurts to ask, and they may even appreciate the request as it shows that your time is important and that you are suggesting theirs is as well, and that by completing the application in advance you are helping them to more closely keep to their schedule. (There is at least one major organization out there that has been known to require all its applicants, except at the very highest levels, to complete the application directly onto a computer! Needless to say, in those situations you will have to visit the organization to complete the application.)

Figure 4-6.

Exhibit 2–2
APPLICATION FOR EMPLOYMENT

APPLICATION FOR EMPLOYMENT

Federal and state laws prohibit discrimination in employment practices on account of race, creed, color, national origin, ancestry, sex, age, marital status, veteran status or handicap.

Last Name, First Name, MI	Date

Is any additional information relative to change of name, use of an assumed name or nickname necessary to enable a check on your work record? Explain.

Present Address (Include Street, City, State and Zipcode)	Phone #

Last Previous Address (if at present address less than two years)

Are you over 17 years of age?	If under 18, do you have working papers?
Are you legally employable within the United States at the present time?	Have you ever been convicted of a crime? Give details.

Have you ever applied to this organization for a job before? If yes, when?	What brought you to this organization?
Were you ever employed by this organization?	☐ newspaper ad ☐ friend/employee ☐ employment agency ☐ on my own ☐ school ☐ other source ☐ state employ. service

Position Desired:	Salary Desired: $

Status (circle one): full/parttime/summer	Earliest start date:

Work Experience—account for all employment since high school or last ten years, whichever is less, with most recent experience first.

From Mo./Yr.	To Mo./Yr.	Employer Name, Address	Principal Duties	Salary Beg.	End	Supervisor's Name, Title, #	Reason for lvg.

Account for all unemployment since leaving school and between positions for the last ten years.

From Mo./Yr.	To Mo./Yr.	State what you were doing	Persons other than relatives who can confirm unemployment (give tel #)

(Continued)

Education Background			
Name	Address	Course of Study	Graduate? If Yes, state degree
High School:			
College/Tech/Bus Sci:		Major: Minor:	
Graduate School:		Major: Minor:	

Are you still in school? If yes, where?

How many courses are you currently taking?   Number of credits:

What is the course of study?

Special Skills (fill in only if job related):

Do you speak any foreign languages?   Read?   Write?

Personal Reference: Give the name, address and telephone number of a personal reference other than a relative or employer.

Name	Address	Telephone #

Employee Responsibility to the organization. (Please read before signing.)

As a condition of my employment, I accept the principle that the welfare of the organization depends upon the conduct and honesty of the members of the staff and upon the trust and confidence of the public. Our customers rightly expect honesty, security and confidentiality in their affairs. I therefore agree to the following:

1. I agree to give no unauthorized information relative to the accounts of the organization or its relation with others, and to discuss no matters of a confidential nature relating to the organization's affairs unless such discussion is in the necessary course of the organization's business and is in accordance with the organization's policy.

2. I also agree to inform the management of the organization, without delay, of any fraud, false entry, substantial error, embezzlement or employee misconduct, which I discover or know to have taken place in any records, property or funds of the organization, and to report any transaction or matter that seems damaging to the organization.

I acknowledge and understand that any violation of this Agreement may result in the termination of my employment.

Name   Signature   Date

Figure 4-6. (*Continued*)

1. *Current (or most recent) job, title, approximate but accurate pay,*[9] *dates of employment—month and year are sufficient.*

[9]Don't lie about your actual current pay. First, it's hard to keep things straight once you start lying—for some organizations the temptation may be to go high, for others low. And beware: any organization may request a copy of your last pay stub as a precondition for employment. I know an organization that employs more than 20,000 people that does.

Please also read before signing. If you have any questions regarding this statement, please ask them of any interviewer before signing.

In the event of my employment with this organization, I will comply with all the rules and regulations as set forth in the organization's policy manual or other communications distributed to all staff members. I understand that such employment is conditioned upon a favorable health evaluation which may include a physical examination by a doctor selected by the organization and to which I hereby assent. I further agree to complete all necessary forms in that regard. Additionally I authorize the organization to supply my employment record, in whole or in part, and in confidence, to any prospective employer, government agency, or other party, with a legal and proper interest.

I certify that all statements made by me on this application are true and complete to the best of my knowledge and that I have withheld nothing that would, if disclosed, affect this application unfavorably. I understand this falsification could result in termination of my employment. In consideration of my employment, I agree to conform to the rules and regulations of the organization. I agree that my employment and compensation can be terminated, with or without cause, and with or without notice, at any time, at the option of either the organization or myself. This is not a contract of employment. Any individual who is hired may voluntarily leave employment upon proper notice and may be terminated by the employer at any time. Any oral or written statements to the contrary are hereby expressly disavowed and should not be relied upon by any prospective or existing employee. I further understand and agree that any employment will be at the sole discretion of the organization. If accepted for employment, I agree to have my fingerprints and photograph taken for the purposes of identification and the maintenance of internal security. I understand that past employers/educational institutions and/or the military will be contacted for references. For reference purposes,

you may ☐   you may not ☐   contact my present employer.

I hereby acknowledge that I have read the above statement and understand the same.

_____
Applicant's Signature

_____
Date

Figure 4-6. *(Continued)*

2. *Name of current (or most recent) supervisor.* Don't be too open here. Ask for the reason, because you may insist on no contact, especially until after an offer has been made. (Even after an offer has been made, a mistake may be made by anyone who hasn't been told to expect the reference check, and the problem may then become yours.) The interviewing process should be a mutual uncovering process, and if they try to jump ahead, you need to protect your references until contact is

necessary. Even if they want to know because they think they know the person, still be cautious, because who knows what might be said? This is never more important than when you are still employed and are actively "shopping" for a new position.

3. *Previous employer information identical to that above.* Here, if a question is asked about the name of a supervisor, you may prefer, again, not to mention him/her, at least not at this time. In that case you could say you had several different supervisors, or that the person you reported to is no longer there (if such are the cases). The answer is an important one, so be prepared in advance to handle it.

4. *What do you know about our organization?* Even if this one isn't asked, create an opportunity somewhere during the interview to show that you have researched the organization—people love to hear about themselves and the organizations they are associated with. Watch out if the person denigrates your comments and/or the organization, and be on the alert to determine his/her agenda. It is amazing how many persons responsible for interviewing make disparaging comments about their organizations. I don't mean to say that the representative of the organization you are meeting with should take a Pollyanna approach and pretend that all is wonderful. To portray the organization in a realistic manner is most desirable; both strengths and problems should be identified, but dirty laundry, personal vendettas, or gossip should have no place in these discussions.

5. *Do you have a business card?* The farther up you go, the more it will be assumed that you have one (even if you are unemployed). If you aren't asked for one, it's up to you whether you want to offer it; but when you ask for the interviewer's card, you should be ready to give one in return. One last note: Keep the word *consultant* off the card, unless you are operating in an active consulting capacity and have other stationery that is consistent. At this point there's nothing wrong with a personal card and your home address.

Those were just some questions to get your feet wet. The interview process can be very superficial, or it can take on all the depth of a therapy session. The following are additional sample interview questions you should prepare to answer in advance.

Regarding the interviewing organization:

Why are you interviewing with us (the organization)?

What do you know about our activities/products/services?

What is our business?

What do you know about the job that we are to discuss?

What value could you add to our organization?

Basic responsibilities:

On what date did you join the organization?

What was your title?

What was your starting salary?

What were your three most important responsibilities on that job?

What important decisions or judgment calls did you have to make?

What achievements are you particularly proud of on that job?

What was the most important project you completed on that job?

How did you feel about the workload in that organization?

Communication:

How important was communication and dealing with others in that job? What role did communication play in your meeting of job goals?

What was more important on the job, written or oral communication? (Several contemporary authors on career counseling say that writing is increasingly important as you climb the career ladder.)

What was the most complex/difficult report you had to write? What made it so? How would you have improved it/made it easier to understand?

How many levels of management did you have to communicate with? What were the issues?

Have you ever had to make an unpopular decision (or an unpopular announcement)? How did you handle it?

What will your boss say when you tell him/her you are leaving?

What was the exact date you left the organization? What was the reason you left?

Were you fired? Why?

Why have you changed jobs so frequently?

Some people say that spending so much time on one job shows a lack of initiative. What's your opinion?

What have you learned from the jobs you have held?

In what ways has your job prepared you to take on greater responsibilities?

To whom did you report? (Give answer by title and function. Then be quiet, unless you want to give out the name.)

Where else are you applying, and for what positions? How long have you been in the job-search process?

What reservations do you have about working here?

What do you like best about this (prospective) job? Least?

What will your references say?

Willingness:

What personal qualities do you think will be needed to make a success of this job?

Describe an incident from your current job that demonstrates your persistence.

How do you feel about your progress to date?

Do you consider yourself successful?

How do you rank among your peers?

What have you done that you are proud of?

What do you consider your greatest strength?

Tell me about a responsibility that you have (really) enjoyed.

Tell me about a project that really got you excited.

Interpersonal skills:

Have you worked with a group like this before? What was it like? How did you handle it?

Did you work alone much on your previous job?

Tell me about a time when you needed to get an understanding of another's situation before you could get your job done. What was it like? How did you handle it? How did you get the understanding, and what problems did you encounter?

In working with new people, how do you go about getting an understanding of them? Are you able to predict their behavior based on your reading of them? Give examples.

What is your role as a group member? Tell me about a specific accomplishment you have achieved as a group member. What was your role in this?

What kinds of people did you have contact with on your previous job? What things did you do differently with each of these different types to get your job done?

What type of person do you get along with best? What types of people do you find it difficult to get along with? How do you manage to get along with these types? Tell me about a difficult situation you had with one of these people, and what happened? What did you learn from this experience?

What difficulties do you have in tolerating people with different backgrounds and interests from yours?

When you joined your last company and met the group for the first time, how did you feel? How did you get on with them?

Define *cooperation.*

How would you define a *conducive work atmosphere?* As a member of a department, how do you see your role as a team builder?

Tell me about an occasion when in difficult circumstances you pulled the team together.

Tell me about a time when a team fell apart. Why did it happen? What did you do?

Have you ever had to build motivation or team spirit with coworkers? Tell me about that situation. Why did your manager allow this situation to arise?

Organizational and management skills:

Do you deal with complex problems on your job? Tell me about a complex job you had to deal with.

What are some of the things you find difficult to do? Why do you find them difficult?

Where/to whom do you turn for help? How do you overcome the problem? Where/when does this situation most commonly arise?

What kinds of decisions are most difficult for you? Tell me about a time when a quick decision had to be made.

How do you organize and plan for major projects?

Do you set goals for yourself? Tell me about an important goal you set for yourself recently. What have you done to reach it? Tell me about a time when you failed to reach a goal.

What did you like about your last job? Dislike?

How many projects can you handle at a time?

Describe a typical day for me (in your current/past job). What problems do you normally experience in getting things done?

Describe a project that required a high amount of energy over an extended period of time. What did you do to keep your enthusiasm up? When you've a great deal of work to do that requires extra effort and time, where does your energy come from?

Tell me about a time when an emergency forced you to reschedule your workload/projects.

How do you organize yourself for day-to-day activities? How many hours a week do you find it necessary to work to get your job done?

Is it ever necessary to go above and beyond the call of duty to get your job done?

How do you plan your day? (Do you use any organizers?)

Tell me about a system of working that you have used, and what it was like. What did/didn't you like about it? Tell me about a method you've developed for handling a job. What were its strengths and weaknesses?

Tell me about a time when you came up with a new method or idea. How did you get it approved and implemented?

Can you think of a time when another idea or project was rejected? Why was it rejected, and what did you do about it?

Think of a crisis situation where things got out of control. Why did it happen, and what was your role in the chain of events?

What's the most difficult situation you have ever faced? What stress did you feel, and how did you react?

Tell me about a directive that really challenged you. How was your approach different from that of others?

What do you do when you have a great deal of work to accomplish in a short time span? How do you react? Tell me about self-improvement efforts you are currently making in this area. Tell me about a task you started but just couldn't seem to get finished. I'd be interested to hear about a time when you couldn't complete a task due to lack of support or information.

Tell me about an occasion when your performance did not live up to your expectations.

Can you recall a time when you went back to a failed project to give it another shot? Why did you do it, and what happened?

What have you done to become more effective in your position?

How long will it take you to make a contribution?

Why aren't you earning more at your age?

What can *you* do for us that someone else cannot do? Why should I hire *you*?

How long will you stay with our company?

Define *challenge* for me.

Are you willing to go where the company sends you? What are your reservations about living/working here? How would working evenings affect you? Travel?

What books have you read that had the greatest effect on your business life? Why and how have they changed you?

How do you define a *successful career?* Is this the type of career you want for yourself?

Manageability:

How do you take direction? Tell me about a time when your manager was in a rush and didn't have time for niceties.

What are some of the things about which you and your boss disagreed?

What are some of the things your boss did that you disliked? (Watch out for "Tell me more"!)

In what areas could your boss have done a better job?

I would be interested to hear about an occasion when your idea or work was criticized.

How well do you feel your boss rated your performance?

How did your boss get the best out of you? How did you get the best out of your boss?

What do you think of your current boss?

Describe the best manager you've ever had. What made him or her stand out? How did you interact with this manager? (Have you ever had a woman for a boss?) How did you react to feedback, instructions, and criticism he/she gave you?

Describe the worst manager you've ever had.

Would you like to have your boss's job?

Tell me about a situation when people were making emotional decisions about your project. What happened, and how did you handle it?

Tell me about a situation when there were objections to your ideas. What did you do to bring management around to your point of view? If I were to say "your solution is too expensive," what would you say?

Have you ever been in a situation where people overruled you, or wouldn't let you get a word in edgewise? How were you able to get your point across?

For what have you been most frequently criticized?

How do your work habits change when your boss is absent? What problems do you experience when working alone?

How do the work habits of others change when the boss is absent or away? Tell me about a time when there was a decision to be made, and the boss was absent or away.

What do you do when there is a decision to be made and no procedure for it exists?

Give me an example of a time when you were told *no*. What did you do in response?

Tell me about an occasion when you felt it necessary to convince your department to change a procedure. How did you go about it? Whose feathers got ruffled?

If you could have made one constructive suggestion to management, what would it have been?

Recall for me a time when those around you were not being as honest or direct as they should have been. What did you do?

What is your general impression of your last company?

Give me an example of a time when management had to change a plan or approach that you were committed to. How did you feel, and how did you explain the change to your people?

Tell me about yourself. What are your pet hates? Why do you feel this way? What situations give rise to these?

When was the last time you got *really* angry? What caused it?

What kinds of rewards are most satisfying to you?

In what ways did your manager contribute to your decision to leave your last job?

In closing:

Are you interested in the job?

What interests you most about it? Least?

How long will it take you to make a contribution?

Should you be offered the job, how long would it take for you to come to a decision?

Why should I offer you this job?

What can you do for us that someone else cannot do?

What special characteristics should I consider about you as a person?

Questions You Don't Have to Answer (and Shouldn't Be Asked)

Employment laws now provide a lot of protection to the applicant so that he/she doesn't have to answer questions that aren't job-related. Unfortunately that doesn't mean you won't be asked non-job-related (and often illegal) questions. What do you do in those circumstances? First, regardless of your willingness to answer, stay calm and hold back any hostile emotions you may be feeling. Then determine how you wish to handle the situation. Is the person asking the question just a poor interviewer who doesn't know what to ask, and who, when he/she ran out of legal questions, moved over to the illegal ones out of desperation? Or is there malice intended (trying to screen out certain types)?

Illegal questions may also be a very gray area. "Do you have children?" is one of those gray-area questions. The supervisor may be asking the question of everyone (male and female) to determine flexibility with working hours, or just trying—believe it or not—to make the person comfortable. It is a poor example of small talk, looking to find similarities. Before answering, probe to find the reason behind the question. "I'm curious as to why you're interested." (They may be trying to boast of their profamily outlook.) You certainly are within your rights to be direct and say "You know that's an illegal question, and I refuse to answer it." The children question is totally irrelevant for the job interview. A more properly worded question and the same question that may get the answer is "Our workloads are constantly fluctuating. There are times during peak periods when we ask all our staff to stay for a seventeen-day period, with no time off, and ten-hour days are the norm at the same time. Will that pose a problem for you, with any commitments you currently have?"

The interviewer should keep all lines of inquiry directly and specifically related to the job. Any questions regarding gender, race, color, religion, national origin, disabilities, Vietnam-era veteran status, or age (40 years of age and over) are forbidden by federal law (except in very specific instances). Protection against certain lines of inquiry exists under state and local laws as well. Questions as to sexual preference is one, and smoking (very rarely) is another.

Remember too that you may voluntarily provide any of this information if you feel it may help your chances. For example, if you do have no outside commitments, including children, or if you do have children, volunteer the fact that they have never been an obstacle to your employment in the past and you don't anticipate that they will be now. If this is the case, by all means say so, because the interviewer may be trying valiantly to find out this information in a legal manner.

The Questions You *Must* Ask

Curiosity is a two-way street. The organization and the interviewer should expect to provide you with information. However, if you're dealing primarily with someone who is intent only on filling in the organization's/interviewer's informational gaps, speak up and ask for needed information. You're not idly trying to impress them with how interested you are (it can't hurt to project interest and enthusiasm). Certain information will affect how you proceed further with the interview. If you feel comfortable pull out a pad and pen to take short notes. (There are those who recommend against it.) Chances are, the interviewer is writing away too!

Here are the questions you *must* ask:

What's the reason for this opening at this time? How long have you been seeking to fill this position?

You (or the recruiter) have given me an overview of the job. Would you please give me more details about the position? What will the primary responsibilities initially be? What major projects are under consideration? What do you view as being an adequate breaking-in period?

Once I start, what will my top priority be?

What do you see as the major challenges of the position? What are the incumbent's prime problems or achievements?

Who will my primary contacts be within the organization? Outside?

On what basis will we (your potential supervisors and department heads) be dealing with each other? Do they prefer the prearranged meeting, formal written agenda, and set time each week? The opposite, or something in between? How often will we meet?

What issues do you expect to be brought to my attention?

On what basis will my performance be evaluated? Pay increases recommended?

How is the organization doing (how's business)? What is its major challenge at this time?

Are you satisfied with your own career progress with this organization? Are you excited about prospects for the future?

What will I like most about my position? Like least?

Knowing what you do about the organization, are there any other areas or problems, organizationally, that I should know about?

Who will make the hiring decision? What is the next step? When will I hear from you?

May I have an annual report/sales brochure/employee newsletter?

Before leaving, remember to ask for a business card. It guarantees you'll have accurate details about the person you're dealing with, when you need to contact him/her. It also shows that you are familiar with the way things are done. Even if he/she doesn't have one, you knew enough to ask, and the very fact that you expected someone at that level to have a card says that you respect them.

Totally Incompetent Interviewers: What to Do about Them

A most frustrating situation is the one you have to face when you realize that the person you must deal with—and who holds your fate in his/her hands—is an incompetent interviewer. In such a situation, the first thing to do is to be sure that your assessment is correct. Maybe his/her style is different, just a way of throwing the applicant off guard.

The telltale signs in this area may be spotted if the person you are facing is

Unprepared

Lacks the ability to link one question with another, or to probe and follow up throughout the meeting

Asks illegal questions

Seems distracted

Makes unrelated statements

Answers the phone continuously

Never looks at you directly (assuming that is not owing to a cultural difference)

Keeps you waiting more than five minutes

Does all the talking

If the person you are meeting with fits all or any of the characteristics mentioned above, he or she may be less than competent as an interviewer.[10]

So what do you do about it? First, you recognize the situation for what it is. Second, you determine how to make the best of the situation. Whatever you do, do not give up, or let up! Treat the person with respect throughout the meeting, and try to mirror their apparent preferences. If the interviewer is not listening for answers, why give long ones? If he/she seems concerned about the time, comment that you will be brief, or volunteer to meet at a more suitable time.

The most frustratingly incompetent interviewer is the one who never lets you talk. You are truly frustrated, because you have thoroughly prepared yourself for this meeting and now you want to show it. That, after all, is the purpose of your being there. But keep in mind that less is more in these situations, and that the less you say the more likely you are to get the job. I personally know of one instance that occurred at a major global bank. The applicant was totally frustrated by the incompetent interviewer, who was a member of senior management and controlled his destiny to get a job in an organization he truly wanted to join. He had been through at least three interviews, and this might be his last. After the meeting, when asked how it had gone, he complained that he had never had a chance during their hour together to say anything, because this fellow did all the talking. Guess what? He was immediately offered the job. He couldn't understand it, but upon reflection he said that he did recall analyzing the meeting as it was occurring. To make the best of the situation, the applicant had consciously encouraged the fellow to continue and had never betrayed his annoyance.[11]

Five Secrets to Winning Interviews

Here are five "keys to life" that must be considered closely if you want to be effective in any interview situation.

---

[10]If the interviewer is in personnel and will not be your immediate supervisor, go with the flow as best you can. However, if this marathon talker is the one you will be directly working for or with, raise the question with yourself, "How could I work every day with this person? Could I accomplish the objectives of my job and be effective, with this person as my immediate supervisor?"

[11]Just to bring you up to date, the fellow accepted the position; reported to this member of senior management for the four years that he was there; enjoyed the organization, but left because of this reporting relationship. After he left, the incompetent interviewer was finally dismissed, although his incompetency as an interviewer was not the issue.

1. *Watch out for the answers you provide to questions that aren't asked.* The best interviewers are those who get answers to questions they never had to ask. Recall that Americans are especially uncomfortable with silence. Our tendency is to fill any silence with noise. Since during an interview our options are limited, if one person isn't saying something the other usually will, even if doing so provides answers to questions that have yet to be asked. Beware of suddenly finding yourself in uncharted territory; breaking new ground and answering unasked questions can turn an interview in entirely the wrong direction.

2. *Never stop practicing effective interview techniques, and interview at every chance you get.* Do it on planes boats, trains, buses, restaurants, parks, museums, and bars—wherever you feel comfortable, and wherever you strike up an acquaintance.

3. *Become skilled in the craft of active listening.* The better you listen to all of the messages any and every person sends (verbal and nonverbal), the more effective you will be throughout any interview process.

4. *Enjoy it!* An interview is always an opportunity to learn, meet someone new, and grow from the experience. Accept it, and look forward to it.

5. *Don't take it personally when you don't win them all.* If you don't get to the next level because you were screened out after an interview, accept that as a fact of life. Always analyze the situation to determine what worked and what didn't, and to decide how you will be more effective next time.

Follow-up

The aftermath of every interview calls for follow-up. The follow-up should be on two levels. The first level should include debriefing, assessment, and evaluation, while the second level should embrace the action plan that was agreed to at the meeting.

The Debriefing

If you were referred for an interview by someone, that person frequently will be interested in meeting with you, or at least in speaking to you after the meeting has taken place. This person may be your initial company contact, a source, or a recruiter from a contingency or retainer placement firm.

You can use the format included in the Interview Journal (Fig. 4-7), which is a variation of the previously used Meeting Log (Fig. 3-5). It's

INTERVIEW JOURNAL

Date of interview _____

Purpose:(exploratory, recruitment, selection, hire)

_____

Organization _____

Locations_____ Department:_____

Name and titles of interviewers:_____

_____

Time of meeting; scheduled _____ actual start _____ actual finish _____

Approximate length of real interview time (total time minus any interruptions)

_____

Describe the setting _____

Describe characteristics of the person(s) you met with _____

_____

_____

_____

List some memorable questions he/she asked _____

_____

_____

Describe yourself during the meeting _____

_____

_____

Figure 4-7.

important that you record the facts (who you saw, where, for what purpose; what information was gleaned from the meeting), as well as the subjective parts: the environment, what "filters" were in play, and any other occurrences worth recalling. This information will come in handy should you come back for a second interview, or interview for

What worked for you? _____

_____

What did you do that you could improve upon? _____

_____

What is the next step? _____

When?_____

On a scale of 0 (lowest) to 10 (highest) what is your feeling of the success of the

meeting?_____

(For a first meeting, what are the chances of a second meeting?)

_____

Comments_____

_____

_____

_____

Source of this contact/referral:_____

Figure 4-7. (*Continued*)

another similar position elsewhere, as well as when it's time to write your follow-up letter.

Sample Interview Follow-up Letters.   You have at least one and possibly two types of follow-up letters to write within the next 24 hours. The first, a thank-you *cum* sales letter, is to the person(s) who gave you the interviews. Send one to each person that you spoke extensively with (not just someone you were introduced to briefly) during the entire interview.

Second, if this interview was the result of a referral or a lead provided by someone else, give them a thank-you also. Unless the source was a very close friend who wants to hear every moment of your experience, or a recruiter who sent you out on the interview (the first might love a telephone call, and the second will expect one), write them a letter within 24 hours.

Some additional sample-thank you letters to be sent out after an interview may be seen in Figs. 4-8 and 4-9. (Also refer back to Fig. 3-6.)

SAMPLE FOLLOW-UP
THANK YOU LETTER AFTER INTERVIEW

[ON YOUR LETTERHEAD]
February 5, 1994

Mrs. Alicia Wethers
Vice President and Controller
Health Care America
550 Second Street
Rockford, Illinois 61110

Dear Mrs. Wethers,

The visit with you yesterday and the tour of Health Care America's facilities was extremely enjoyable and informative. I was particularly taken with the state of the art patient accounting system recently brought on line. You are understandably anxious that this particular area be under the daily guidance of someone as committed as you are to detail and performance.

Although I have worked in several smaller health care institutions, the last one was brought from the dark ages of manual accounting into the daylight and future of computers while I was the department manager. This task required the support of the entire staff to ensure its success. Like yourself, I was excited beyond measure when the system went "live" and management was finally able to keep a closer tab on costs, patient services, and billing.

With all the effort that has gone into setting up your patient accounting department, I appreciate your wanting to ensure its continued success. I believe that I am that person because of my love of the work itself and my prior achievements in that area. With all that said, I look forward to hearing from you in the next two weeks to discuss the position of department head of patient accounting further.

Wishing you continued success,

Figure 4-8.

Week 4 Checklist

☐ Considered the various elements of interviews.

☐ Reviewed the dynamics of communication and interviews.

☐ Assembled all the items on Interview Checklist prior to each interview.

☐ Either reviewed sample application form, or completed actual application to be submitted to the organization.

SAMPLE FOLLOW-UP
THANK YOU LETTER AFTER INTERVIEW

[ON YOUR LETTERHEAD]

February 5, 1994

Mr. Randy Garcia
President
Health Care America
550 Second Street
Rockford, Illinois 61110

Dear Mr. Garcia,

Thank you so much for spending time and meeting with me yesterday. Alicia Wethers gave me an enthusiastic and informed tour of your entire facility but my personal highlight was the visit to the new patient accounting area. To see such a state-of-the-art system humming with life and being an integral part of the entire facilities management information system was very exciting.

As I mentioned, my efforts to modernize the accounting system at my former employer without a drastic loss of jobs (it was a major local employer) was featured in the *Cleveland Press*. One reason I was able to be so successful in that project was the support of management combined with the local community's response to a major job training effort at local community colleges. Everyone wanted to learn to work on the computers! I have enclosed a copy of the article for your files.

I wish to thank you for your words of encouragement concerning my job search. If I can answer any questions raised by the enclosed article, please contact me.

Warmest regards,

Figure 4-9.

☐ Reviewed the list of Sample Interview questions, and developed answers for each; rehearsed responses prior to interview.

☐ Completed Interview Journal after the interview.

☐ Wrote and mailed thank-you letters after the interview (within 24 hours).

Week 5

Headhunters

Fact and Fiction

Day 29

Already Week 5! What have you to show for it? As I have said many times before, feel good about all the "seeds" you have planted previously, because now they should be demonstrating results—a bit at a time. Remember, you were taking this in a logical sequence of steps. First you were targeting potential employers and performing research, as a salesperson would any sales prospect. Second, you had to evaluate the potential of each. Third, you made the contact with a letter. Fourth, you followed up with a phone call. Fifth, you had the meeting to explore job possibilities together. Then there was the recruitment interview, and next the selection process. Depending on the time cycle of each of these avenues of pursuit, you are somewhere along the route by now with different stages of development on several prospects.

Go ahead and feel guilty if there are no results to show, if you haven't been as focused as you should have been in the previous four weeks. If you fell out for just a week you are probably only a week behind, but if you got distracted for a longer period of time, now is definitely the time to rally and make up for lost time, to generate interest and get some meetings to take place.

By this time too you should be getting unexpected calls, because of either indirect referrals or some other twists of fate that have arisen as the word has spread that you are looking for a job. Don't stay home, though, waiting for the phone to ring. Go out and continue to make things happen. The calls and meetings you are getting now are due to past efforts. You need to sustain those efforts now, to generate more leads for the upcoming weeks just in case the efforts to date have been slow in yielding results.

What if you have been "focused, focused, focused," and you still have nothing to show for it? *Nothing*—no meetings, no phone calls, everything is "dead." What's going on? See if either of these possible solutions applies to you. First, keep putting in the research time, but on the Effort Analysis Worksheet (Fig. 5-1), monitor your activities to

Figure 5-1.

EFFORT ANALYSIS WORKSHEET

DATE COMPLETED : _____

ANALYSIS BEING PERFORMED FOR THE PERIOD _____ to _____

    Number of days covered _____.

    Average number of hours spent each day during this period _____.

    Typical day started at _____ ended at _____. Deduct any breaks _____.

    Then determine total daily average hours _____.

PART ONE: Quantitative Analysis (The job search is a "numbers game." How many people are you reaching?)

<u>SECTION A - SCORECARD</u>

A. The number of telephone calls I made last week _____

   The number of meetings I arranged from those calls: ____

B. The number of letters I wrote last week: ____

   The number of meetings arranged from those letters ____

C. The number of people I contacted/met during the past week (not already included in A and B

   above. ____

D. Any other developing situations worth noting? _____

_____

_____

_____

_____

E. Success Ratio: (Here, to determine how successful you have been, divide the number of meetings by the number of telephone calls made and do the same for meetings generated from letters sent.) The ratio can never be greater than one (1.0) - the point at which all calls for example would lead to a meeting.

Success Ratio for telephone calls is _____   Success Ratio for letters is _____

(Continued)

F. Once the data has been provided, then you, the applicant, must determine first if the volume of phone calls, letters, and contacts is sufficient to generate the serious leads and contacts to find potential job openings. If the calls, letters and/or contacts are too few, you need to identify opportunities and a course of action for generating a higher number on a daily basis.

G. In an effort to increase my calls and letter generation, I plan to do the following and will start today:

1. _____

2. _____

3. _____

4. _____

　　　(If you haven't identified at least four opportunities and/or action plans to build volume, feel guilty; then go back and try again. Don't take a break until this exercise is completed.)

PART TWO: Qualitative Analysis (It is not enough to have the quantities of contacts but they must be quality contacts. There is one simple standard to measure quality: Do they have the ability to get you job leads?)

A. In this section of the worksheet, taking each category in Part One into consideration, analyze each call and letter to determine the "quality" of the contact. Fill in each box so that the information is here and readily available. Include the source of the contact and the outcome to see which ones lead to any additional steps. Once you consider what took place, if anything, then evaluate the quality of the contact, using A for top prospects, B for those having a lot of potential at this point, C for those with some potential but not very promising, and D for those that were a complete waste of time.

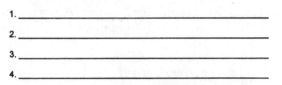

TELEPHONE CONTACTS

DATE	NAME	ORGANIZATION	TITLE	PHONE #	SOURCE	OUTCOME	RATING

Figure 5-1. (Continued)

ensure that you're being great in the effort category, even if low (nonexistent) in results to this point. It may be a slow time cycle you are dealing with. Don't assume that, though; analyze your efforts. Remember what I said earlier: the job-search process doesn't necessarily link a successful job search with *dedicated* effort. The successful job search is the result of *effective* job-search efforts. Hard work never guarantees success; effective performance does.

LETTER CONTACTS

DATE	NAME	ORGANIZATION	TITLE	PHONE #	SOURCE	OUTCOME	RATING

DIRECT CONTACTS
(People met at seminars, workshops, traveling and other places)

DATE	NAME	ORGANIZATION	TITLE	PHONE #	SOURCE	OUTCOME	RATING

Figure 5-1. *(Continued)*

Second, analyze your approach to determine what is causing the lack of results. If warranted, restructure your activities and try some different approaches. For instance, if you have been looking for a position in the not-for-profit sector, consider a change of focus to either the profit or the governmental sector. Also consider taking a temporary job while you continue the job search, to take some pressure off and build some confidence. Lastly, consider some tactics that you may not have tried before. Examples might include going into business for

B. Now identify 5 sources from each category that have been effective contacts and determine
what you can do to concentrate more on those sources. If your lists in A indicate you have yet
to identify **5 effective sources** in each category, then revisit this exercise each week while
keeping careful records of each call made, letter sent, and other direct contact made.

Telephone contacts

1. _____

2. _____

3. _____

4. _____

5. _____

Letter contacts

1. _____

2. _____

3. _____

4. _____

5. _____

Other direct contacts

1. _____

2. _____

3. _____

4. _____

5. _____

Figure 5-1. *(Continued)*

yourself by starting a business, or buying an established organization
either on the market or through a franchise arrangement. One more
new tactic to consider is using "headhunters."

The "Glamour" Side of Recruiting: The "Headhunters"

Some would argue that making use of the "headhunting" industry is
the most obvious route to take when considering a job change. But just
to scare you a little bit, note that a recent *Wall Street Journal* article stated that for the last year figures were reported, more than *11 million*
resumes were sent by applicants to recruiters in response to only
around *14,000* positions available through the executive recruiting
firms nationwide that participated in the survey.

The key reason for including this chapter in the book is to gain a greater understanding of the role of the recruiting industry, so that when you wish to consider using their services you will be able to determine whether they will be helpful in your search for a job.

Employment Agencies and Executive Recruiters: Two Different Things

Before you decide whether you will seek the services of an executive recruiter or an employment agency, first try to understand what is their primary source of income. The role they could play in your job search effort will then be more discernible.

The term *headhunter* is known all over the world. In fact once, coming back from a vacation in the Caribbean, an executive recruiter was talking to the person next to him on the plane. The fellow who initiated the conversation started off by asking if the executive recruiter would mind if he practiced his very poor English on him. The recruiter said absolutely not, and the conversation commenced. The more the fellow tried to speak English, the more the recruiter realized that his English comprehension was barely elementary. With much difficulty, the man then asked "What do you do?" Making a great effort to be understood, the recruiter went to great lengths in a very slow, detailed explanation. The other fellow perked up and said in his broken, highly accented English, "Oh, you're a headhunter." This really proves the point that the term is known the world over, not just in the English-speaking countries.

To take what is definitely a minority stand, I think the expression is a terrible one. The implication is that recruiters look for bodies (or more specifically, body *parts*), and the image definitely is dehumanizing. Nonetheless, it's a popular and standard one, and therefore will be used here.

The point is that the term really clouds the issue. Even though the term *headhunter* is the one most commonly used for everyone in the recruiting profession, actually there are different types of recruiters. The biggest distinction is between the executive recruiting firm and the employment agency. Let's consider each in turn, because your appreciation of the difference between the two will make it clearer what each is and is not able to do for you.

Initially, *headhunter* was a term confined to those senior members of the executive recruiting profession who made the biggest deals by working for corporate clients at the highest echelons of the largest organizations to fill key posts—both as executives and board members. The more attractive, visible, and glamorous the headhunter's reputation became, the more his/her title and legend spread. Now it's difficult to find anyone in the recruiting industry who wouldn't use the title to describe himself/herself. Actually the term only confuses things, for there are two approaches that organizations use when they try to fill a position with a recruiting firm's help. Either an executive recruiting firm or an employment agency will be sought out. As I said, it's important to know the differences, because you will certainly be treated differently by each, regardless of approach, though both are to be considered separate parts of the recruiting industry. For what a recruiter can do for you refer to Fig. 5-2.

The Executive Recruiting (Executive Search) Firm

The executive recruiting firm (often called an *executive search* firm) that is truly an executive recruiting firm is *retained* by an organizational

WHAT A RECRUITER CAN DO FOR YOU

Practice interview skills.
Critique interview techniques.
Critique resume.*
Identify potential job prospects.
Develop a contact for networking.
Sharpen job focus.
Practice telephone courtesy skills.
Practice active-listening skills.
Strengthen self-evaluation skills.
Practice meeting skills.
Indicate follow-up practices.
Demonstrate courtesy and etiquette.
Improve pathfinding skills.
Force you to get dressed and get out.
Locate job openings.
Unlock doors to interviews.
Lead job offers to you.

AND MAY ALSO

Waste your time.
Sap your energy.
Pigeonhole you into existing job orders.
Never call you back.
Deflate your ego.
Lead you on.
Distract you from your focus.

* Watch out for retainer recruiters (heavy hitting "Headhunters")
They are not known for their patience for free advice. If you are
in need of resume advice, tread carefully.

Figure 5-2.

client in the governmental, not-for-profit, or profit sectors, in an effort to fill a key post. The process is a formal one that commences with a face-to-face meeting. A written proposal for the organization from the recruiting firm then follows. To say that the recruiting firm serves in a consulting capacity would be accurate, because in this situation the firm making the most successful proposal will be retained by the client to meet a specific need (namely to fill one or more specific positions) and will serve the client for the duration of the search.

The search firm promises to conduct a thorough search of the field of relevant professionals. To avoid a conflict of interest they promise not to "raid" current clients' organizations. The impression they convey is that they will conduct a complete and thorough search to unearth candidates. Implied in this promise is the uniqueness of the search; therefore any earlier rejected candidates from other assignments may be rejected as damaged goods. They go out looking for candidates anew each time, regardless of all the prior searches, so previously received resumes are for the most part ignored.

The client is expected to pay the search firm for retaining them—whether or not a successful candidate is found. In other words, they get paid regardless of whether a candidate is hired, and even if the search is canceled for any reason including a withdrawal of the vacancy. A portion of the fee (usually a third) is expected to be paid upfront, usually when the proposal is accepted. At that point the engagement begins and the search commences. A second payment is expected midway through the search, and the final settlement is made usually at the end of the second or beginning of the third month, regardless of the progress level of the assignment.

Fees usually are a percentage of salary, and while that percentage is negotiable it generally runs around 35 to 38 percent of the anticipated first-year salary of the successful candidate, plus all expenses that the search firm incurs. Those expenses can be quite sizable, and include advertising, transportation, and hotel and meal expenses, as well as office overhead expenses (to include but not be limited to phone calls and copying). Sometimes the fee may be a flat amount rather than a percentage (although expenses are always additional), as was the case when IBM used a search firm when looking for a chairman. Actually in their unique situation they hired two firms; in the event that either firm had a conflict of interest with current clients, IBM would be assured that the entire field would be searched. It has been reported by the press that in that case the fee was a flat $1 million, to be shared equally by both of the firms IBM had retained.

The key to the success of the great recruiters is their ability to obtain retainer assignments. No specific personnel or human resources training or background or experience is necessary. Those out front who actually do the calls to get the assignments need to be effective sales-persons. If they don't get the business, it doesn't matter how good they are in finding candidates. Those responsible for "research"—that is, those doing the background work to identify likely candidates for the applicant pool—are usually bright people who are not able to command high salaries elsewhere, and therefore are willing to take these assignments to learn the business. Such jobs also allow the freedom for individuals to pursue other interests; for example, a single parent can make the phone inquiries from home while caring for his/her child; or an actor can create a schedule of making calls at off hours while still being available for daytime auditions.[1]

The tone set by the caller is elitist and exclusive. This alternative is presented to the client as a one-stop solution. The executive recruiter has an organization staffed by senior professionals with worldly contacts in the field (in addition to the research staff), and each time called upon the search firm will conduct a customized campaign to find the ideal candidate.

Because of the freshness of each search, it is not to be accomplished quickly. Usually a timetable is established, with an anticipated completion date of 90 days. The rationale is that a start-from-scratch search will require time to comb the relevant marketplace, screen candidates, and conduct thorough reference checks. Additionally, because of the retention of the search firm for this assignment, the client need not worry about considering alternative recruiting sources. In fact, if anyone surfaces directly with the client, the client will ask the search firm to follow up as part of its search effort.

The search firm usually guarantees the successful placement for six months of the person who finally is offered and accepts the job. The guarantee period may vary, but six months is quite common. There was a legal search firm in New York City that for several years had guaranteed its placements for one year, but when a placed attorney passed away well into the seventh month of employment, the firm reduced its guarantee to six months! What the guarantee means is that the search firm will try to replace the candidate hired at no additional fee other than expenses.

What would make an organization agree to the terms mentioned above that are demanded by the search firm? What does this all mean to you and your job-search effort?

First, there continues to be a bias that the best candidates for any search assignments are those who a) are not looking for work (reminds one of dating, doesn't it?), and b) are currently working. From time to

[1]It is not out of the question to consider recruiting a career opportunity or training/apprenticeship program for one looking for a job.

time there will appear an article in the newspaper, or a person on TV, announcing that the "stigma" of being unemployed and searching for a job has been removed, due to the long and widespread period of unemployment we have been experiencing here in the United States. The point here is that if you have never had a job, or are currently out of one, you most likely will not be considered a potential candidate. Needless to say, the same goes for career-changers.

Another key point to remember is that you should never contact the executive recruiter. If you contact a recruiter, he (or perhaps she, although it is still very much an old-boy profession, with women more likely to be found in the support roles—administration, research, and other junior positions) usually will be put off. The very fact that you are initiating the contact means that you are looking for a job—hence the automatic disqualification. Talk about a "Catch 22"!

What If an Executive Recruiter Contacts You

First, you must determine whether the "executive recruiter" is truly an executive recruiter. Frequently any person engaged by a recruiting firm or employment agency refers to himself or herself as a "headhunter." Watch out; usually this is a tip that the caller is working for an employment agency. Second, keep in mind that the caller usually is the one doing the preliminary screenings, so don't get too excited. They're trying to build a pool from which the senior recruiter who deals with the client organization will be able to screen the most appropriate candidates. That's the very first step in the process. The next step will be setting up a meeting so that they may view you and make a more detailed determination regarding your continuing viability, on a person-by-person basis and in comparison to the market and whomever else they have been able to identify.

Take copious notes of the phone conversation. Get details, such as the name of the person, phone and fax numbers, organization he/she is representing, and whatever specific detail about the client and the position that the caller is willing to share. At this point the client will not have been identified, but use your probing skills to try to narrow down the organizations that could be the likely client. Be at your phone and interview best, because if you aren't this may be the last you'll hear from them. The caller will go through the motions of asking you to send your resume. If they want it faxed, that's usually a good sign, but they may only be requesting this because it's the thing to do (pretend urgency). Remember that each and every step going forward will only mean more work for you, so the more you qualify the caller up-front, the more you will be able to determine whether the person at the other end of the phone truly has the ability to land you a job. If he/she can, then all the time you spend will be a wise invest-ment, so be enthusiastic. If he/she can't be of help, be polite and cour-teous, because you may underestimate him/her otherwise. Even if this isn't the appropriate position for you, you will be remembered for your professional demeanor, and should another assignment develop that is more to your liking and ability, the time spent on the first dis-cussion will be of benefit then.

Lastly, get closure. Ask quite specifically what to expect as a next step. Who will call? When will that be, and would the caller like to meet? If the response is even a weak yes, try to get a meeting with the caller and another more senior person in the firm responsible for this assignment. If finding a mutually convenient time proves difficult, suggest that you meet early or late in the day, in the evening or even on the weekend. Sound cooperative and enthusiastic, but not difficult or desperate.

Be flattered. Whatever you talk about, do not under any circum-stances ask, "How did you get my name?" To create and sustain a feel-ing of attractiveness, you must convey the impression that you get these calls all the time and agree to pursue only a select few, if any at all. You are "impressed with your [the caller's] approach, and intrigued at the description of [the organization] and [the position portrayed]."

Get off the phone as quickly as possible. You want the caller to be left hungry to find out more about you. If all is disclosed over the phone, or if you're better in person, aim to get that chance. Impress, but don't overwhelm (either positively or negatively). You are a busy person who has a full schedule: "Can't talk now, but let me know what you need, and when, and you'll have it." Then make sure you produce as promised. Consider the telephone conversation in its entirety as a preselection/screening interview, and the entire presenta-tion as a quiz. So pay attention to what you're saying, and don't deliv-er anything (e.g., resume, work sample) in a less than perfect format. You need to impress this gatekeeper if you're going to get anywhere with this lead.

Try to subtly determine the source of the referral. The more you can identify sources, the better idea you will have of which of your activi-ties are producing results. Since this is Week 5, it's especially impor-tant to start pulling this information together, if you haven't done so already. Another reason for identifying the source of the referral is to consider thanking the person. It's amazing how many times people, especially during the search effort, forget the little courtesies.

After you get off the phone with the recruiter, log in the call (using the Job Search Log in Fig. 1-19) and write down all the details (using the Meeting Log in Fig. 3-5). Then research the organization and the recruiter. The place to start is with the *Directory of Executive Recruiters*. It is a comprehensive listing of both contingency and retainer firms that is updated on an annual basis. If they're listed, then you know the firm has been around at least for a while. If they aren't listed, mention it when you meet, to see what they say.

Research the organization by visiting it and evaluating its premises. Try to determine by asking them directly (or by asking around with your contacts, or both) who their primary client base is. What is their reputation in the marketplace, both from the client as well as the candidate side? Also, try to find out if they have a reputation for "shopping" resumes, i.e., for doing their own "mass" mailings in the hope that at least one will "hit," even though they have neither a job assignment nor the applicant's permission to share the resume. Lastly, evaluate your contact person for the organization, because he/she will be your primary contact. Determine quickly what their role will be with you (researcher, preliminary screener, or what level of recruiter?). You need to know if the position they are discussing with you is for their client or someone else's. You should know how long this person has been in the business, and what they did before they joined this organization.

The Employment or Contingency Agency

When you get a call from someone at an employment agency (as opposed to a search firm), he or she may say that he/she is a "headhunter." For starters, they usually give their professional name, which is invariably a simple, friendly name, generally composed of two monosyllables (John Jones, Kate James). Some even have different names for different assignments! If the executive search firm is looked upon as the prestigious side of the recruiting industry, the employment agency is seen as the seamier one. The businesses are small, and more often than not the counselors are paid on a commission basis. Here accounts are needed, and the goal is to get people to work in the business who have contacts and who know how to sell. This is unique selling, because it takes a double sale to complete the transaction. First the recruiter must convince the organizational client to use his/her services and give his agency job orders to fill. Then the recruiter must convince the applicant to first go for the interview to be considered for the job, and later to take the job when offered.

The first "sale" involves getting job orders. Without them, the counselor[2] has no jobs to fill. Even when he/she has job orders, they may not be very meaningful. Organizations are contacted by the counselor or designated sales representative. If the agency is big enough it may have both, but usually, because of the nature of the sale, the recruiter is responsible both for getting the job orders and for making the placement, because he/she knows both the organization trying to fill the position and the applicants.

Two characteristics of this industry complicate the nature of the process further:

1. Contact is most frequently made by phone, and the way to get the job order is through the placement of a lot of calls on a regular basis.

2. There is a great deal of uncertainty as to the recipient of the call for a job order. It could be the person responsible (at some level, including clericals) for human resources or a specialist for one of their activities, such as recruiting, or it could be someone in any other department. At this point it takes a knowledgeable person on the selling end to determine whether the person on the other end of the phone is

   Authorized. The person dealing with the recruiter must have the authority in his/her organization to "make a deal" by giving out job orders to agencies that will be getting a fee for their services.

   Knowledgeable. The person taking the call must understand a) that the agency is providing a service and b) the rules for engagement in dealing with that agency.

   Professional. The person in the organization must be realistic about the organization's need, and determine whether this sales call will be a service that the organization will take seriously, rather than just casually agree to accept resumes because they have nothing to lose, aren't assertive, and don't want to say no to anyone.

What all of this means is that the counselors must know their clients; the job order may be real, or late (they are just about to make an offer,

---

[2]In referring to people who work in contingency recruiting firms (employment agencies), I will use both the terms *recruiter* and *counselor*. You may meet either, when dealing with these organizations. A recruiter is one who actively solicits applicants, using a variety of sources and contacts to find suitable candidates. The counselor, on the other hand, defines his/her job more in *terms* of waiting for the applicants to find him/her. If you are dealing with a counselor, he/she will most likely be sales-oriented, but frequently will lack the nuances and sophistication of an experienced recruiter. Titles, however, are to be monitored carefully, because the titles may be nonnegotiable; the counselor may be a very talented and effective recruiter, but the persons responsible for dispensing the titles may be unwilling to give the appropriate one.

but if someone "really knocks their socks off"), or nonexistent ("we aren't interested in hiring right now, but let's see what the quality is out there; we might change our minds").

Job order in hand, the recruiter must then locate the candidate, and do it before the client learns of this candidate ahead of anyone else. Then the recruiter must convince the targeted person to be interested in the position. In other words, the recruiter must make a second sale[3] or he/she will not get paid.

It gets a little more complicated on this end. Usually there's intensive competition in this industry. In addition to everything just mentioned, there are a couple of other characteristics that must be considered. First, the fee is more negotiable than on the search side, and second, there is more of a feeling of informality, which is further complicated by the fact that not everyone understands the rules of engagement. For instance, what comprises the "contract"? What is the basis for getting paid? And who is responsible for paying the agency: the job applicant or the organizational client?

Until the most recent recession, it frequently had been estimated that because of the explosive growth of the seventies and eighties, the number of employment agencies exceeded 600 in New York City alone. Consider the job market from a buyer's and a seller's view. Who each is. Think of the buyers as the employers with the jobs. They needed to attract the talent to sustain growth in the labor-intensive industries located in the New York City area. Think of the sellers as the people looking for a job. There were less of them than the markets demanded, so for them it was a dream come true. The situation was such that employers in several industries were even taking a page out of the professional baseball player's book, as they began to offer "sign-on" bonuses. As long as the economy was growing and there were more jobs available than applicants, it was a seller's dream but a buyer's nightmare.

An industry that thrived on just this scenario was the recruiting industry. The selling point they were able to make to employers was that it was so tough to find candidates that the best thing for the buyers to do was to pay a fee. For their part, the recruiters, especially on the contingency side of the street, needed job orders, so they put a premium on those who could deliver job orders and identified the key skill to be sales. The problem with this arrangement is that the recruiting industry—on both sides of the street—didn't give enough attention to the unique features of the industry. (For example, it is one of the rare instances in life where it is necessary to have a double sale

---

[3]In an executive search, the firm would get paid whether or not the position was filled, and regardless of the origin of the referral.

before any deal is ever made.) Not only is it enough for the recruiter to identify business opportunities by identifying organizational clients willing to pay the fee, but once the job order has been obtained it is necessary for the recruiter to convince the applicant to go on the interview ("strictly exploratory" is the phrase still heard today).[4]

Keep in mind that during the past several years of turmoil in the job markets, there has been major change in the recruiting industry both for retainer and contingency firms. The resulting fallout has left fewer players, and the ones who have stayed are the ones who were able to stay in business in a shrinking, increasingly competitive environment. For most locations and industries, it has turned around into a buyer's market, with many sellers offering their products.

Even though the numbers are certainly still big enough to support normal curve aggregations (you have a small number of great, many average, and a few poor recruiters and counselors), the remaining organizations are a cut above the "make a quick buck" operators that populated the industry in the past. So your chances of dealing with a reputable firm have vastly improved.

Should You Pay a Fee to an Employment Agency? In some communities today, there are instances where the employment agency still obtains the fee from the applicant. In your community, when you're dealing with a contingency firm, don't take anything for granted, including the fee arrangements. Ask up-front, "Who pays the fee?" Make sure having the applicant pay the fee isn't a practice of any agency that you consider asking to help you find a job—unless of course you see the value of paying it.[5] When people are desperate, they are more likely to accept terms, including a fee payment. If the relationship deteriorates because you're losing patience and not finding a job after a fee has been paid, the energy expended, and the time and additional costs involved to reach a settlement with the organization with which you have the dispute, will be an even bigger drain and cause more headaches than if you had put the time and effort into the job search directly through other sources.

---

[4]All the more difficult, because the organization client frequently will send the recruiter on a wild goose chase, because the client doesn't understand the requests made by their own department managers. Or even if the applicant is an appropriate candidate for a real opening, very often the HR "gatekeeper" will impose rigid demands. These demands will require the applicant to go on the interview at great risk to himself/herself, because the people interviewing want to see the candidates only between 9 and 5, with no interviews between 12 and 1.

[5]If you are interested in paying a fee to have someone help you to find a job, research the organization before you commit to any fee. My suggestion—*never* pay to get a job. *Never!*

What All This Should Mean to *You*

Remember the complicated business for what it is and why they are reaching out to you. The key to keep in mind is who is paying them. Obviously not you (I say "obviously," because I strongly recommend that you do not pay an agency in the hope of finding a job). However, when the organization is providing a service to you, especially when in-depth counseling is involved, perhaps a fee is appropriate.[6]

Remember that any fees should be worked out in advance and documented in writing, no matter how close the relationship. By putting the agreement in writing, you are seeing on paper exactly what you are being offered for the fee that you are paying. Under no circumstances is it in your interest for the organization to get a fee both from the organizational client and from you.

Whenever you deal with an executive search firm or employment agency, know the recruiting organization, and most importantly your contact in it. Go to the offices and evaluate their sophistication, professionalism, and decor. The better you get to know the organization, the more likely it is that you will get a feel for the type of client it serves. Consider the contacts you have made. What recruiting firms were used? What was their level of satisfaction?

Don't be put off—if you know the client, make the contact with the organizational decision maker. I know a woman who was not presented to a banking client of one of the largest and most prestigious of executive recruiting firms. The fellow who was responsible for this particular search assignment had been known to her on the client side (in plain English, she had been the one authorized to retain him when she'd had a previous job in personnel). She learned that he had this assignment, so she contacted him. He was serving as the gatekeeper, but she felt he was unwilling to present her as a candidate. She identified a person in the organization as a possible entry point, because she knew him slightly. Once the introduction had been made, she got the job, and with absolutely no help from the executive recruiter!

In all fairness to the executive recruiter, oftentimes the recruiters—and this is so frequently true for the people responsible for the recruiting function in the personnel department of any organization as well—are unwilling to send candidates as applicants because they feel they will be rejected by the corporate client. But needless to say they are not always right.

---

[6]Career counseling firms will charge you a fee because that is the service they provide and *you* are the client. Outplacement firms are career counseling firms that accept a fee from the organization and the employee sent becomes the client.

Other Types of Recruiters

Contract recruiters are becoming increasingly important figures in this changing job landscape. More and more organizations are becoming more dependent on a "supplemental" work force—that is, a group of people who are able to give any organization the support it needs as business requires it. This approach is also considered a *temp* (for temporary) approach. The term *contract* is used, because the recruiting firm works under contract to provide an employee to the client organization. The advantage to the employer, in addition to an immediate supply of workers whenever required, is the reduced cost in terms of no severance, COBRA, or pension when the assignment ends. For its service through the contract, the agency is frequently able to give as much as a 50 percent mark-up. For that fee, the employee will be on the contract agency's payroll while on assignment to the client organization, and therefore all taxes and other mandatory contributions are paid through the agency as well.

Contract agencies had been the hangout in times past of the free spirits of the organizational world. Oftentimes actors and dancers would work through these agencies, as a loose opportunity to obtain extra cash when the need was there. Also, it was easy while working to get time off to audition whenever the need arose.

Technical recruiters can be found on both the permanent and temp sides. They may also be working on a retainer or contingency basis.

Consultants also are available as recruiters, whether for a fee or as a favor to their clients. Regardless of the circumstances, if a consultant gives you a lead for a job, he/she will be hoping that you will be able to return the favor.

Recognize that other opportunities for temporary or even permanent work may come from employee leasing and outsourcing firms. An *employee leasing* firm is one that leases employees to organizations that wish to keep these people off their payroll, either because the assignment is temporary or because they feel that their costs are higher when they carry these people on their payroll. The organization may be very generous with its benefits, for example, whereas the leasing firm would be much more cost-conscious.

Outsourcing firms are another form of nontraditional arrangement. Here, an organization determines that it is cheaper to go outside for services that don't fall within the organization's area of expertise. For years, payroll has been an outsourcing activity before the term was ever used. Outsourcing firms frequently are in a growth mode, because organizations seem to continue to be interested in reducing their own head counts. In employee-leasing arrangements, the outsourcing arrangement depends on the organization's ability to continue to retain the contracts it already has, while trying to get others.

Networking with Recruiters

Find the opportunity to network with recruiters. The telephone book or any business meeting are both fertile hunting grounds. *The Directory of Executive Recruiters* provides a breakdown of both contingency and retainer recruiting firms throughout the United States. The book is quite helpful, too, because there are breakdowns both by industry and by geographical location.

It's a small world out there, and to know recruiters is helpful. Let me share a story with you to emphasize that last point. There was a fellow who badly wanted to work for the Japanese. One day not too long ago, he learned that a position was available. Not knowing anyone inside the organization to contact, he called two recruiters from two different organizations to see if either would be willing to make overtures for him and market him to the organization. He called two recruiters simply because the first was unable to help him at all. The second got him the interview, and subsequently the job. Moral: Keep the recruiting pipeline open!

The Key to Finding the Right Recruiter(s)

As with all aspects of your job search, to find the right recruiter you must perform vigorous research. A strong recruiter who has the jobs will certainly help you to find a job.

The Directory of Executive Recruiters is a good place to start. Find the firms that recruit for your industry and occupation. Be mindful of territorial considerations as well. In addition, *The Job Hunters Sourcebook: A Gale Career Guide* lists recruiters that specialize in particular fields, such as health care, information systems, and human resources.

The local newspapers are another source, because you'll identify firms that are advertising. If they are, then they can *afford* to—and of course they have positions available—why else run the ad?

Talk to any of your prior employers. If they use recruiting firms, see if someone in Personnel/Human Resources will make an introduction.

However you find recruiters, try to meet with them at their offices. It's good to know there really is an organization out there, and you need to "kick the tires" and to see how they treat their own people.

How to Get the Recruiters to Work for You

In the story told regarding the applicant and the Japanese firm, it's easy to see the role a recruiter can play if he/she is going to truly work for you—and well he/she should, since he/she needs you to collect a fee.

What you need to determine is the function the recruiter will play in helping you to find a job. Consider the following:

1. *What will make the recruiter want to spend time with you?* Put another way, how will he/she see that time with you represents money in the pocket? And why should he/she spend time with you rather than with someone else?

2. *Is the recruiter competent?* Groucho Marx used to say he never trusted any club that would let him be a member. Should you be suspicious that with all the people out there looking for a job, a recruiter is interested in spending time with *you?* Don't think *nice* here, think *self-interest.* You should be spending time with a recruiter only if there is a good chance that that time is likely to lead to results. Don't worry that you're thinking self-interest, because the recruiter is too. Quite frankly, there is nothing wrong with that.

3. *Ask the right questions.* Interview the recruiter as well as the firm. The firm is only as good as the recruiter that you have access to, but the reverse is not necessarily true, so remember both sides. Find out who the firm's clients are; they may not share specific names with you, but they should tell you at least by industry and hopefully with a little more description (for example, big companies or small, by size of staff and revenues). Also consider the recruiting firm's own length of time in business and the size of their staff. Where does the name come from? Who are the principals? How long has your recruiter been there? Where did he/she come from before this? How about the ambiance of the office? Is the receptionist a bear (i.e., unbearable)? What did the other applicants look like? Has your confidence been compromised by the treatment you've received, the forms they've made you complete, or the time they've made you wait? Do you know anyone who has obtained a job through their services? If you have any HR friends, do you know any that have used (or even know the reputation of) the firm? How do they get paid? What tests do they give? What about the quality of those tests? Are they up to date? Relevant? Appropriate?

Determine on what basis you will agree to proceed. What will the method of follow-up entail? Does he/she plan to circulate your resume without sharing the organization's name with you? If you want control over resume distribution, now is the time to learn the recruiter's opinion. Many just send them out, and it's gotten even worse since the invention of the fax machine.

Then follow up. Don't be the person who could win the Guinness World Record for persistence with recruiters, for spending all the time you can calling for follow-up because it seems they never return your phone calls. Don't forget that more often than not the only reason the recruiter isn't calling is that he/she has nothing to report or, worse than that, only bad news (the client isn't interested in meeting with you, or there's no position available, contrary to what the recruiter and you had been led to believe). Any recruiter who spends his/her time seeking out potential candidates could easily occupy his/her time handling follow-up calls from people whose credentials they consider too weak to be worthy of serious consideration. Better to save the calls for a live and real assignment, and make sure the recruiter can reach you in a timely manner if need be. Remember that their goal and basic requirement is to fill each position with the candidate most suitable to the *client*.

Tips on How to Size up Recruiters Quickly, and Steer Clear of the Losers

Listen carefully when you call a recruiting firm, to determine their level of professionalism. Does whoever answers your call put you on hold and never come back on? Do they seem to find it impossible to pronounce your name correctly? Are they pleasant on the phone? When you call at different times (for example, really early in the morning, like 7:30 A.M., and after 5:00 P.M.), what kind of treatment do you get? Do they seem eager for your business?

Visit the firm. This goes for executive recruiters and contingency firms alike. How's the location? What's the building like? How are the facilities themselves? What's on the walls—artwork, or testimonials, or pictures of the firm's principals with a variety of political figures, or underwater photography? Russell Reynolds, one of the premier executive recruiting firms, has antique French taxi horns throughout their offices. They say that in the firm's earlier years, every time a placement was made the horns were blown.

How is the reception area? The receptionist? What's the reading material like? The better firms have current periodicals that in several instances are a reflection of the industries their clients come from (a banking recruiting firm will have financial publications, a Pacific Rim recruiter may have Australian and Asian periodicals). How high is the level of confidentiality? How do they respect your time and show appreciative awareness of your presence? Are applicants all forced to stay in a public area, or are they discreetly greeted and given a quiet area in which to wait and be met? Are interviews conducted in a quiet area, or in a work area reminiscent of the vast public areas of nineteenth-century offices? What are the application and tests like? Does the application seem current? Is it in compliance with the law? Does it ask illegal questions? (For instance, "What year did you graduate from high school?" "Have you ever been arrested?")

If a PC test is given, does the equipment seem well cared for? Are the tests relevant and appropriate, or are all candidates given the same "find the misspelled word" test, regardless of applicant and level of position applied for? Do those responsible for giving the tests know how to administer them? Are they helpful and polite to the applicants? Are they timely in completing the process? If any refreshments are offered, what is the condition of the area reserved for refreshments? What about printed information—do they have any to offer you? What image are they trying to cater to: the subway masses, the Wall Street elite, or something in between? How is their correspondence with you? Is stationery altered (e.g., old name/address stamped out and new name/address provided), and quality of printed work acceptable? Lastly, do they deliver what they promise? Do they call you back as they said they would? Will they give your resume to a client only after obtaining your approval? Do they check (and later provide) references?

Traps to Avoid

Regardless of whether you are attempting to establish a relationship with a contingency firm or an executive recruiter, be careful to make a meaningful contact and develop an effective relationship. Keep the following tips in mind.

Avoid the trainee at the search firm. Unless you're already known in your particular field, you need to get past the researcher more often than not. The researcher is the advance person who uncovers those candidates who later are screened out by the recruiter. Don't write anyone off, but try to diplomatically determine which person knows the client. That's the key person to seek out, because he/she will be the one to determine if you pass muster. The sooner you find that person, the sooner you either have a "go" or know for sure that it's a no-go.

On the contingency side, you also need to evaluate your contact to determine their experience level. How to do that? Simple: do a little interviewing yourself. Most people love to talk about themselves, and recruiters are no different. Especially on the contingency side, recruiters are always under the gun to produce. A friendly face that shows respect and appreciation for the work he or she does will pay dividends, and help the person you are dealing with to remember you.

But keep in mind that making yourself endearing should be an effort reserved for those from whom job openings can actually be obtained. Test the recruiter out quickly, to determine if he/she has the same values as you, and to determine whether he/she will be able to find you a job. Watch out for recruiters that are doing no advertising— either they have a tight network, or no assignments. Listen to ensure that they are listening to themselves—if not, they display poor interviewing and sales skills, which are necessary to their function.

Lastly, consider longevity. How long has he/she been with this firm? You don't want to have a different recruiter turning over in the same firm every two months.

Week 5 Checklist

☐ Completed Effort Analysis Worksheet.

☐ Using the form below, list the recruiters you have been in touch with. Mark each with an "R" for retainer firm, and "C" for a contingency agency, and "?" for don't know.

RECRUITER'S NAME AND CONTACT PERSON	TYPE (R, C, OR ?)	SUBMITTED RESUME (DATE)	MET WITH RECRUITER (DATE)	SENT ON INTERVIEW (DATE AND EMPLOYER)

☐ Which of the above recruiters appears to be most helpful and effective?

_____

Why? _____

_____

Week 6
Working Smarter, Not Harder

Or, Effort Doesn't Guarantee Success

Day 36

At this point in the search, where are you? Thirty-five days have passed, and if your earlier efforts have been effective, you are now seeing the results of your search. Your daily activities should include

A steady flurry of telephone calls, both as follow-up for meetings that have already taken place, follow-ups for resumes mailed, and initial telephone calls to prospects in search of additional meetings

Telephone calls (returns) from those whose calls you may have missed regarding meetings, resumes

Telephone calls from the "grapevine," those who have heard about you and your job search

Looking for new opportunities to identify possible leads and contacts

Attending periodic luncheons, association meetings, seminars related to your chosen field

Writing thank-you notes after meetings, assistance, and referrals

Writing marketing letters to new targeted organizations, as well as to friends and referrals

Updating your Meeting Journal, Job Search Log, Resume Log, and Monthly Cash Budget

All of the above activities are designed to help you to focus on your objective, obtaining a job within the next 54 days! However, whether you deem your job search on target[1] or not so far (unless you live in an area devoid of humankind), you probably have also been party to some of these not-so-helpful activities:

- Telephone calls (or worse, drop-in visits) from folks who heard that you "were home" and might be available to chat for a while (everyone else is "old news," and you *are* home!)

- Visits from neighbors who either saw or heard you at home, and thought that since you were there, would you mind looking out for the UPS delivery truck while they run down to the market?

- A telephone call from a distant relative who wanted to give you a lengthy pep talk. ("Talk about job searches, my friend looked for 17 years to find just the right job! You've got plenty of time.")

- Requests from immediate family members to "let the plumber in," or "drop this off at the post office," or "meet the school bus"

- Any actual or near medical emergency, involving anyone who knows you at all

Given the fact that you don't wish to appear totally heartless (and you do live next to or even with some of these people), on those occasions where you feel you must become involved in the problem, take a consulting approach. Try not to take on the problem as your own, but rather point the person in the right direction and then follow up with a brief telephone call to ensure that all went as planned. This approach will accomplish several things:

You're solving the problem, so you're practicing creative problem-solving skills.

You're performing as a consultant by intervening in a situation whereby the person you dealt with can learn how to solve the problem should it arise again.

You're sending a signal to the person requesting assistance, "I am concerned, and I will help you this time, but in such a way that *you*

---

[1]On the average, you should expect to schedule at least one meeting each week. These may be exploratory or job interviews, or even just to look for leads. You cannot locate your new job by staying at home and just answering classified ads! You should also aim to contact by telephone or letter five new names daily, to request a lead, referral, job opening, or interview.

can learn what to do next time." The second message they will get is that you value your time (you are "working" not just "at" home) and you are not available for every problem.

You will feel more in control. By saying no, you reinforce the idea that you control what you do and don't do with your time. Additionally, your confidence is bolstered by the fact that you have stayed focused on your objective.

Taking Stock: What Has Worked, and What Hasn't

In the normal course of employment, most employees are given periodic performance appraisals. These reviews are made in the interest of providing specific feedback and highlighting those areas where further improvement is called for. Your situation is no different. There is a management approach called Management by Objective (MBO), in which employees list specific goals they are to be held accountable for ($50,000 sales level each month, 2 percent increase in productivity, etc.). You already have an objective—a new job—but checking out your performance along the way is essential to keeping a well-focused and action-oriented job campaign on the right track.

Use the Week 6 Review Worksheet (Fig. 6-1) to see how well you're really doing. Refer to your Job Search and Resume Logs, your appointment book and journals, to see how active and effective you have been over these past five weeks. "What have you been doing?" Have you been spending too much time answering ads, and not enough reaching out to friends? Now, look over Fig. 6-1 and give your efforts an honest appraisal.

Has the trend been toward "doing more," "doing less," or "doing about the same" each week?

_____

Can you identify any reason/distractions that may have had a negative influence on your time and efforts over the past five weeks? _____

_____

What have you done, or what can you do, to eliminate or minimize the problem?

_____

Figure 6-1.

WEEK 6 REVIEW WORKSHEET
Refer to your Job Search and Resume Logs, as well as your Appointment Calendar to determine your activity levels

	WEEK 1	WEEK 2	WEEK 3	WEEK 4	WEEK 5
NUMBER OF RESUMES SENT					
*TO BLIND ADS					
*TO REFERRALS					
NUMBER OF MARKETING LETTERS SENT					
* SENT COLD					
* REFERRALS					
NUMBER OF TELEPHONE CALLS MADE					
* COLD CALLS					
* REFERRALS					
NUMBER OF MEETINGS SET UP					
NUMBER OF JOB INTERVIEWS SET UP					
NUMBER OF OFFERS RECEIVED					

(Continued)

How many situations are now "pending" (require another telephone call, a letter, a visit)? _____

Have you scheduled these activities for today? _____ This week? _____ Later? _____

REVIEW WORKSHEET, PART 2

How effective have your various approaches been? To be deemed
effective, your objective (get a lead, interview) must have been met.

	WEEK 1	WEEK 2	WEEK 3	WEEK 4	WEEK 5
RESUME RESPONSES	X	X	X	X	X
*TO BLIND ADS					
*TO REFERRALS					
RESPONSES TO MARKETING LETTERS	X	X	X	X	X
* SENT COLD					
* REFERRALS					
RESPONSES TO TELEPHONE CALLS	X	X	X	X	X
* COLD CALLS					
* REFERRALS					

EFFECTIVENESS ANALYSIS

In the past five weeks (Weeks 1-5) of your job search, what generated the
greatest responses?

Resumes mailed to blind ads or to referrals?_____

Marketing letters mailed "cold" or to referrals?_____

Telephone calls made "cold" or to referrals?_____

Figure 6-1. (*Continued*)

Which of these "pending items requires action from you: new stationery, business cards, book or magazine you're waiting for,
etc. _____

_____

_____

Are all of these noted in your appointment book for follow-up actions (e.g., date stationery is to be ready)? _____ If not, do so now.

Are any items time-sensitive (listing of job openings, publication date of magazine or journal, day person you are trying to reach returns from trip)? _____ Be certain these are clearly noted in your appointment book.

What has been the most effective contact method (resumes mailed, marketing letters, telephone calls) in obtaining your stated objective? _____

_____

_____

Why do you think this has been so effective (your skill, the people you've been contacting, or a combination thereof)? _____

_____

After this eye-opening look at your performance, is there anything that you'll do differently[2] this week? _____

_____

At the end of each week you should review your past week's efforts, with the same eye for keeping up with all the details and making notes for what to do the following week.

Working Hard, or Hardly Working?

Think back to your last job. Remember the coffee breaks, personal telephone calls, meetings without a purpose, gathering around the proverbial "water cooler"? What about the late nights, bringing work home, deadlines?

How does your present workday stack up against your prior work habits? Today, log in your activities for each time period of your work day on the daily planner (Fig. 6-2).

Now, has this been a typical workday for you, or did you do more because you were more conscious of time passing while filling out the hourly log? If the latter is the case, perhaps you should utilize an hourly planner to keep track of where the time goes each day. If this was pretty much how you spend your days, are you using all the time

_____

[2]If it ain't broke, don't fix it! If you have a successful strategy, keep it up just as long as it works.

8:00	
8:30	
9:00	
9:30	
10:00	
10:30	
11:00	
11:30	
12:00	
12:30	
1:00	
1:30	
2:00	
2:30	
3:00	
3:30	
4:00	
4:30	
5:00	
5:30	
6:00	

Figure 6-2. Daily planner.

available and using it wisely? As I said before, working for yourself may be the hardest work you have ever done. Give yourself a performance rating on the form shown in Fig. 6-3. Be specific, and cite details.

Recent Achievements

Earlier, in Week 1, you completed an Achievement Worksheet (Fig. 1-5). You were asked to list 10 accomplishments that you were proud of, and to determine what skills had assisted you in reaching your goals.

The time is right for repeating the exercise, but only looking at your accomplishments of the past five weeks! This isn't an easy process, as progress may be subtle. As you have seen by the exercises that you've completed so far this week, working hard and working smart may yield results in time. And then there are those golden moments of inspiration! Following the instructions given next, fill out Achievement Worksheet #2 (Fig. 6-4).

First, address your successes. The toughest part may be for you to recognize your accomplishments. That's why I strongly suggest you

PERSONAL EVALUATION FORM

Date completed:_____Period being evaluated: From_____ to_____.

Regarding efforts displayed by me, I would say that I:

_____**Works hard.** Specifically I put in ____ hours per day, ____ days per week.

Exceptions:_____

_____**Works effectively.** I have accomplished the following results to date:

Number of face-to-face meetings: Completed_____ scheduled_____.

Number of offers obtained: Orally_____ in writing_____.

Number of future offers anticipated as of today_____.

List below all offers made or anticipated by the date of the offer (received or

anticipated); the name of the organization; the name and title of person making the

offer; the name of the positon being offered; the title, location, salary range or amount

associated with the offer:

_____

_____

_____

_____

_____

_____**Could do more.** I could use my time more wisely, as follows:

_____

_____

_____**Needs improvement.** My specific goals for improvement this week is:

_____

Figure 6-3.

consider them first. Too often we dwell on our losses, and then they become self-fulfilling prophecies. You need to identify what specifically has worked, so that you can duplicate those successes. You must become a *conscious competent*—i.e., know exactly what you are doing that works.

ACHIEVEMENT WORKSHEET #2

**List at least 10 achievements you have made during your job campaign.
Identify the skill(s) that helped you reach your goal.**

ACHIEVEMENTS	SKILLS
1	
2	
3	
4	
5	
6	
7	
8	
9	
10	

Figure 6-4.

Give yourself credit for the basics of a job campaign. Have you worked fully, every/almost every business day, in trying to find a job? That in itself (given all the potential time-wasters lurking out there) is an achievement.

Have you identified and followed up on leads? Turned any possibles into probables? Have you been diligent in doing follow-up telephone calls and thank-you letters? What accomplishments have you made in tracking down resources to network with? Have you actually attended any meetings or scheduled any in the near future with new networking resources? What other sources have you identified for further research?

Look ahead. What do you have "in the works" in terms of contacts, leads, prospects, meetings, interviews? All this took your constant focused effort to achieve. Glance through your logs, journal, and appointment book to identify those instances where you set yourself a goal or objective and met it. How many people did you have to go through (call-screeners) to get the name of the one person who would be most helpful? Give yourself credit. Just because you have not reached your final objective—a new job—doesn't mean you haven't been successful and made progress. It's as important to analyze why something went *right* as to be the Monday morning quarterback when things went wrong.

Second, can you pick out any specific skills that you used to achieve these recent successes? For example, did you use your college reunion to network with both fellow classmates and academic staff? Very creative. Have you been getting good response to your marketing letters? Writing skills are very positive. These are the skills that you should push forward on.

And on the Down Side...

Not every letter gets a response. Not every person you contact is helpful. Not every telephone call is returned promptly (if at all). There are bound to be instances where you wish the tape could be rewound and you could do the entire interaction over. What could or would (there is a difference) you have done differently?

Recently a colleague in human resources related an incident that addresses just this type of situation. A woman was trying to separate herself from internships (frequently poor or nonpaying jobs couched as entry-level or apprenticeships in the not-for-profit sector) by finding a paying job in her sports marketing field. She had gotten a great contact through a professor colleague at the university where she'd obtained her degree.

Despite the long distance she had to travel to meet this contact, she took the entire process so seriously that she took the entire day off to make the meeting. In spite of all this effort and a strong desire on her part, the recruiter felt the day had been wasted. It happened at the start of her interview. "What do you know about our organization?" His organization was highly visible, and there was no excuse for the woman to have had no information and be unprepared for that basic question.

The most frustrating part about the whole interview is that it left them *both* wounded. He could not ignore the flustered effect on her whole presence that permeated the meeting. He also felt annoyed with himself for disarming her; he had thought it a perfect question to draw her out. She, of course, realized that she had come in poorly prepared, and panic set in.

If, when she returned home and turned her mind back to the day's events, she had analyzed the situation (similar to the exercise that you will do next) and realized her mistake, she could have determined what steps she might take to prevent this from occurring ever again.

Now it's your turn. Hopefully there have been no major faux pas, but if so you lived through it, and now you can learn from it. Using the Near Misses Worksheet (Fig. 6-5), list those times when things did not go quite as you wished. Missed telephone calls. Ineffective cover letter. Nervous telephone calls. Sweaty palms and lots of "umm's" in a meeting. Not having *any* answer, not to mention the right one. Totally wrong appearance for a meeting. Mispronouncing a key person's name, or forgetting it. Missing a meeting entirely.

Use as many lines as you need—no one else will read it. Next to each, write down exactly why you think things didn't turn out as you wished. For example, you were very nervous for an interview, and your voice betrayed your anxiety; why? Did the interviewer look like your old homeroom teacher? (Oh, nightmare!) Or did you get confused at the last minute in the reception area, as to what job opening you were interviewing for at which organization?

Now comes even a harder part: realizing what part you had (if any) in the problem. You can't control all the outcomes of every event. However, some problems are of our own making, to a greater or lesser extent. There is a wisdom that comes from experience and that teaches us what we can and cannot change; the wisdom comes in recognizing the difference. Perhaps your nervousness at the interview was due to the manner in which the interview was conducted (myriad interruptions, so you couldn't hold your train of thought; condescending interviewer), or perhaps you were nervous simply because interviews make you nervous.

List on the worksheet what you *might* have done differently if you *could* have. You can only deal with those variables that are under your control. After you have listed all the suggestions for do-overs, ask yourself whether you have also identified any areas (telephone skills, your resume, marketing techniques) that need work. List them:

1. _____

2. _____

NEAR MISSES WORKSHEET

**List at least 10 incidents that you feel did not go as you wished during
your job search and what you would do differently if you could.**

What went wrong	What you would do differently
1	
2	
3	
4	
5	
6	
7	
8	
9	
10	

Figure 6-5.

3. _____

4. _____

5. _____

Working Smarter, Starting Today

Assuming that you're not perfect, and that you've identified at least one area that needs improvement, how are you to go about improving? What are the skills needed for a successful job campaign? Sales skills, product development, organizational skills, and marketing—identify opportunities in each of these categories for immediate improvement. For starters, and for no additional monetary expense, a trip to the library may yield a bunch of books and videos on all of these topics. Don't plan a self-help film festival, though; be ruthless in determining the quality of each approach, and jot down tips that you will need to immediately practice.

Sales Skills

How are you meeting prospective "buyers," through the mail, in person, or over the telephone? Each technique is used to a different degree of effectiveness, and each requires a different approach.

Letters.   These must be concise, attention-getting, and geared specifically to the reader and the purpose of the meeting. Do yours fit the bill? If not, Figs. 6-6 and 6-7 show you two sample marketing letters.

The Telephone.   How are your telephone skills? It's easy to ignore a letter, but not so someone on the telephone. If you want to stand out from the crowd, make recruiters get to know you by religiously doing follow-up telephone calls. A prospective employer on the other end of the telephone is somewhat a captive audience, so you must quickly make it clear that you have something to offer; you are looking for a mutually beneficial relationship (you can add value, they can give you a job). You must be brief and to the point. One recruiter says that if his interest isn't grabbed within the first 30 seconds, he moves on. Be prepared when you call; be pleasant and courteous. Have a specific goal in mind. (Are there any job openings? Did you get my resume? Can you suggest someone I could call for job openings? Can we meet?) Your objective should be to obtain either an interview or a referral.

Are you calling the right person? Can you get through all the "call-screeners" who protect the movers and shakers in the organization? You must determine who is the "hiring authority" (the person who decides who gets the job) and is most likely the head of the department in which you are seeking to work. This information usually is

SAMPLE FOLLOW-UP LETTER
AFTER A PRESENTATION

[ON YOUR LETTERHEAD]

October 19, 1994

Ms. Jacklyn O'Neill
Greyson Design Associates, Inc.
6 Pearl Street
Rome, Ohio 44298

Dear Ms. O'Neill,

On Friday, October 18th I was fortunate to attend your presentation on "Networking —How to Make It Work For You" at the Rome Chamber of Commerce luncheon. You were particularly helpful in giving me insight into ways to approach those people with whom a business relationship might be forged. I did note, however, the importance of networking all the time, not just when assistance or information is needed.

One circumstance you did not delve into is the situation I find myself in. I am about to graduate next June from Ohio State University with a B.A., majoring in business and minoring in art history. My objective is to obtain a position in an art gallery as a prelude to either eventually opening my own gallery or being a curator of an art museum. My problem is finding contacts in those major cities where art circles mean big business. For example, I subscribe to Gallery Guide covering New York City exhibitions. On my budget I find it difficult to travel to New York, Chicago, or Los Angeles to attend openings and build contacts.

I have applied for summer internships and have worked and volunteered in various art projects, so I am not totally without a local network. Can you provide any suggestions for me to obtain entry to the larger art world? If you would care to be my guest for either breakfast or an afternoon coffee, it would be my pleasure. Should your schedule not permit a short visit, I hope you can spare me a few minutes on the telephone. I will call you on Tuesday, October 29th at 10:30 AM. If you would care to reach me before that time, I can be reached at the above telephone number every afternoon from 3:00 to 5:30 PM.

Again I thank you for a most informative presentation.

Appreciatively,

Signature

Figure 6-6.

available from the organization's headquarters. Be certain you get the right spelling, pronunciation if possible, and title, in addition to the mailing address. Then you must leap the hurdles to get to this hiring authority. Don't call and say you sent a resume. Instead, try something like this:

SAMPLE FOLLOW-UP LETTER
TO A CONSULTANT

[ON YOUR LETTERHEAD]

August 5, 1994

Mr. David Lui
Assistant Vice President
Halting, Weinstein and Tully, PC
90 Wethervale Lane
Arlington, Virginia 93650

Dear Mr. Lui,

Eight months ago you gave a series of management training sessions at Arlington Electric, Inc. and I was fortunate to be one of the participants. In the time since my sessions with you I have found many occasions to use some of the techniques of team building and communication skills that you introduced me to. It gave me a sense of confidence and control to know that, together with the members of my department, we could meet and exceed any goals set for us by senior management.

Life is ironic. Never before has my shipping department performed better than the past six months; productivity soared in a weak economy. However, the overall performance of Arlington Electric did not quite keep up the pace and last week it was announced that the company would be closing in one month because of adverse economic pressures.

Mr. Lui, you were so helpful in the training sessions and I seemed to really be able to use your advice in a hands-on capacity. I am looking for a similar position in another manufacturing business located within a 90-mile radius of Arlington's location. I do have excellent references, having worked myself up in the organization from a shipping clerk in 1989 to department head in 1992. I was responsible for innovations in the department, including a computerized package tracking system that not only increased productivity 12% in the first year but also saved the company $85,000 over an 18-month period.

I have enclosed a current resume that I would greatly appreciate your comments on. On Wednesday afternoon, August 12th I will telephone you to discuss it. I look forward to any assistance you can render.

With best wishes,

Signature

Figure 6-7.

"Is Chris Jones available? This is Pat Smith calling. I sent some information last week, and I'm certain she'll be familiar with it."

"I'm sorry, she is in a meeting. Can I take a message?"

"Thank you. Please tell her that Pat Smith called, and that I can be reached at _____ until _____ o'clock today. If she's unable to call me back today, what would be a good time for me to reach her tomorrow? I don't want her to have to chase me down."

"I know she'll be in early tomorrow, around 8, and then she'll be gone most of the afternoon."

I'll try around 8. Thank you—you've been very helpful."

All of that is truthful (your mailing to her was your resume), but you have planted the seed that Ms. Jones is anxious to talk with you and that you're trying to make it as easy as possible for her. Mutual benefit! If in your case there's a bear guarding access, try early (before 9 A.M.), after 5 P.M., or during lunch, when the hiring authority is likely to be in and the call-screener not.

How are you once you get through to the right person? Time is in short supply, and you must win them over. You must be prepared to sell yourself quickly. Don't try to always rely on thinking on your feet—write out several versions of a short script of your opening statement. And practice saying it out loud:

"Hello, Ms. Jones. My name is Pat Smith, and upon the recommendation of Bill Black of XYZ Co., I sent you my resume last week. I've been employed as a graphic designer for the past five years, and I've worked on several CD covers. I know that your company has several recording companies as clients. I'm calling to see if you received my resume, and whether you have an interest in my background."

In a few short sentences you have told her why you're calling her, that you know what her company does, and given an indication that you can add value to her organization. If she is receptive, remember that your objective is either a job interview or a referral.

"Presenting Applicant X..."

When you write letters or telephone, you want to stand out and be noticed. But when you meet face-to-face, you don't want to "stand out" due to your personal appearance. Consider your appearance at meetings or interviews (or even seminars, luncheons, association meetings); has your attire meshed with that of your peers?

For example, are you the only one in a three-piece suit while the others are in sports jackets and dress pants? Or the only one wearing a tailored suit and high heels, while the others have adopted a more casual approach? You want to look as if you work there already when you go on an interview. Again, the solution to not being uncomfortably surprised is to do research. If necessary, be near the entrance of the organization on a nonmeeting day, and observe the employees coming to work.

One last statement on your attire. Whatever you deem to be appropriate dress, wear something that makes you feel comfortable and confident. Whether it's an old outfit (still in good shape) or a bought-special-for-interviews outfit, be sure you feel like a million dollars in it. An important interview is no time to be tugging on collars, or at fabrics that will not stay put. If it's a new purchase, take it out for a dry run first. Can you sit in it comfortably and reach and shake a hand?

Lastly, how are your interpersonal skills when meeting face-to-face? Do you show up having done your research, and having reviewed all your answers to possible questions? When the other person is talking, are you an active listener, or are you just waiting for your chance to speak? Look over your meeting logs; do you seem to come away from these meetings *with* information, or are your predominantly interested in *sending* messages?

How's your speaking voice? Do you talk in a clear, confident manner? Is your speech interspersed with "like," "ummm," or other space-fillers? Do you maintain eye contact with the interviewer? Are you a fidgeter or squirmer? Do you smell of tobacco smoke, or of what you ate for lunch? What nonverbal messages are you sending? Do you sit with good posture in your chair, hands relaxed, or are your arms crossed tightly? Body language—gestures, posture, eye contact—can either reinforce or detract from the image of a confident, capable, potential employee.

Follow-up Techniques

How successful have your follow-up strategies been? Do you have established follow-up strategies? Calling someone you already have spoken or written to is easier than making a "cold" call, in which case you're dealing with a stranger who has no idea who you are. Following up on people you have been referred to by mutual friends or business contacts, whom you have met at seminars or luncheons, or to whom you have sent a letter, will require a slightly different approach, depending on your objective (a referral, an interview).

Resume and/or Marketing Letter Follow-up

After you send your resume with a cover letter, or a marketing letter alone, you must telephone to determine if there is an interest in your expertise. If you leap this first hurdle and they want to have an exploratory meeting, get as much information about the position over the telephone as you can before you show up for the meeting. This is all research for your presentation at the interview, and will help you to position yourself. Some possible questions:

Who does this position report to (functional or corporate title)?

How long has there been a vacancy?

What happened to the prior employee (promoted, quit, fired)?

What are the prime responsibilities of this position?

If no interest is shown, ask if they will keep your resume on file should the situation change. (Fat chance, but test their reaction anyway.) Do they anticipate any job openings in the near future? When could you call back? If the outlook is bleak at that organization, express gratitude for their assistance and ask if they know of any similar openings in other organizations, or any other names they could refer you to. If this works, ask if you can use their name when you call their referral. In any case, if they do provide you with any referrals or leads, write a short thank-you letter after you have followed up on their lead.

Meeting Follow-up

Whether you met formally (a meeting that was arranged) or informally (at a business seminar or luncheon), identify yourself and "remind" the person where you last met. Then inquire, as you did after a resume follow-up, if there is any interest in someone with your background. If there is interest, determine if the proper course of action is a formal application (directed to whom?) or if the next step is an interview. Again, find out as much as you can about the position. Of course if there is no interest, seek a referral and ask if there might be an opening in the future. Send a thank-you letter if they have provided you with additional information.

Interview Follow-up

After each interview, send a thank-you letter expressing appreciation for their time and information, and stating either that you will look forward to hearing from them within the next few weeks (or whatever time frame was indicated in the interview as an appropriate interval for them to make a hiring decision) or that you will call them on such and such a day (again, whatever is an appropriate time frame) to learn if the hiring decision has yet been made. (If it had been made, and you were the choice, they would have followed up and called you.)

If no decision has been made yet, inquire as to when the decision will be made, whether there will be further interviews (callbacks), and if you should schedule your interview now. What if the decision *has* been made, and it wasn't you? Ask the hiring authority for constructive criticism ("Was there something you wished to see in my background that wasn't there?" "Is there anything I can do to make a stronger presentation in the future?") and for any possible referrals to prospective employers. You should now send a thank-you letter (again) after you have followed up on their advice or referrals, so that you can be specific in what you are thanking them for. It's a small world in employment circles, and it never hurts to leave fans in your wake. Chances are competitors know who is hiring, and your name may pop up; you always want to create a favorable impression even *in absentia.* Your job-search campaign is heavily reliant on public relations and goodwill; leave some goodwill behind you after every encounter.

Referral Follow-up

Begin by identifying yourself, and explaining how you got their name. Proceed to see if there is any interest, and press for an interview or a referral. Send a thank-you letter if they have been helpful.

Staying Motivated, and on Top of Everything

By repeatedly reading this chapter! Seriously, it's done by reviewing your successes, seeing what's effective and what isn't, and giving yourself feedback (positive and negative) on every phase of your search. Confidence comes from knowledge: knowing that you have been working all your contacts, following up on leads, and revising your approaches as necessary.

Remember that you're keeping your eye on your budget, and should now begin to have some idea as to whether you can live within it. If you can't, revise the Monthly Cash Budget (Fig. 2-2) to reflect an accurate level of cash income and outflow.

What are you doing *for yourself?* After a hard day (and sometimes evening) of job hunting, reward yourself. Continue to pursue those pleasures that were part of your life before the job campaign. Take advantage of not having to get up at dawn or return late after a long daily commute; get up early and enjoy the morning hours by leisurely reading the paper and having a second cup of coffee, or by going for a bicycle ride or talking casually to family members (they're not used to you *not* rushing out the door each morning). Of course, you'll be rushing out some days for interviews and meetings, so enjoy your flexible time when you have it. You will work happier and harder if you physically and mentally refresh yourself!

Fallback Position Review

Depending on both your progress to date and your financial picture, you may have to more seriously consider alternative income sources. This may include "dipping" into savings or short-term investments, forgoing some planned expenditures, or accepting temporary or part-time employment. Some choices were discussed in Week 1 under the heading Fallback Options (Alternative Work Arrangements).

If this is an option you must now actively pursue, you will be looking for two jobs at the same time until you have a secondary job in place. While it may relieve some pressure from financial worries, it will require you to be even more focused and organized in your job campaign, and you will have less time available to do it. There is a tradeoff, however; your temporary or part-time job may unearth an entirely new, unmined selection of leads and contacts to pursue. And your search for a supplemental job may also produce leads. Consider also any organizations that you may have targeted and interviewed at (or where you have an interview scheduled); if there's no full-time position at this time, would they consider a temporary or part-time assignment? If you really like the organization, this could solve your immediate cash-flow problem, as well as get your foot in the door. If worse comes to worst, you at least have a part-time job while you continue to search for full-time employment; you have met one of your immediate objectives.

Week 6 Checklist

☐ Reviewed Job Search Log.

☐ Reviewed Resume Log.

☐ Reviewed Meeting Journal.

☐ Reviewed Interview Journal.

☐ Reviewed appointment book.

☐ Completed the Week 6 Review Worksheet.

☐ Completed the Daily Planner (hourly work log).

☐ Completed the Near Misses Worksheet.

☐ Analyzed areas and skills that need improvement.

☐ Mailed thank-you letters.

☐ Identified at least five new names to contact each day.

   ☐ Contacted these five new names each day.

☐ Reviewed and revised, if necessary, Monthly Cash Budget.

☐ Reconfirm your job objective. Full-time/part-time/change of career? State here.

_____

_____

☐ Reconfirm your employer profile (refer to Work Environment Survey, Fig. 1-8). Describe below.

_____

_____

Week 7
Keeping the Momentum Going

Networking Adjustments

Day 43

You are nearly at the midpoint of this 90-day job search campaign. You should have collected a storehouse of contacts and leads that you have followed, and some that you are continuing to keep on top of. You should also have considered and reconsidered organizations and jobs that are of primary interest. At this point, you may feel that nothing seems to be leading to any results. But as the song says, "What a difference a day makes." Success is hard to gauge, because one telephone call can change a dead lead into a job offer. In fact, this week is a crucial one for keeping yourself focused. You have been planting a lot of seeds, but they need watering and more attention so as to not only lead to results but also keep you focused.

How would success be measured at this point in your job search? Obviously, landing a new job would be 100 percent success. How can you evaluate your progress to date? If there were a magic number that would ensure success ("You should have sent x number of resumes by this time." "What, only y number of telephone calls made?"), you would not need this book, only a sheaf of paper or a telephone book. However, you should have at least a few exploratory meetings under your belt.

Special Tricks for Keeping
Your Enthusiasm Up

The following are several "calls to action" to enhance your creativity and to have some fun with too. If you haven't gotten out as much as you should have (Are you taking those early-morning walks, or some other form of healthy exercise recommended in Week 1?), this is an opportunity to "think outside the box" and brainstorm a bit.

1. Visit a retail organization, with the thought of exploring it as a potential employee. Do this, even if your last thought would be to join a retail organization because your vision is one of low pay, long hours, and boring work. Test that hypothesis. Take a road map (or city public transportation map) and draw a circle around the area you live in, encompassing the distance you would gladly travel to work.

Use the chart in Fig. 7-1. List at least five national retail organizations with at least one outlet in your area.

Now conduct some basic research; include recent help-wanted ads, advertisements, and other business information or recent news.

2. Do the same for manufacturing facilities. Use the form shown in Fig. 7-1 for this and following suggestions.

NATIONAL RETAIL ORGANIZATIONS
LOCATED IN MY AREA

NAME AND ADDRESS	TARGETED OBJECTIVE

Figure 7-1.

3. Do the same for not-for-profits.

4. Do the same for governments (federal, state, local—and don't forget authorities and local boards). Watch for the opportunity to take civil service exams.

5. Do the same for service organizations.

Now if that wasn't fun enough, let's try something else! Identify some opportunities that may be enjoyable for you that are low in cost (both time and monetary expense). A time-management workshop, a briefing in your profession, a discussion of hidden career opportunities. You need to get out! Do something that's job-related, but that also puts you into a situation where you will meet others who hopefully are *not* looking for jobs too.

Target Objectives. In each category, identify at least one objective to achieve this week. It could be to seek job openings and referrals or an informal walk-around visit (store or service outlet). See what ideas develop, and what contacts/leads you can pinpoint.

How to Develop More (and Targeted) Contacts

After six weeks of exercising your mind and building your networking and sales/interpersonal skills, you have become, I have no doubt, very proficient at it. You have also become accustomed to it (it has become part of you), and hopefully you're enjoying using those skills because they're skills that you can use the rest of your life. With this as the reference point, consider the following as a source of opportunities to develop more (quantity) and better (quality) contacts to enhance your effectiveness.

Power and Contacts

What does power have to do with contacts? Plenty. Power helps to build contacts, and those contacts, either directly or indirectly, will lead to job leads if not to jobs themselves.

Power means having the ability to influence others so as to get them to do what we want. Yet too often we fall into patterns of behavior that lead us down the path of increasingly powerless activities, and the spiral continues in that downward direction. Not having a job is one event in our lives that definitely contributes to that feeling of pow-

erlessness ("The fear of unemployment makes cowards of us all"—
from the movie *The Abilene Paradox*), and we need to identify and contain it. In our society the idea of *power* is loaded down with a heavy
negative overtone, and many people consider the use (abuse) of power
to be unethical or immoral. Let me ask you to look at it in another
way.

Would you rather have people do things your way, or would you
rather do things their way? If you're puzzled by that thought, let me
ask which way is easier for you. Oftentimes in our society, where
altruism frequently is touted as a preferred value, we feel guilty about
putting ourselves first. But to be effective, we need to ensure that our
frame of reference begins with ourselves (even if we agree to be altruistic!), and this is true certainly of your job search as well.

How Do You Get Power?

Being on the "asking" end of every conversation may not imbue you
with a sense of power. Frustration, rejection, telephoning and calling
day after day—all these can leave you feeling powerless. But you are
not without power: you are taking control, reviewing your options,
and maximizing every encounter.

Here are some suggestions as to how you can get power, both now
and after you have started in your new position.

Act "as if" you had power. If there's an attribute you wish you had,
act as if you have it. That self-confidence will in itself project a powerful image. If you wish that people would like you, go into a meeting
reminding yourself that everyone *does* want you to do well. Everyone
is a friend; they just may not know it yet.

Don't lose your cool. When you're faced with people who are less
than professional (stand you up for meetings, are rude to you on the
telephone), take a mental or physical walk; distance yourself from the
situation, and don't take on that person's problems as your own (you
didn't make him disorganized; you're not the reason she was rude).
Then go on and treat everyone as you wish to be treated: professionally, and with courtesy.

Never close your mind or your ears. Listen. Pay attention, so that
you can discover what it is that others want, what is their message.
Empathize with others, and to the degree that you give them what
they're looking for, more often than not you will find them reciprocat-
ing.

Try for win-win situations. Don't always view life as a battleground
of winners and losers. If everyone comes out of a transaction a little

bit ahead, then everyone wins. *Draw* people into agreement with you—remember President Eisenhower and the piece of string? Pull, don't push.

Be able to *surprise*. Don't leave yourself without a backup plan. If someone can't make a meeting, is there another time? Someone else who can act in his or her stead?

When you do win, win *quietly*. Recognize all those who helped you, in big ways and in small, to achieve your goal. Share the spotlight.

Align Yourself with Power

Look at the time you've spent so far. Examine your list of job-search contacts and leads. Are you dealing with "haves" or "have-nots" in terms of power? If you feel there's a definite power shortage in your search, you need to become more power-oriented.

Avoid places/circumstances/people that drain your energy, and over which or whom you have little or no control. Gravitate toward circumstances/people/places where you can exert a lot of control.

Call in your chits. Identify who to go to, to find a job directly (the best and least time-consuming approach) or indirectly. Starting today, identify opportunities to build future obligations. The past is past, so don't call in chits if the person wasn't aware of a "this for that" arrangement, but otherwise start to do so immediately. It doesn't hurt to cash in some chips—or at least to try to, and see what happens. (It doesn't hurt to ask, and you will be building an assertiveness skill in the process. How can you lose, even if your request isn't met?)

Change Your Daily Routines, Open Yourself Up to New Encounters

Avoid driving to destinations alone if you can avoid it. Car-pool, whether with people you know or don't know; take a commuter bus or train. For longer trips, take a train or a plane. On a plane take a middle seat—it gives you two chances to meet someone (one on either side). If there is reason to change your seat, try to do so. Reasons for seat-changing include: counterculture individuals (unless of course you're looking for a job in an industry that hires many of them, or caters to them), students, retired people, and adults with small children. This isn't to say that no adult with a small child will ever help you to find a job, but on the other hand the likelihood (should you be able to catch and retain their attention long enough to engage in a grown-up conversation) is quite small. Likewise for those very senior citizens—although you can never tell what positions they might have held in the past, and what contacts they might provide. If you can afford to do so, and it's consistent with the level of people you need to meet to help you find a job, fly first or business class.

Always "dress for success" when you travel. If you can get an invite into one of the airline's member lounges, by all means do so. Also, if you have a chance to fly direct, or in two or more stopovers, take the stopovers. The trip is as important as the arrival. The more opportunity you have to interact with more people, the more your chances of making valuable contacts increase.

If you're a single parent, try to mix opportunities and have some fun too. In New York City, the exclusive toy store FAO Schwarz has the reputation of being a great place for single people to meet on Saturday afternoons. At least one woman's how-to-find-a-man book suggests it as a place to go, because the men there who are unattached are being generous with their kids and they can afford to be so toward a new friend as well. There's no harm in visiting a place like FAO Schwarz, for several reasons:

1. The kid(s) will like it.

2. If the retail outlet you're visiting is in the industry you're interested in pursuing, there's nothing like field research to expand your knowledge base.

3. Even if it's *not* a targeted organization or industry (or even if it's one of those organizations you think you would never consider working for), check it out. You never know.

4. If you're looking for a date, then you have that opportunity to pursue as well!

5. If it gets you out of the house on a Saturday or a Sunday, that's all to the good, because on those days there's little chance of a business meeting in most professions and industries.

Tips on Meeting as Many Helpful People as Possible

To be successful in your job search, you need to meet as many helpful people as possible—wherever and whenever you can. By "helpful" I specifically mean assisting you in reaching your goals and objectives.

No matter what your performance has been up to today, here are some tips to become more effective.

Always be ready. Wherever and whenever an opportunity presents itself, jump in. The more you practice, the more comfortable you will be when it counts. The other day a family from Sacramento, California, was on a train bound for the suburbs of Connecticut, when in fact they were trying to get to the U.S. Military Academy at West Point, New York. Evidently, when asking for directions prior to boarding the train, the person they had asked heard "Westport" (which is in Connecticut) for "West Point" (which is not)! Sitting next to this family was a person who put his conversational skills to work. He obviously enjoyed meeting these people, and they certainly enjoyed it and minded less the fact that they had been misled. So who was helpful? The person who gave directions, or the person who chatted the time away on the train?

Be sure to have business cards made. The business card is a subtle touch that says a lot of positive things about a person. It also serves a very practical function—as a "tickler" to use when you want to follow up with a phone call. If you have never felt comfortable in the past passing out business cards, now is the time to change that attitude. Always have them ready in case they're asked for. If you don't have one, then you need to promise the requesting party that you don't have any on you at this time, but that if they give you their cards you'll certainly see that they get one. Of course that takes time and energy, so avoid the need for that follow-up by having the cards with you.

Stay flexible. There's an old saying, "When life gives you lemons, make lemonade." If you're not able to reach a contact person in an organization despite repeated attempts (he apparently travels a great deal), ask who is in charge in his absence. This may be the helpful person you need. If you're all prepped and geared up for an important interview, only to find, once you arrive, that their office has been trying to contact you to reschedule, put on your best face and whip out your appointment book. (Better yet, call before you leave for the rescheduled meeting, to confirm the time!)

Don't be unidirectional and succumb to saying "Hi, My name is Matt, and I'm looking for a job" as your constant opener whenever you meet someone. That's the quickest path to becoming a bore, being avoided, and missing opportunities. Consider what the other person may want from the conversation, and then try to address that first. As you move forward conversationally, determine the appropriateness of your current plight and your wish to determine whether the person you are talking to is a job-search prospect. If not, don't break off the conversation immediately just because this person won't be of use too you. But also don't linger any longer than the situation demands, because you need to "work the room" and locate more likely prospects.

Enjoy the process. Interpersonal skills are needed in every career (well, maybe not for a lighthouse keeper...), and usually one can spot those people you meet who seem to genuinely enjoy talking and meeting others. Don't become the job-seeking equivalent of a gold-digger, only interested in what people can do for you. You may miss out on developing some new friendships and learning a lot about human nature. Granted, you're in the midst of your job campaign, but you're entitled to some enjoyment at the same time.

Practice small talk. If your nose has been buried in research and classified ads, you are turning into a very dull person! In addition to your job campaign, it's essential that you have a *life*. Maintain as many of those interests and activities you enjoyed before commencing your job search as is practical. The more interests you have, the more interesting you become. And "small" talk can play a very big part in your search. In interviewing, usually the first hurdle to be leaped is to make the interviewer comfortable with you. This is done by revealing yourself to be someone with similar ideas, interests, goals, and background. These can be explored during small talk. ("Did you get to see much of the Olympics?" "Why does it seem that all the nice weather only occurs during the week and the rain on the weekend?") Subjects like the weather, current (nonpolitical) events, the occasion you're meeting at, books or pictures decorating the office where you're interviewing, and music or movies/television can be safe yet interesting topics. Don't merely wait for a chance to speak, really listen to the other person. You need all the practice in listening skills you can get.

Have an agenda (what I have to give versus what I want to take—a job!). This involves some "sizing up" of the situation and of the person you're meeting. What could I give this person? What is he/she "buying"? For example, don't disregard those lower on the job totem pole, people who could possibly work for you. They may have contacts (their boss's ear) and may know all the unofficial information about an organization. Network "down" from time to time. Let them talk about their jobs—what they like, what they don't—and file it away for future reference if you ever interview at that organization. What you have gained is an understanding of another position that could impact on yours while you let someone talk about their favorite subject: themselves!

Get out, and stay out all day long. Cluster your appointments whenever possible. There's nothing worse than getting ready all morning for an afternoon meeting and using up the entire day unknowingly. (There will be, however, those interviews where some last-minute rehearsals will be essential.) When you're traveling to another part of town or another city, at what other places can you call while you're in the area? Visit a local research library. Make some follow-up appointments in the area.

Keep your eyes and ears open. Look for notices of gatherings on a variety of issues, including a new job. If you live near a college or university, get a copy of their calendar of current events. Oftentimes they have career days or nights, where a panel of experts in a particular field discuss job opportunities and are open for a question-and-answer period. You may make new contacts, either in the audience or on the panel. Local Chambers of Commerce, houses of worship, or other civic groups may have similar training sessions or discussion groups. A catalog from a specialty paper company advertised a free series of all-day seminars on doing presentations (ostensibly using their products, but that's okay). Part of this trick is to "act as if" you had the job you want, to read the papers and magazines that would keep you current in the field, and to attend any events you can that people in your chosen career path normally would. Join groups that cut across many career paths, such as NAFE (National Association of Female Executives). Do some more research on associations you could join.

Follow-up Drill

Look at your Job Search and Resume logs, together with your appointment book. Track some of the people and/or organizations that you've been in touch with. It may have started with a letter, then a telephone call. Audit all your entries, to see if any have fallen through the cracks (you owe them a letter; they should have called you back) and to determine what action is needed.

Go through all your correspondence. Are there any names or organizations that could be reapproached? Do some look better now, with the passage of time?

Go through your collection of business cards. Is there someone you can call today? Sort through the collection of articles, magazines, and brochures you have collected regarding your profession and industry. Are any names mentioned (of persons or organizations) that you have not contacted recently? What about all those lists: membership lists of professional organizations, attendees or presenters at seminars or luncheons; whom can you call? Lastly, look through your appointment book, going back to the beginning of your job search (and look through your calendar for the three months before that), and see if any names come to light that you owe a lunch to, or to whom you can send a short note.

What Others Have to Say

As a break from listening to *me*, here are some quotes from others in the job-search arena, either players or successful job finders.

Leslie Prager of the Prager-Bernstein Group, a career counseling firm: "The one constant in the nineties is the change in our work lives and career shapes. The days of the one-company career are over. Our new career shapes will include full-time work, as well as consulting, home-based businesses, telecommuting, part-time work, temporary work, and entrepreneurship."

Edwin Sultan, a recently displaced executive, says that the six job search basics are

Perseverance	Being insistent but not abrasive
Patience	Being able to endure hardship or inconvenience with calm assurance
Passion	Being fired with intense feeling about the work you most enjoy
Persuasiveness	Enlisting others (your network) to support your goals and objectives
Preparation	Organizing your search campaign so that you're in position to recognize and seize opportunities as they arise
Package	Being computer literate; writing a compelling resume; tuning-up social skills; smiling

John Janowski, a career military officer who decided to seek a civilian occupation: "If you do not like what you are doing, no matter how secure it is, then you owe it to yourself to make a change that will provide happiness....People love to be asked to help. One of my best contacts was a paper route customer who remembered how reliable I was 10 years ago. The key is to get your foot in the door."

Week 7 Checklist

☐ Visited new locations and venues. Obtained _____ new people, places and/or organizations to contact.

☐ Identified _____ powerful people you're presently in contact with, or who you will contact this week.

☐ Long shot: Identify five people whom you would like to meet who are prominent in your profession. Write them a brief yet concise letter stating why you feel they are so effective, and close by asking for advice on your job search. Research them and their organizations (refer to recent newspaper or magazine articles). Ask a specific question that you really do wonder about.

☐ How many new people did you meet this week ?_____

☐ Completed a follow-up drill and identified persons and situations that you can contact this week.

☐ Keeping a record of all job-search expenses and related receipts for tax purposes.

☐ Inventory check of supplies: stationery, business cards, stamps.

Week 8

Resume Adjustments

What's Working, What Isn't

Day 50

This week marks the point at which you have approximately 30 business days left to land a job. If one or more offers have already come in, you're way ahead of schedule and should move on toward closing the deal if you haven't done so already [see Week 12—Evaluating the Offer(s)]. If not, this is a time to continue the exercises we discussed in Chapter 7 last week, to identify and exploit opportunities to their fullest. The emphasis last week was on improving networking and contacts. This week the emphasis will be on changes to the resume.

Resumes are the bane of those looking for a job. Frequently they represent that foot you must get in the door. Bureaucrats in any organization, executive recruiters, educators, politicians, corporate chieftains—even friends, neighbors, and otherwise helpful relatives—all seem to have been born with the words, "Send me your resume" in their mouths.[1]

The typewriter has been the chief culprit in keeping resumes from being truly effective. Invented in the 1870s along with the eraser-topped number two pencil, the typewriter went on to stifle the greatest office minds for more than a century, and continues to do so because of the difficulty in making any changes and the effort it takes to move

---

[1]With a nod to technology, *Fax me* your resume" is being heard more and more!

things around (a total retype, unless you have great cut-and-pasting skills—and even that takes a great deal of time and effort). Linked to the typewriter's productivity deficiencies was the copying technology that went along with it. In the world before the arrival of photocopiers, each of us had to go to a printer to achieve a truly "professional"-looking resume. Not only was there a direct expense which involved cash outlays, but a certain amount of lead time also was required. There was then a delay in getting the resume "in hand" so that something could be done with it—namely, forward it to any one or more of the parties mentioned above so that they could do something about it. In those days, even though at times that job market was an improvement over this one, I never would have agreed to write this book, because of the difficulty and delays one had to expect with regard to the availability of the essential ingredient in any job search: a resume.

As I asked in Week 1, can you get a job without a resume? The answer is yes, and if you're aware of such a situation, by all means go get that job without one. But it's far more likely that you'll be required to provide one upon request.[2] The most important way to think of a resume is as a sales tool. It is the advance copy, the package labeling that will lead the employer to "buy" your total presentation. The question to ask yourself when putting together a resume is, "What is there about my experience that will make the reader want to see more, and specifically to want to see *me*?"

Just as most job ads are written from the perspective of the employer, because that's who's putting the ad together,[3] so too most resumes are put together from the viewpoint of the person writing it. What's wrong with that? In both instances, plenty. The point to be made here is that knowing who created the ad is important, because that person is the interviewer, and you can gain a great deal of insight into his/her perception of the position. However, the ad may have been written by the human resources department with no (or hardly any) input from

[2]Don't forget that, even if it's not required, a resume is a good, basic, skill and experience inventory tool. We don't accurately remember dates, places, and accomplishments over any period of time. Even when there's no other reason to do so, a resume should be put together as an opportunity to recall what's been going on most recently professionally. Updating the resume periodically is a way of eliminating the risk of forgetting what has occurred to you most recently, and what you have successfully completed.

[3]Sometimes the recruiter, instead of writing the ad themselves, will have the vendor responsible for placing the ad write the copy. At other times, if a search firm is involved, they will write the copy. Lastly, sometimes organizations insist that the advertising or marketing department write the ad. Each of these instances represents opportunities for the ad to take on the bias of the direction it's coming from, but in all other circumstances—I believe by far the great majority—the recruiter writes the ad.

the manager or other department employee responsible for filling the position. If you address such an ad, you may be addressing a perspective which may be different from the decision maker's. (By the way, note that most classified ads have very little white space. The thinking here is to cram all the words in, because the person writing the ad is paying for it and wants to show all that is important about the position.)[4]

The more words there are in an ad, the more insight you will get into the person who wrote it. And, if the creator isn't the person doing the hiring, then don't be surprised during one or more interviews to find the position to be significantly different from the one described. (Whatever happens, and regardless of who's responsible for the wording of the ad, don't get into an argument begun by your saying, "That's not what the ad said!") It may be useful, if not crucial, to consider the parameters written into the ad, when writing a cover letter and even before you submit the resume.

I mentioned earlier in this book that resumes are considered by many to be the junk mail of the nineties. The major reason that appears to be true is that so many human resource professionals, in organizations and recruiting firms as well as employment agencies, have to contend with so many resumes whenever they try to use the media to identify candidates. When you look at the resumes submitted, it's difficult to determine the link that the submitter saw between his/her experience and the particular job advertised in the first place.

The first point is that they are written from the *submitter's* perspective, and the second that they seem to have been "mass-mailed." These applicants get the idea that if you send out enough resumes, one or more will *have* to lead to an invitation to visit. I don't know why that's such a prevalent notion, or where it originated. Granted, from time to time a "How to Find a Job" book comes out with the formula that the more resumes you get out, the more likely it is you'll get interviews, and the more interviews you get, the more likely it is you'll get hired—and then adds the warning that the reverse is also true (the only word not included is *beware*).

In all fairness to that school of thought, they do imply (unfortunately, not strongly enough) that those resumes must see the light of day to have any chance, but the more selective the sender, then the more likely the appropriateness of the reply. Now there are even organiza-

[4]There's a professor who teaches Human Resource courses at New York University. He loves to shock his students with the challenge of adding more "white space" to their ads. He says ads loaded with small print words are ineffective. He is pleased when, time after time, a student who happens to be a recruiter in a day job tells him after the fact that he/she surreptitiously tried more white space, with fantastic results!

tions advertising in *The New York Times* and *The Wall Street Journal* that promise you success by taking responsibility for the mass mailing of your resumes with a cover letter. They include testimonials from people who doubled and even quadrupled their salaries. My strong suggestion is that you consider "micro-marketing" instead, and that is the approach suggested here.

The hypothesis is as follows: To get a job, you need to get an interview with someone who has some influence in the hiring process. To get that interview, you need to identify the most likely opportunity to obtain that interview, and the way to do that is to find the right person. Communication is best as face-to-face contact. When that's not possible, the telephone is next; when that's not possible, then written communication will do. Notice, though, that written communication is only the third best alternative.

As far as your approach is concerned, if you can see someone and get them to agree to an interview on the spot, by all means do so. If all it takes is a telephone call to get an interview, by all means do so. When neither of these two choices is available, or even if you were successful using the face-to-face or phone technique, there is still the possibility that a resume and/or letter will be required.

Think about the resume from the reader's perspective. The PC and photocopying machines make it a requirement for you to move your resume into the nineties if you want to find a job, especially in just 90 days, because you're competing with a small but growing group, all of whom realize that that is what *they* must do.

A Change Is Gonna Come...

Now's the time to make resume additions, deletions, and major revisions. No resume should be etched in stone. Throughout the search, consider it as a working document, constantly available for refinement and adjustment.

At this time be brutal in your review of your resume. Look over your notes for any comments you have gathered from others regarding your resume. Consider the source, but note the comments. Everyone has an opinion on two things in life: the ideal picnic, and the perfect resume.

Your Resume: Up Close and Personal

After you have considered everyone's comments, go to the best version of the document and take up a pen. Ask the following questions, and try to make this "best" version even better.

First, look at the resume as if it were a picture—without looking at the words. (Turn it upside down, even.) How attractive is it to look at? Is there enough white space (just as I mentioned previously about ad copy, white space provides a pleasing contrast to the eye)?

What about an objective? Do you need one? You have to decide, and in fact remember that the resume is a *personal* statement and therefore no particular format is required. Granted, there *is* a general style that is generally accepted in our country, but within that framework the choice is yours. It's up to you to determine whether you want a chronological resume, a functional resume, or something in between. One of the decisions you must make is whether you want to include an objective on your resume.

You will need an objective on your resume when

You are switching careers

You have worn several different hats and played several different roles

You have just graduated from school—high, college, or university, or even technical, trade, or other school

You are looking for the same job in a different organization

What if you have an inside track on a position? Even though a meeting (and serious consideration) is guaranteed, you may consider including an objective on your resume, if it is extremely targeted and focused.

You should *never* consider an objective when the resume is not even requested until well into the selection and interviewing process. Why? Because you don't want to blow it now! Don't give nay-sayers or bureaucratic (or any other) delayers, with a variety of possible objectives and agendas in mind, the opportunity to sabotage your candidacy. "Well, he says he wants to _____. What made him consider our job?" "She says her goal is to join an organization that _____. That characteristic certainly can't be applied to this organization."

You also should not consider including an objective when it is an exploratory or courtesy interview.

How's My Objective?

Once you have decided to use an objective, you need to look at it carefully. Ask yourself questions like, "Does the objective state clearly what my job goal is? Is the job goal writer- or reader-directed? Does it say something like a `self-driven individual who wishes to join a management training program' or `a person with hard organizational skills that will contribute to the growth of any organization'?"

Other examples might include "A results-driven salesperson who seeks the challenge of a new product," or "A proven project manager ready to apply those tested skills to an organization going through a major transformation," or "A PC-literate secretary with strong interpersonal skills, ready to apply them in a fast-paced, customer-driven environment."

The key to writing an effective objective is to remember its underlying purpose: to be a "grabber." Research indicates that people spend approximately 25 seconds reviewing any resume. In that brief period of time, the better job you do of making the reviewer take notice, the more likely it is that the interview will unlock the door that gets you an invitation for an interview. The objective should be to get the reader to say, "Hmmm—let me see more."

Consider the Ad

If you're responding to an ad, you may want your objective to contain a statement that is a paraphrase from the ad. Here's an actual ad from *The New York Times:*

ADMINISTRATIVE ASSISTANT

Construction firm in midtown Manhattan seeks responsible person who can take control & do it all in small but busy 2 person office. Previous experience in construction a must. Fax your resume to...

Working from that ad, you get: "OBJECTIVE: To utilize managerial and organizational skills obtained in large metropolitan construction concern in a smaller, more dynamic `hands-on' environment."

Here's another ad:

COLLEGE GRAD
NOTED AUTHOR-LAWYER

Looking for very intelligent, driven assistant to work in small eclectic exciting office to research and write scripts for TV, handle public relations, work on legal/client matters & handle phones, travel scheduling, etc. Must be articulate, caring, personable and a self-starter. Send cover letter and resume to...

Here are two different approaches to this striking ad. The first speaks to the tone of the ad, while the second mirrors some of the terms directly used in the ad. They are both "customer-driven."

Objective: Avid writer and editor of college newspaper seeks a unique position utilizing my superb personal and organizational skills in a nontraditional setting, while enabling my continuing evening studies in pre-law.

Objective: Seeking a unique position that will make the most of my varied writing, research, and organizational skills, in a nontraditional setting requiring a self-motivated, personable worker.

How Many Resumes Should You Have?

Different organizations don't necessarily warrant different resumes, but there are good reasons to customize your resume to a specific reader. At this juncture, many potential employers out there still see the resume as etched in stone. If your resume appears on the desk of someone who still sees it that way, that person will surely be impressed that your resume lists the specific attributes and/or experiences mentioned in the ad.

Tailoring a resume makes you sharper. By making the extra effort (not all that much is required), you are targeting your resume and in the process giving more attention to the specific organization you're attempting to get a job from. This is a customer-driven (reader-driven) approach that allows you to stay focused and be more effective.

Samples of different versions of the same resume are shown in Figs. 8-1 and 8-2.

Additional Sources to Consider for Resume Hints

There are as many opinions about what makes a good resume as there are people. Get as many informed opinions as possible. The one that matters most is the person's who will be reviewing your resume to determine whether he/she is interested in seeing you. Find persons who are similar to that person (in that profession, in that industry) to review your resume. Consider also any corporate communication that is created and distributed by the organization. Try to incorporate a "feel" that is consistent with the "hot buttons" of the organization to which you are applying.

Also, try to get the opinion of the "pros." Recruiters frequently are willing, if they already know you, to provide you with suggestions or comments; counselors in outplacement firms also can be most helpful. The resume in these instances may also be helpful in providing a non-threatening situation for you to practice interviewing and networking skills (and the other person won't mind if you refrain from saying, "Now, how about a job?"!). The resume in Fig. 8-3 was reworked with the assistance of a contingency recruiter.

Don't just take my word for it. As I said a moment ago, there are as many different opinions as to what makes for an effective resume as

Melissa Parker
221 N. Bainridge Road
Corte Vista, California 40528

Home: (612)858-7113
Office: (612)921-6000

Summary: Experienced human resources professional with a take-charge attitude, team building approach, quality commitment and results orientation.

WORK EXPERIENCE

1990
to
Present

Grundel Corporation, San Francisco, California
Director of Human Resources and Payroll

Reporting to the Vice President of Finance and Administration; provide leadership in both Human Resources and Payroll for this fast-paced, high tech, software manufacturing start-up. **Major accomplishments** include:

* Total commitment to total quality initiatives in the human resources function through team-building, benchmarking, and process re-engineering that led to 25% improvement in delivery time for recruitment services at an annualized savings of more than $400,000 in real dollar costs.

* Redirected human resource staff focus to a customer-driven delivery system.

* Organized a task force to determine organizational information requirements in human resources and payroll that resulted in the installation of an integrated, user-friendly system for both functions that eliminated data redundancies, created an error-free environment and allowed management to access and use information required in a timely manner.

1987
to
1990

California First Bank, San Diego, California
Personnel Administrator

Upon completion of college was hired by this major Southern California bank to provide administrative support for a regional human resource office. Reported to the manager of the unit. **Primary accomplishments** included:

* a service provider approach that included resolving any staff-related concerns in a 72-hour turnaround time.

* instituting a customer satisfaction survey program that was expanded to include payroll-related services.

* a complete review of all human resource forms to eliminate redundancies and obsolescence while redesigning several forms, totally with internal resources and software, in an effort to obtain required data in a more effective manner.

EDUCATION

Costa Mesa University, Costa Mesa California, Bachelor of Arts Degree

SKILLS/ACTIVITIES

PC literate in standalone and LAN environments. Software: ABRA Pay, LOTUS 1-2-3, Fox-Pro, Word for Windows, LOTUS Notes. Spanish. Member, Society for Human Resource Management and American Payroll Association.

Figure 8-1.

there are people. The resume should be a reflection of *you*. So get as many people's opinions of what constitutes a good resume for you and your job goals as you can; then separate what seems to be the good advice from the bad. However, keep in mind throughout the process that 1) the purpose of a resume is to get a job, and 2) whatever you do, you shouldn't use the creation of the "perfect resume" as an excuse to delay finding a job.

Melissa Parker   Home: (612)858-7113
221 N. Bainridge Road   Office: (612)921-6000
Corte Vista, California 40528

Summary: Experienced payroll professional with a take-charge attitude, team building approach, quality commitment and results orientation.

WORK EXPERIENCE

1990   **Grundel Corporation**, San Francisco, California
to   Director of Payroll and Human Resources
Present

              Reporting to the Vice President of Finance and Administration; provide leader-
              ship in both Payroll and Human Resources for this fast-paced, high tech, soft-
              ware manufacturing start-up. **Major accomplishments** include:

              * Total commitment to total quality initiatives in the payroll function through
                team-building, benchmarking, and process re-engineering that led to 40%
                improvement in delivery time and at an annualized savings of more than
                $250,000 in real dollar costs.

              * Redirected payroll staff focus to a customer-driven delivery system.

              * Organized a task force to determine organizational information requirements in
                payroll and human resources that resulted in the installation of an integrated,
                user-friendly system for both functions that eliminated data redundancies, crea-
                ted an error-free environment and allowed management to access and use in-
                formation required in a timely manner.

1987   **California First Bank**, San Diego, California
to   Personnel Administrator
1990

              Upon completion of college was hired by this major Southern California bank to
              provide administrative support for a regional human resource office. Reporting
              to the manager of the unit. **Primary accomplishments** included:

              * a service provider approach that included resolving any pay discrepancies in a
                24-hour turnaround time.

              * instituting a customer satisfaction survey program that was expanded to inclu-
                ded human resource services as well.

              * a complete review of all payroll forms to eliminate redundancies and obsoles-
                cence while redesigning several forms, totally with internal resources and soft-
                ware, in an effort to obtain required data in a more effective manner.

EDUCATION

              Costa Mesa University, Costa Mesa California, Bachelor of Arts Degree

SKILLS/ACTIVITIES

              PC literate in standalone and LAN environments. Software: ABRA Pay,
              LOTUS 1-2-3, Fox-Pro, Word for Windows, LOTUS Notes. Spanish. Member,
              American Payroll Association and Society for Human Resource Management.

Figure 8-2.

Where Can You Get More Ideas about Resumes?   In addition to the
obvious sources—your spouse, the kids, neighbors, friends, the person
referred to you who happens to be a senior consultant in a major outplacement firm—consider the perhaps not-so-obvious ones. For example,
anyone who works at an employment agency. If you evaluate the person
as being competent, ask for his/her frank opinion about your resume.
Take notes, and rush back home so that you will not only have time to

Harry Smith
264 West 213rd Street Apt. 3A
Cleveland, Ohio 41234
(216) 864-5181

EXPERIENCE

7/88 - Present **Fuller Bank,** Cleveland, Ohio
Mail and Office Supplies Supervisor
With staff of three, provided leadership for coordination of mail and
distribution of supplies for the bank. Responsibilities include
vendor contact, pricing and purchasing recommendations for
stationery, office equipment, and computer supplies. Facsimile,
photocopier, and telex equipment located in Mail Department
facilities.

4/87 - 4/88 **Independent Television Sales, Inc.** Toledo, Ohio
Production Sales Assistant
Responsible for the daily operations of the Mail, Printing, and
Shipping Departments; also responsible for supply inventories and
re-orders. Company went out of business.

8/82 - 4/87 **Garretto Co. Inc.** Toledo, Ohio
Mail Department Supervisor
Responsible, with a staff of ten, for providing the leadership and
coordination of daily activities; developed procedures that
enhanced the department's effectiveness and improved the quality
of services provided.

1/81 - 4/82 **Hapatics, Inc.** New York City
General Assistant/Driver

1976-80 Served as **Mail Clerk** for **Lincoln Dime Savings Bank** (1976-79)
and **Tostner Construction Company** (1979-80)

EDUCATION **New York Community College**
Graduate, **Springfield Gardens High School**

OFFICE Xerox 9500/1075, Pitney Bowes Meter Machine 435, IBM
EQUIPMENT Telecopier 495, Canon Rotary Microfilm 700P, and folding
machinery

REFERENCES References are available on request

Figure 8-3.

consider the notes you have obtained but also the opportunity to determine what you liked about the comments.

Keep in mind two things, however. First, most counselors fall in a
middle category; they're not the best and not the worst, so consider
what they say but take that as just one of the many opinions you
obtain. Second, they have a vested interest. The more the person serving as your counselor tries to impose his/her will, the more likely it is

that you will rebel and probably avoid that counselor. A lot of "counselors" will try to get you to reshape the resume, whenever possible, and they may leave you wondering why, after you agreed to make those major revisions to your resume, it now does a poor job of representing you. Frequently, a counselor will try to reduce your significant contribution(s) so that you can be pigeonholed into filling a job they have an order for.

Here's a list of possible sources of resumes, critiques, and advice:

College placement offices

Outplacement groups

Public library seminars or workshops

Church groups

Professional associations

Adult education programs

Department of Labor, Unemployment Service

Other not-for-profits in the job development industry

Techno-Resumes

A new twenty-first century method for sending out resumes and answering ads has arisen in some cities. This new method falls somewhere between a targeted mailing and responding to blind ads. *The New York Times* (and I'm sure other big-city newspapers as well) has introduced a membership program ($6.66 per month, or $40 for six months of unlimited use) that combines your resume, their classified ads, and a push-button telephone. This program, called FasTrak, is guaranteed, with membership fees refunded at any time without question.[5]

Here's how it works. You send in your resume (or they create one for you, from submitted information on your registration form). As you watch the display and classified employment advertisements, you note the FasTrak number on the bottom of any ad of any participating employer of interest. By using your telephone (a combination of your ID number and the ad's code), up to five employers at a time will receive your resume electronically.

Before signing up for this electronic wizardry, if it is available in your area or in a city to which you wish to relocate, size up the ads in advance. The key word in such a program is *participating* employers.

---

[5]At this time *The New York Times* has canceled this service, but I am sure it will commence again.

Look to see how many ads that have the code are ads you would be interested in applying for. This program was introduced in mid-December of 1993 by *The New York Times,* and there are quite a few coded employment advertisers. Depending on how these ads were distributed in your job-objective target area, and if you're still interested in answering blind ads, this may be an option to try. Given the cost to you, in time, of writing a letter, addressing an envelope, and mailing it, a telephone call seems painless.

If you do opt to try this program, keep a close tab on what ads you have answered in this method, and on your response rate. Keep in mind that these are long shots, and that less than 5 percent of your time should be devoted to such high-risk endeavors.

Week 8 Checklist

☐ Reviewed Job Search Log and Resume Log.

☐ Updated appointment book for all follow-up activities.

☐ Reviewed Meeting and Interview Logs for comments on resume.

☐ Revised current resume.

☐ Revisited job-hunt objective to ensure continuing *daily* effort to obtain five more contacts (people, organizations) for job leads.

Week 9
Follow-Up Strategies

Day 57

At this point you have slightly more than 30 days to reach your objective of obtaining a new job within 90 days. You are two-thirds of the way there, in terms of calendar time. How is your progress in terms of the more important job-search time? If you're on target, and on or close to schedule, your job search should be displaying certain characteristics.

Week 9 Signposts

First Meetings. You should have experienced several first meetings with persons in organizations that have jobs to offer, and jobs for which you have been given specific indications that you are a candidate. If you need a benchmark number for these "in the works" opportunities, at least eight (or one per week) would be a comfortable margin. Five or less is definitely on the weak side. You need these meetings to kick off the process of receiving a job offer. Without the meetings, you can't proceed. You can't work in a vacuum.

Number of your "first meetings" to date? _____

Interviews. You should be committed to at least five interviews for first meetings during this (ninth) week. These meetings should be with persons whom you feel can meet your objective of having an appropriate job opening, or lead to a job opening.

Number of your interviews to date? _____

Contacts.   You should be continuing to make five new contacts a day now, by telephone, to discover new contacts or more job-prospect meetings.

Average number of daily new contacts you made last week _____

If your individual performance is less than that you've just indicated, you need to look back at the last few weeks to determine where you've been spending your time, and to analyze why you haven't been getting results. If it's merely the fact that you must put in more time to make contacts that can lead to meetings, concentrate on that objective this week. If you have been putting in the time but not getting the results, this is the week to improve your follow-up techniques.

Two elements that are essential to finding a job are *activity* and *observation*.

Activity.   You need to put the time in, take care of the sometimes tedious details, and be relentless about it. This doesn't equate with "going through the motions." You must work hard—*and* work smart.

Observation.   You work smart only when you look at what you're doing each day and determine what's working and what isn't, and why. Then, after observing, you take appropriate action to improve your results.

Key Steps to Ensure Effective Follow-up

1. *Keep one calendar (appointment book).*   Woe to the person who keeps more than one calendar (one for the pocket, one at home, one for the job search)! Unless you're obsessively detailed and organized, sooner or later a follow-up or appointment will be missed. Why chance it? Be disciplined about marking down all your meetings, things to do, telephone calls to make, and keeping track of how you use the hours in each job-search day.[1] Keeping a second calendar is just more work, and that you don't need.

---

[1]Don't forget all the job-search expenses. Keep track of all your mileage, fuel, and tolls, if you travel by car; rental receipts, if you lease a vehicle; and all surface and air transportation ticket receipts. Even if you don't qualify to deduct these expenses on your tax return, in terms of your budget it's necessary to know where the money is going. Depending on how expensive it has been for you so far in this job search, this is certainly a factor to be considered when you're weighing other alternative job situations.

2. *Check your calendar at least twice a day.*   Check it late each day, to determine what you must prepare for with regard to the next day's activities. Do you have all the materials you require (updated and customer-driven resume, research notes, telephone numbers) to start the day promptly? Check it also early the following day, to see how you're proceeding on your "to do" list and follow-ups; afternoon activities; letters to mail; meetings to schedule and research to perform. Put all pertinent follow-up data from your resume and job-search logs into your calendar to "tickle" for additional action.

3. *Practice active listening skills.*   Use these skills to ensure that you're recording accurate information (in person or over the telephone), but also, in the feedback mode, to be certain the person you're dealing with is noting the correct information. Don't assume that everyone is a good listener, or even a better listener than you. It's hard enough to find leads and set up appointments, without the complications resulting from incorrect information.

When you're speaking to someone who doesn't appear to be an active listener, periodically elicit responses from your statements: "Is this what you mean?" "Do you have a similar situation here?" Or even just stop talking once you've made a point. Most people can't stand silence, and unless you start rambling, chances are the other person will speak to fill the silence. This will encourage the other person to "take turns" sending and receiving messages.

4. *Always reconfirm appointments.*   The day before, always call to reconfirm, because there's always the possibility of last-minute cancellations, and you can at least take a preventative step if you're dealing with a disorganized person.

5. *Always write a thank-you letter within 24 hours of any meeting, interview, and referral given.*

6. *Always write an individual thank-you letter, specifically mentioning some details from the meeting.*   If you met with a group, each person gets their own letter; no group letters, please. With a little thought and reference to your Meeting or Interview Journal, these brief missives can remind the reader of your good points brought out at the meeting, and also of whatever other actions were promised or indicated: "I look forward to meeting you and the department head at our next meeting, scheduled _____." "As you said you thought you would fill the position within a month, I will telephone you in three weeks to determine the status of the opening, as you suggested."

Another benefit of sending these thank-you letters is that so few people do so. If you have created a favorable impression at the meeting, the thank-you will surely enhance it. If the meeting was only so-so, a brief, to-the-point, thank-you may move your chances up a notch or two. In any case, it will keep your name in the person's mind while he/she is perhaps seeing others.

7. *Keep in touch.*   If you have an answering machine and you're out at meetings, call in frequently to retrieve your messages; then make prompt callbacks (make sure you have a pocketful of quarters, or a telephone charge card). Should you get the complaint, "I tried to reach you, but your line was always busy," and you *are* on the phone a lot (as you *should* be!), investigate the call-waiting option from your local telephone company, or an answering service that takes a message whenever the line is busy.

Common Courtesies to Keep Your Name Visible, and Accomplish a Whole Lot More

In addition to thank-you letters, there are several other action steps to be considered that will leave a favorable impression, not just during your job search but on your whole reputation, both personally and professionally. Don't forget them in the midst of the stress and distraction of a totally focused job campaign.

Don't Forget Business and Professional Courtesy.   There was a recent *Wall Street Journal* article that dealt only with manners. The article was an interview with Miss Manners, author of *Manners in Contemporary American Culture.* There's an expectation in the marketplace that you will know how to deal with social situations and the amenities, in and out of the business arena. If you have the slightest doubt as to what is appropriate behavior in terms of opening doors, elevator etiquette, ordering in restaurants, and addressing others, immediately obtain (purchase, or take out a library copy) a book on business etiquette. Any old book of manners will *not* do; how to address wedding invitations is not as important to you as how to order at a business lunch! Look for a book that deals exclusively with business-related situations. Even if you consider yourself to be the master (mistress) of propriety, it would do you good to review current practices; there may be a few new wrinkles out there that you're not prepared for. You must be able to be sensitive, and to extend all courtesies in a wholesome and confident manner.

Practice.   You need to exercise your personal and professional skills as often as you can. To use a sports analogy, you have to play the game on a regular basis. Get out. Be involved. Don't discover that you're rusty just when your big moment has come. Telephone calls and letters are important, but the advertising is never as important as the product. You are selling *yourself*, and you must be out in the marketplace in order to close a sale. If you are doing volunteer work, take that opportunity to "interview" others, exercise your small talk, and practice active listening skills.

Don't Apologize.   Without self-confidence, you're doomed. When questioned about your skills, experiences, choices of schools or workplaces, *never* give excuses! Always put a positive spin on any aspect of your prior experience. When asked, for example, why you picked a particular college or university, don't say "My parents wanted me to go there," or "It was the only one I could afford." Those statements may be true, but they will hardly enhance your reputation. Don't cast yourself as a "victim" of parental choice, economics, or poor high school performance. Use these opportunities to state something positive about the school and your experience there.

"I'm surprised you've never heard of _____. It has a reputation in the state as being an excellent school for journalism. I found the instruction to be top-notch, and since the classes weren't overly crowded, I had the opportunity to really work closely with the teachers. In fact, I was able to work on several extensive projects."

"Yes, I suppose taking a year off from college and completing my education later on in evening classes might be viewed as taking the long way around, but I was very anxious to delve into the real world of banking. A great opportunity presented itself, and I grabbed it; it was the best move I ever made. I always intended to get the necessary credits to graduate, and when I attended evening classes I was so much more motivated, and I had a lot more in common with the other students who were also out there working. In fact, I hope to attend more classes in the evenings so as to obtain my MBA."

The same goes for former employers: *never* degrade them, regardless of the circumstances. All places of employment were great places to work until it became time for you to move on.

"XYZ Inc. had a terrific financial department that I've been lucky enough to work in for the past three years. I was able to assume more responsibilities and expertise on the job. When they were bought out by ABC Company six months ago, ABC had a completely different financial approach, as well as a larger finance department. They preferred to use their own staff, and there wasn't a similar position in the company that I could see myself moving into. I've really enjoyed my job, and I look forward to finding a similar position." That's one way to put a positive spin on the brute fact that you were excess baggage.

Plan What You're Going to Say in Advance of Being Asked.   We all put our feet in our mouths sometimes, and it's easy, when you're still burning with outrage and frustration over losing your old job, to let slip a few cheap shots at your old boss. But it sure won't help you in the long run. One way to avoid these gaffes is to rehearse your answers, with regard to jobs and experience, as suggested in Week 4. What you *don't* need is excuses: rather, you need to project the image of being an able and confident potential employee. These meetings and interviews offer an insight into your character; let yours give evidence of strong leadership, the ability to bring new ideas on board, and initiative. Remember, you give others insight into your loyalty, motivation, goals, and energy, when you speak about choices you have made in your life. Portray yourself as a winner who always looks for the best opportunity.

Be on Time for All Meetings.   Plan your route ahead of time, because "when you're early, you're early." When you're ahead of schedule, buses fly through traffic, trains arrive on time, and you always find a parking place right next door to your appointment. Unfortunately, the opposite is also true. It's when we are hoping to gain every single minute en route that we run into total gridlock, overcrowded elevators, and the bus that crawls along the highway. Of course when the unmentionable does happen, regardless of all your planning, and you see yourself running late, by all means telephone and ask if the meeting can be moved back (half-hour, hour?) or if they can reschedule. Unless you have been totally undone by whatever happened to make you late, cross your fingers that they'll say they can take you a little late.

Be Neat, Organized, and Effective.   You are working for yourself (the hardest boss you'll ever have, I hope), so you have to do all the filing, letter writing, proofreading, and follow-up. There's an old saying, "if you don't work with your head, you have to work with your feet." To paraphrase, use your head and do it right the first time, because it's a lot more work to have to correct it and do it over.

Mndjnfhffff, or "What?"   On the telephone (and of course at all times in person), leave the food, gum, cigarettes, and music for off hours. You wouldn't do those things on the job, so don't do them now. If you're working out of the house, it's very easy to adopt a casual demeanor. Wrong! Have you ever spoken to someone over the telephone, and you knew exactly when they took a drag on their cigarette, or chomped down on a carrot? Take a regular lunch break instead.

Watch How Others Do It.   In any gathering, be very observant of all those around you. Spot confident, powerful-looking people; determine their "manners" ratio. Do they "lord it over others" by demeaning those around them, or are they gracious? Whenever possible, seek to align yourself with these praiseworthy professionals.

A Creativity Exercise to
Identify More Job Sources

Here we go again. You'll never exhaust your ability to identify additional job sources, as long as you don't confine your thinking within the "box."

What is the *least* likely place to go to look for a job lead or a contact? Some might identify the zoo, a ballpark, a movie. Think of five others. What makes you think they are poor opportunities?

1. _____
2. _____
3. _____
4. _____
5. _____

Next, think of the five most unlikely friends or adult relatives to help you through networking. How so?

1. _____
2. _____
3. _____
4. _____
5. _____

Now, what if those were the only five places you could go, and the only five people left for you to contact? Can you reevaluate, and find any overlooked opportunities there?

1. _____
2. _____
3. _____
4. _____
5. _____

A Review of Current (and Not So Current) Prospects

This is your opportunity to evaluate all those prospects you've identified over the past three weeks, to be certain that none fell through the cracks, to consider their potential and quality, and to see if you can use them more effectively.

Use the Prospect Analysis (Fig. 9-1) to make a list of the current prospects. List each name, title, organization, telephone number, and last contact date. Write down the objective of each contact: lead, further prospects, job opening. In the column next to Objective, rate each prospect from 0 (long shot) to 5 (a very viable prospect with a high potential for success).

Once that's done, look to see if you do have all the information needed to make the follow-up (address, telephone number). If any items are missing, fill in the blanks now.

Review each prospect line by line, and be satisfied that your qualitative evaluation was correct. Next, identify what action must be taken for each prospect this week, and allocate a day and time in your appointment book when you plan to do it.

Using Prospect Analysis #2 (Fig. 9-2), repeat the exercise for all the other prospects you have identified since you began your job search. Evaluate their current status, and identify the best avenue to approach them again. With the passage of time, some of these prospects may have become viable. If so, determine the actions you must take this week, and mark these down in your appointment book. Don't give up. There is a fellow who had impeccable credentials and wanted to join a major outplacement firm. It took him 19 tries.

Meetings

Do you have five interviews lined up at this time for the week?

How many are lined up for the upcoming weeks? _____

List all your interviews scheduled for the next few weeks. Using the same 0 to 5 rating system, with 5 being the one with the most potential, rate each. Use the Interview Analysis form (Fig. 9-3).

PROSPECT ANALYSIS

List your current prospects identified over past three weeks.
Rate their potential, "0" for long shot up to "5" for high probability of reaching your objective.

NAME	TITLE	ORGANIZATION	PHONE #	CONTACT DATE	OBJECTIVE	RATING

Figure 9-1.

PROSPECT ANALYSIS #2

List your older prospects, those identified since beginning of job search.
Rate their potential, "0" for long shot up to "5" for high probability of reaching your objective.

NAME	TITLE	ORGANIZATION	PHONE #	LAST CONTACT DATE	OBJECTIVE	RATING

Figure 9-2.

INTERVIEW ANALYSIS

List all your interviews scheduled for the next three weeks.

Rate their potential, "0" for long shot up to "5" for high probability of reaching your objective.

NAME	TITLE	ORGANIZATION	PHONE #	LAST CONTACT DATE	OBJECTIVE	RATING

Figure 9-3.

Prospective Employers

In Week 2, you completed a Work Environment Survey. In light of the places that you have interviewed, and the interviews that you have scheduled, has your employer profile changed? Is there more than one profile of an employer that you would be satisfied with? Have you also reevaluated your choice of position sought? With all the contacts you have made, have any new possibilities surfaced?

Write down what your job objective(s) are at this time. If you are looking at more than one option, list all that you would consider.

_____

_____

_____

_____

What is your present employer profile? You may wish to trade off some facets, for example a longer commute, in exchange for flexible hours, or to reflect the reality that you probably _will_ have to travel more than you had originally desired.

_____

_____

_____

_____

As you cover more territory in your job campaign, it's important to take periodic reality checks and determine if any readjustments are prudent. With the previous objectives (position and employer) in mind, identify at least 10 new organizations that you can approach in your job search. Do research and find out the hiring authority for each, their telephone numbers, what makes you interested in them, and what value you could bring to them as an employee. Transcribe this information into your Job Search Log, and follow up with dates and times in your appointment book to pursue these leads.

1. _____

2. _____

3. _____

4. _____

5. _____

6. _____

7. _____

8. _____

9. _____

10. _____

Week 9 Checklist

☐ Reviewed number of first meetings you've had.

☐ Reviewed number of interviews you've had.

☐ Reviewed number of contacts you've made.

Rate your effectiveness: ☐ Excellent ☐ Satisfactory ☐ Needs Improvement

☐ Thank-you letters all written. ☐Within 24 hours?

☐ Reviewed answers on Sample Interview Questions (see Week 4) for able, confident tone (no excuses, please!).

☐ Re-rehearsed answers to most-asked questions.

☐ Identified further names and organizations for networking activities.

☐ Reviewed and rated prospects.

☐ Reviewed and rated interviews scheduled.

☐ Reviewed and confirmed job objectives and employer profile.

Week 10

Advanced Networking

Just When You Thought You Knew It All...

Day 64

Sixty-three days down, and just twenty-seven to go! At this point in your search you should be hitting certain benchmarks. First of all, you should be just about ready to get at least one offer (if you haven't already). Also, there should be at least a few follow-up meetings scheduled for the coming week, and you should also be searching for and identifying new potential prospects. It's crucial at this point to continue the pursuit constantly and actively, because situations have a way of changing. If you're feeling any disappointment because a job offer has fallen through, remember that you have several other prospects in various stages of the process. Don't, in other words, put all your resumes in one basket.

Have you still not received a single offer? (Pendings don't count, in your answer here!) If you haven't been given at least one offer, don't panic, but reexamine what you've been doing. Ensure that your focus of activities is as targeted as it should be. At this point, *after* you have gone through the exercise of making today's telephone calls so as to generate more prospects, you need to sit somewhere in silence—preferably out of the house (get out, and make things happen!)—and perform an analysis of what's working and what isn't. Figure 10-1 provides you with a Job Search Effectiveness Worksheet to fill out.

JOB SEARCH EFFECTIVENESS WORKSHEET

Today's Date _____ Date Search Began _____

Number of actual working days to date devoted to job search efforts _____

Progress Report

List below for each of the past nine weeks the number of telephone calls or visits to those persons that fall into the following categories:

WEEK #	1	2	3	4	5	6	7	8	9
Was of no assistance:									
Offered information or assistance:									
Agreed to a meeting:									
Made a commitment for more meetings:									
Had additional meetings:									
Gave you a job offer:									

Figure 10-1.

If you have gotten an offer—either just gotten, or received and rejected a while ago—I suggest you too complete the worksheet. If you have an offer in hand and are deciding whether to accept it, you have more to do, but that's okay, because it's this type of "problem" we all should be striving for. Go to Week 12 to perform an analysis, to determine whether this offer is acceptable. Then turn back to this week to complete the Job Search Effectiveness Worksheet (Fig. 10-1) to review what efforts and results you have obtained, as one more barometer of the viability of the offer you have received.

Of the "no-assistance calls," identify the ones that were handled ineffectively by you. Use Fig. 10-2 to list a few of them, and to note how you would do them over again if you could. If these calls were mostly in the early weeks rather than more recently, then your prowess in identifying leads, or your ability to get others to render assistance, has greatly increased. If the contrary is true, it's even more essential that you identify why these were negative. Was it the choice of the person whom you contacted (misidentified a lead), or the method of the contact (shouldn't have called; should have written a letter first), or something else?

Check Your Sources.   Check your newspaper/periodical clippings; have all been followed through? Identify each clipping to be used for future reference—include any ads clipped. What have the results been? Refer to both your Job Search and Resume Logs (Figs. 1-19 and 1-20). Use Fig. 10-3 to analyze where you've been getting your contacts from, and which type(s) have been most successful.

The Medium Carries the Message.   How have you been reaching out to these leads? By telephone? By letter? Using Fig. 10-4, analyze the Job Search and Resume Logs again, by the type of media used. In terms of

"NO ASSISTANCE" CONTACTS	"WHAT I COULD HAVE DONE DIFFERENTLY..."
1	
2	
3	
4	
5	

Figure 10-2.

SOURCES OF LEADS	# OBTAINED OBJECTIVE	# NO HELP GIVEN	# STILL PENDING
1			
2			
3			
4			
5			
6			
7			
8			
9			
10			

Figure 10-3.

MEDIUM:	# SUCCESSFUL	# UNSUCCESSFUL	# PENDING
COLD TELEPHONE CALL			
REFERRED TELEPHONE CALL			
COLD VISIT			
BLIND AD LETTER			
REFERRED LETTER			
OTHER			

Figure 10-4.

resumes mailed, what portion were for blind ads, and what was your response rate?

List here your most effective methods of getting responses (the response is that which met the objective of your call).

Most successful contacts were referred from (sources, either names or type):

_____

_____

Most successful method of contact:

_____

_____

Least successful contacts (sources or names):

_____

_____

Least successful method of contact:

_____

_____

Why do you think you were successful or unsuccessful, in each case?

_____

_____

_____

On the "unsuccessful" list, can you identify any leads that you can turn around, and where you can try a new approach or a different tactic?

_____

_____

_____

Major Network Adjustment and Review

Now that you've taken a few minutes to analyze the effectiveness of your opportunities, it's time to turn your attention to your networking activities.

Rank in descending order the five networking sources (friends, former employers, business associates, neighbors, etc.) that you are using the most.

1. _____

2. _____

3. _____

4. _____

5. _____

Of those, which do you feel are proving to be the most helpful? Most effective?

_____

_____

In those categories that you feel have been the most helpful in leading you to contacts and/or job openings, how many *more* names can you think of that you have yet to schedule a contact for?

_____

_____

_____

_____

Put these names/organizations in your Job Search Log to contact this week.

What meetings or seminars or business meetings, of organizations or associations, have you attended in the past five weeks?

_____

_____

_____

_____

Have any leads or contacts been generated from these activities?

_____

_____

_____

If none, why do you think this has happened?

_____

_____

_____

Looking for New Sources

Identify five new networking sources, in an effort to uncover major opportunities for more contacts. To accomplish this in a major-sweep fashion, but one that continues your targeted marketing approach, you will need to identify friendly sources for names from which you will be able to select and choose the most likely sources for leads or jobs themselves. You need to take the time to test the list for accuracy, and you also need to keep a brief but detailed log to determine the list's effectiveness.

You may ask, "What are we doing here that we haven't done before?"[1] The answer is that this is an opportunity to locate and use *secondary* sources. What makes a source secondary? Simply the fact that you didn't identify it as a primary opportunity when you compiled your list the first time. Will all of us always have the chance to identify secondary sources? The answer is a definite yes, but for some it will take more creativity to come up with them. To jog your mind, consider the following examples.

---

[1]Calling friends and acquaintances is easier for some than others. Look back at the list you prepared during Week 1 (Lead Organizer, Fig. 1-8). Are there any that you have avoided calling? If you need any motivation, most experts agree that 75 percent of all new jobs come from friends or friends of friends. Don't feel that you are using your friends; give them something—an article, a book, a lunch, a compliment, an ear for them to talk to. Don't be embarrassed (see the same reasons for not apologizing in Week 9). Put a positive twist on it. "I am giving myself the chance to grow professionally by looking for a company I can grow with. I am so excited." Don't write letters to those with whom you would be more natural and comfortable talking. Be yourself—that is who you are selling. If you cannot practice your selling skills on friends who want you to do well, how can you be confident selling yourself to strangers? Go back over your lists. Do not forget your relatives and parents!

College Lists.   Go to colleges and universities where you did *not* go to school, and look at and work with their alumni directories and (more importantly) placement offices. I assume you already have and are using your college alumni directory, but usually there's a reference copy in the library.

Public or Research Libraries.   While at the library, consider other references that have lists of names, such as some type or other of "Who's Who." They're of varying quality depending on the publisher, but if they give you accurate data that helps you in your search, you've accomplished your stated objective. Browse any library for magazines and other periodicals as well as lists to use, sources that you weren't previously aware of. In Week 5 you were encouraged to use *The Job Hunters' Sourcebook: A Gale Career Information Guide* to locate professional organizations that will lead to opportunities for sources. Go back and see if there were any other listings, or other reference books for your particular industry, that could be of help. Look for organizations that cross over into several career paths. There are also very specific groups organized along gender or other special-interest lines. One example is NAFE, the National Association of Female Executives. They have local network connections and specializations (minorities, women in computing) and provide monthly newsletters, business breakfasts, and low-to-no-cost seminars for members. This group can lead you to other networks. So go back to the library and search out every group that touches on your job objective(s). There are even associations for people who work at home! So if you're considering other options, now is the time to reach out to groups that can place you on the inside track.

The College Placement Office.   Even if it's not your own school, many placement offices will allow you to look around and use whatever information is available for their students and alumni. One human resource manager, located near a medium-sized private university, posted some open positions with the placement office. He received five responses for one of the openings, and not one of those five people had ever attended the school!

Alumni Lists from Employers.   Many larger organizations have lists of former employees, with updated information on how to contact them. Included with the contact information is of course the most recent title and organizational affiliation. Here you aren't going after the organization but after the list of its former employees, now in positions of authority at organizations you may not have heard of.

Electronic Bulletin Boards.   Even if you aren't technically inclined, roam the "information highway" with someone who is PC-knowledgeable, in search of jobs. One of the complaints of those who access electronic bulletin boards and resume services through their computers is that only technical workers apply. Here's an obvious advantage for the non-techie. Make an effort to understand the population using the service, and to determine whether there will be job opportunities there. It takes time, but do reach out and get help. You win in three ways:

1. You are growing more technically proficient, and learning a new skill.

2. You are building a relationship with the person upon whom you are depending for help (and using/sharpening negotiation skills in the process, without even thinking about it).

3. You are uncovering new sources that will mean more opportunities for meetings, interviews, and offers.

Job Fairs. Get copies of local college and university event calendars so that you can watch for job fairs or industry presentations that may provide information or leads.

Corporate or Organization In-House Newsletters and/or Annual Reports. Either call or visit the headquarters of any large organization, and ask for a copy of their latest annual report (if they're a public company) or their newsletter. *Always* ask for copies of these when you interview or visit. You can find names, news tidbits, and information about the company, all of which can make you more knowledgeable when you interview or try to find contacts.

Sources You Should Usually Avoid

Outplacement Network Meetings. These are not only outplacement organizations and religious groups that have offered their facilities for their congregations, but any other informally arranged gatherings of out-of-work people as well. These could be arranged by a profession, or by the displaced workers of an employer who, by themselves, agreed to form the group; the former employer may even have agreed to provide facilities.

The primary purpose of these meetings is to network for support. The second reason is to share leads, especially those that someone has identified but that aren't right for him/her. There is some good to be obtained from these sessions, and I know of a few instances in which a person got a lead that turned into a job offer. The problem I have with them is with the composition of the gathering itself: a group of people who are themselves looking for work. To put yourself in that environment may only lead you to frustration, concern, or worse. Many of those people will have "more experience," "better skills," or both, or something else "more/better than me," and it's just a step from that to the positive conviction that "I'll never get another job."

My suggestion is that you surround yourself with people who feel powerful and positive and have success stories to tell, because in that kind of setting, your thoughts turn to success. You ask, "What are they doing that I'm not?", and the results are more positive in tone and are proactive. So if you have the time and want to include such gatherings as one more source, give it a try, but establish specific targets as the reason for your participation and identify what you're willing to offer in exchange for what you're going to get.

Volunteer Outplacement Firms.   Avoid these, unless you're unable to get the information you need, and are sure you won't get bogged down in time-consuming commitments. Remember to make a contribution if you do decide to go this route, and even offer to be an active member *after* your job search has ended.

Cold Call Strategies That Work

They're called "cold" calls, but you should warm them up a bit and *never, ever* go in "cold"—i.e., without basic information. When you're in the library, go to the periodical section and the Periodical Index. Look up your industry. Look up the large companies that are the leaders in your field. What's been written lately? Who's been in the news? Can you pull a question from the articles that will be a grabber when you call or write? If your field is computers, and a certain company has announced a major transition to a different system, write a letter to one of the key people mentioned in the article. Ask an opinion or fact-finding question. Relate it to something in your background. Close with a request to meet, and a promise to call. Don't try to be funny; you want a job, not applause for your wit. Don't be arrogant, or boast that *you* never would have gotten their company into its present predicament!

What *does* seems to work when it comes to "breaking in" to new organizations? Appeals to their ego by means of compliments ("What a terrific marketing approach!") sometimes strike the right note. Trading on industry information ("When I was at XYZ Co., I was part of a team that introduced...") may get their attention. Sell your accomplishments. If you're in a field where creativity is highly prized, let yourself go and try several *different* approaches—don't let yourself get bored. And *always* follow up with a telephone call, as promised.

How's the Money Holding Up?

Ten weeks have passed since you began your job search in earnest. How are your finances? Have you been adhering to your budget? If your fiscal resources are still intact, and your efforts are producing interviews and offers, you're extremely blessed on both fronts.

However, if either your funds are running low or you haven't turned up enough prospects and interviews to generate job offers, and if you don't feel this is going to change next week, you must seriously consider alternative employment solutions.

You must restate your primary job objective at this time, but you may still retain your original objective as secondary, for the time being. That doesn't mean that you're giving up on finding that new job you've been looking for so hard these past 10 weeks, just that you are facing up to the realities of your situation. You're taking control. You're being proactive. You're continuing to search for options, and will duly consider all opportunities that present themselves. You're simply reordering your objectives at this time.

Primary job objective: _____

Secondary job objective: _____

Of the following possibilities, which do you feel are most viable at this time?

Part-time employment _____   Consulting _____
Unrelated employment _____   Buy a business _____
Start own business _____   Temporary work _____
Other _____

If you must explore another area of employment, go back to the first weeks and prepare lists of prospects, marketing letters, and a resume that will target those jobs. Ideally, if you're merely switching gears into consulting or part-time employment, you can use your same resume and many of the contacts. You can also expand into agencies and employee leasing (outsourcing) firms for leads. List at least 10 contacts that you will pursue this week, in support of your restated job objective.

1. _____
2. _____
3. _____
4. _____
5. _____
6. _____
7. _____
8. _____
9. _____
10. _____

Working at Home

You may already have been working out of the home for the past 10 weeks. Has the thought crossed your mind, "This is great! How can I ever go back to having a boss?" Maybe you have picked up some assignments along the way to tide you over, to do a friend a favor, or just to remain active in your field. Assuming that this is something that has been in the back of your mind for quite a while, ask yourself the following questions, to gauge your chances of being successful working out of your home.

Do I have a highly marketable skill, service, or product? Do I know where and to whom I can market my skill, service, or product? Do I have the materials needed?

Am I disciplined enough to set and adhere to a schedule? Do I mind working long hours and working alone?

Am I willing to learn new skills, do new things? Am I flexible?

Can I manage my own finances, taxes, and expenses, until payments come in from my clients?

Is my family supportive of this enterprise. If need be, can I pay for child care?

Do I really want to do this?

The greater number of "yeses" you have given to the above questions, the greater your chance of success.[2]

---

[2]The U.S. Small Business Administration (SBA) has development centers and seminars that provide advice. Call 800-8-ASKSBA.

Week 10 Checklist

- ☐ Completed and analyzed Job Search Effectiveness Worksheet.
- ☐ Completed "No Assistance" analysis.
- ☐ Analyzed sources and effectiveness of contacts and leads.
- ☐ Analyzed the media used to reach contacts.
- ☐ Reviewed financial situation and monthly Cash Budget.
- ☐ Restated job objective.
    - ☐ Identified prime objective.
    - ☐ Prepared list of contacts.
    - ☐ Revised resume for new job objective.
- ☐ Sent marketing letters to at least five contacts.

Week 11

Progress Review, and More Adjustments

Day 71

Down to the wire—just 20 days to go! If you've received one or more offers by this point, don't give up now, unless the offer is (1) attractive, and you're certain you're going to accept it, and (2) there is absolute certainty that the job offer will turn into a real job. The point is, you must be careful when offered a job that no circumstances develop to turn the firm offer into vapor on Day 1, when you've been scheduled to start. (See Week 12 for further discussion on offers, and the unsavory but necessary subject of offers that turn out not to be offers.)

Even though you have a deadline that is rapidly approaching, take a reality check at this point to determine what your status and prospects are today. Whether you haven't received any offers, have no offers you wish to accept, or are considering an offer but haven't yet accepted, there is still more work to do. You must reevaluate what is working and what isn't, and what to do to increase your effectiveness.

Review It All Again

Use the by-now-familiar format (you used it in Week 6) found in the Review Worksheet (Fig. 11-1) to count up and analyze how much and

WEEK 11 REVIEW WORKSHEET
Refer to your Job Search and Resume Logs, as well as your Appointment Book to determine your activity levels

	WEEKS 1-5	WEEK 6	WEEK 7	WEEK 8	WEEK 9	WEEK 10
NUMBER OF RESUMES SENT						
*TO BLIND ADS						
*TO REFERRALS						
NUMBER OF MARKETING LETTERS SENT						
* SENT COLD						
* REFERRALS						
NUMBER OF TELEPHONE CALLS MADE						
* COLD CALLS						
* REFERRALS						
NUMBER OF MEETINGS SET UP						
NUMBER OF JOB INTERVIEWS SET UP						
NUMBER OF OFFERS RECEIVED						

Figure 11-1.

how effectively you have been working. It's important to periodically review performance, for if you were employed now, someone would be monitoring your performance and giving you feedback as to how to avoid mistakes and improve your work. Since you're working for yourself, it's all up to you. Besides providing you with needed feedback so that you can do more of what's working and look to change what isn't, self-criticism is a skill that will keep you in good stead no matter where you find your new position. Doing well will build your confidence, and the ability to stop and improve in other areas will give you a sense of control.

After you have referred back to your numbers from Week 6, update the worksheet to include your efforts from the past five weeks (Weeks 6 through 10) in the areas of sending resumes and marketing letters and making telephone calls. Also, track how many meetings, interviews, and job offers occurred during each month. Is a trend visible? Are you keeping up a steady effort?

Look back to your results for the first five weeks. Have you improved in those areas that you felt at that time called for a stronger effort? _____

If not, do you have an explanation for why your efforts have fallen off recently? _____

_____

Looking at the last five weeks, where do you find your greatest success(es)? _____

Why do you think this has happened? _____

_____

How do those "successes" relate to the areas where you have made the most effort? _____

This month, what will be your prime objective in the way of improved results? _____

In Week 10, you reexamined your job objectives by the light of both your progress and your financial situation. Are you comfortable with the decision you made? _____

Are you pursuing two job objectives at the same time, with one being a priority? _____

How has this altered your job campaign? _____

_____

_____

Key Readjustments

There are five readjustment steps you should take to become more effective and *get that job!*

1. To be more assertive, and to get the meetings that will accomplish something, *practice your phone techniques.*

2. *Utilize advanced time-management techniques.* Use the daily planner format (Fig. 6-1) in your appointment book to determine time-wasters (things, activities, and/or people) who detract from the project at hand. At the start of each day, establish the uninterrupted total time you will devote to your job search on that day. Establish the number of effective calls you plan to place, and to make them even more effective, think in terms of results rather than the final goal, the job. This is "processed-based" planning: "Today I will make x number of telephone calls." Set the goal of establishing one meeting per day. Keep calling until you get that one invite. Then establish other job-search strategies—such as finding a new source from which to get referrals to make more telephone calls to set up more meetings.

3. For those positions you have a genuine interest in, *attempt to determine the organization behind the listing of a blind ad.* One way is to read the ad for clues—the description, for example. When the description of the organization is of a "major downtown hospital," the hospital may be one of just two. Go after both. Call human resources, and speak definitively of the fact that you're interested in the ad; you wish to discuss the matter with the person responsible for screening the calls for the position. If that doesn't work, ask for the name and title of the person that resumes should be sent to. Follow up with phone calls to set up a meeting.

4. If you're having a hard time getting through to someone who may be a source, a contact, or even a bona fide job lead (as suggested earlier), *call at imaginative times.* Try first thing in the morning at a work number (7:30 A.M. may be convenient and appropriate, particularly, if that's the time the hard-to-get-a-hold-of person is answering his/her own phone). For latecomers, consider them as potential stay-laters; when to call them? Try after 5 P.M., and keep trying until you're sure they must have left for the evening. For both early and late calls, you need to do advance work to get a direct phone number, because more often than not the main number will be voice

mail, with instructions to dial the person's number directly—*if* (a big if) you know it.[1]

5. *Think about networking in a downward direction.* This seemingly unthinkable piece of advice has been suggested by veteran recruiter Gil Tucker, a principal in the recruiting firm The Bankers Register located in New York City. He says that, especially for the mid-level career person, the doors this approach can open are almost endless, and that it represents a great deal of potential. What does he mean by "networking downward"? It means that you should consider the people who worked below you in the organizations where you worked as sources for leads. Is this such a strange idea? Why does it never seem to be mentioned as a suggestion? Sure, networking contacts from organizations in which we have worked include peers and colleagues, supervisors and members of senior management. But what about the secretaries, clerks, and receptionists who served us so well? Where are they now, and do they represent possible contacts for leads? Think about it. What about the people you worked with in your most recent organization, the ones with whom you developed a nice rapport? Are they to be considered a possible source for leads and contacts, and even a job? Is one of them now a secretary in another organization who has a good rapport with his/her current boss, and would be happy to make an introduction?

When you're considering old contacts, also try to look up persons in positions below yours. In five years someone may have really found a niche in some organization, and is now in a position to hire you. Be sure, though, that you can accept the fact that this is the same person who used to report to you and whom you coached through his/her most insecure days.

Extend the thought, as well. Many people tend to be "elitist," especially when it comes to work. Review your list of "nonbusiness" contacts. Are they limited to those you considered "above" you or on a par with you socioeconomically, or by level of education or by profession? Ask yourself if there's a neighbor or friend (or relative, for that matter) whom you had previously thought would be of little or no help in linking you to a specific position. Use the Lead Organizer (Fig. 1-9) to look for any categories or individuals you may have missed. One way to organize such a search for contacts is to think of all the "hats" you wear. You may be a parent, a son/daughter, a home owner, a commuter, a patient, an employee. Count how many hats you

---

[1]There are a few state-of-the-art phone systems that offer an alternative to the extension number requirement: the option to dial the person's last name.

wear, and how many people you know that can be considered sources of possible leads.

Reference Check-up

Rethink your references. If you've made it though the interview stage but never made it to an offer, consider any names you may have given as a reference, personal or professional. Have you had occasion to speak to these people, and were they ever contacted by any of the organizations you approached? If so, ask for a brief synopsis of the conversation, or for a copy of the letter if the contact was made in writing and if you feel comfortable doing so.

Just as you have had to consider your own telephone and writing skills, reflect now on how your references may come across on the telephone or in a letter. They may be terrific people, and they may know you inside and out, but they must also be able to "sell" you. If their interpersonal skills are somewhat lacking (no matter how difficult it may be for you to acknowledge this), seriously consider *not* giving them as a reference.

Can you "trade up" your references? Are you using the most powerful, the most prestigious people you know, as well as people who are able to accurately describe your skills and the value you can add to any (particularly the calling) organization? Don't forget that this job search is essentially a public relations and a selling job. Review your references with that in mind.

Four Successful Follow-up Strategies

1. Call when you promised to.
2. Adjust your approach when the situation requires it.
3. Keep a record of what's working in follow-up, and what isn't.
4. Remember to cut your losses.

Fallback Review, and Radical Alternatives

For 70 days now you've been seeking new employment. Consider this question very seriously: Do you have any promising prospects at this point? If so, jot them down on Fig. 11-2. Write next to each prospect the date by which you will have an answer.

PROSPECT REVIEW

PROSPECTS	ESTIMATED RESPONSE DATE

Figure 11-2.

Be cautious here, because even as many as five prospects may be too few, and all five may elude you in the end. What should you do if you're concerned that your efforts are causing you to put too much time into activities that are yielding so little in terms of result? You still need a job (perhaps even more than before, depending on the state of your finances), but nothing is working. Your review of your progress by using the Review Worksheet (Fig. 11-1) has added to your concern. Your concern may be very realistic, and you're wise to address it at this point. But keep in mind that financial considerations may be an impetus both to "keep on pushing" and to consider different approaches.

What about setting up your own business? What are the steps required? Investigate franchises, particularly in a service business such as our old favorite, a recruiting firm. In every instance, the consideration requires a block of research time and attention. You need to consider the situation in terms of what it will cost to get started, both in terms of time, expertise, and cash. What amount of revenue will you need to sustain yourself, and how soon must that level be reached? What is the worst-case scenario if the business folds?

Training for a Different Career (and Profession)

If the notion of a total change in jobs has only just now occurred to you, it's probably a thought born of desperation. In order for you to make as major a change in your life as a career change, several steps must occur.

1. *The idea must have been somewhere in the back of your mind already.* You may be unaware, or not aware enough, that there is a definite problem with your present career choice, or else you may simply be refusing to believe it. For the past few weeks, a nagging doubt as to whether you are looking in the right area (despite your having reconfirmed your job objectives twice in the past week) has been haunting you.

2. *You now recognize the problem, and acknowledge the dissatisfaction.* You grow more aware of the need to "look around" to see if there are other choices you should explore.

3. *You start to poke around.* You find yourself reading articles about other professions, other organizations involved in other activities. You may look up some friends or associates in these other careers to see how they're doing, whether they like what they're doing, what job prospects are like in that field. This information will either confirm you in your decision to look further in this direction or lead you to think that "the devil you know" is better than "the devil you don't know," and thus to discontinue your explorations.

4. *You are convinced that action is necessary.* Information and research have led you to believe that both the time and choice are right: you should actively pursue a career change. You begin to evaluate your skills and experiences in relation to this new possible career. You investigate what additional training or skills are needed; are there organizations with entry-level training programs, or should outside sources (evening school, seminars) be considered?

If you're at this point, to some extent you must go back to Week 1 and rewrite your resume, redesign your marketing letter, and develop another set of sources for leads, contacts, job openings. It's a radical step to do a 180° turn at this point, but it's plausible only if you've been half-considering it in your subconscious all the while. And just because you didn't succeed with your first job objective doesn't mean that this reincarnated job search also will be a failure. No one ever said that your first, second, or third choice of a job had to be the one to last you your entire life.

Go for it! Stage a full-tilt job search in another direction. Use all the skills you've developed so far to carry you forward.

A Complete Career Change Too Radical?   What about a job to carry you, while you continue to pursue your real hope? If it fulfills your financial requirements and it meets some (but not all) of your career objectives, there's no harm in accepting it and keeping an active eye out, both inside your new organization and on the outside.

How do you convince your prospective new organization that you really want to work there, that it's not just a stopgap? Remember, they're looking for the best candidate for the job. Act "as if." After all, this may be your job for a while, and this organization may turn out to be full of hidden opportunities. Keep your thoughts positive, and tailor your resume and cover letter to this particular job and organization. Act "as if" this is what you wanted all along. You never know. And *do* keep on looking, discreetly.

Week 11 Checklist

☐ Completed the Week 11 Review Worksheet.

　　☐ Identified the following areas that need more effort:

_____

_____

☐ Identified pending prospects and possible job offers. List them below, and rank 0 for a long shot and 5 for a very probable.

Prospect or Possible Job Offer   Rank

_____   _____

_____   _____

_____   _____

Prospect or Possible Job Offer   Rank

_____   _____

_____   _____

_____   _____

_____   _____

☐ Reviewed Lead Organizer (Fig. 1-8) and identified at least five new contacts.

1. _____

2. _____

3. _____

4. _____

5. _____

☐ Reviewed references.

Week 12
Closing the Deal

Don't Blow It Now!

Day 78

This is the second-to-last week. By this time, I hope, you're about to close the deal. You're waiting for your next meeting, and someone has said, either directly or not (they may have intimated), that you will be returning to meet with Mr./Ms. X, who likes to see the final candidates before a final decision is made. But you're told not to worry, X really just wants to say "hello" and to extend his/her greeting to you. You are not to worry.

Watch out, if you're told those exact words, or anything similar. Even though the offer is "in the bag" according to whomever you have been dealing with, always assume that it isn't until you've actually been made an offer. This "don't worry about it" meeting may be just a ruse to get you to drop your defenses. Depending on the organization and the level you're looking to come in on, some people do play hardball. Some managers hire inept interviewers, advocate stressful interviews, and play games about who actually makes the hiring decision right up to the last minute. Even if everyone and every part of the process has been professional and above-board, the thing to remember about this process is that, given the volatility of American organizations today, the person who has become your strongest advocate may be on the way out, or may not have been able to share with you information that might cause you to seriously question the viability of the offer.

Keep Your Defenses Up. Therefore, when you do go to that final meeting, be prepared for any twists (and issues) that may hit you. Don't assume that the offer has been made until you actually have it in hand, and in writing.

Traps to Avoid with (or without) Dessert

Each get-together with your potential new employer is loaded with potential traps, and the greater the number of meetings, the more you have to make a very conscious effort to avoid those traps. Be particularly watchful at social situations where, caught unawares when you have been coaxed into a false sense of security, you let your guard down. Heed these tips.

Avoid Alcoholic Beverages.   Don't start celebrating yet. If you can't avoid a business meal, don't forget that it's not about eating. This isn't the time to order lobster, or to try to make up for all the hectic, grab-a-bite-and-run meals that you endured during the search.

Watch Your Requests.   You may think this is true love, but in fact you're still dating; the wedding is a ways off. This isn't the time to wonder if the walls have to be that shade of beige, or whether the rug is just too dreary. And why must you start at 8:45, when 9:00 is so much more civilized? If you have a major question, by all means raise it, but don't get entangled in knots of little details. Try to determine the culture of the organization. For instance, if you're expected to work some late nights periodically, a safety question as to transportation accommodation is entirely permissible. To idly wonder if anyone ever gets to ride in the boss's limousine, is *not!* When it comes to attempts at humor, do you really know what these folks consider funny at this point?

Separate real requirements from fluff.   Of course, if you're being wooed and the suitor is waving enticements such as a renovated office and other perks, act as if it's your due and not the "deal breaker." If you sense that your prospective employers have shifted roles dramatically from the "buyer," trying to determine why they should want you, to that of "seller" of the organization and all its trimmings to you, then you must be very careful to send and receive accurate messages. This is negotiation-skill territory. In all these "courting" conversations, you must let the other side see what will get you to say yes. What are your "must haves" in relation to this particular job and organization? This is also the opportunity for the organization to let you see into their appraisal of the situation. This give-and-take, or evaluation of feedback, is what will lead both of you down the path to an actual offer.

Negotiate Now

If you do not get a written (or verbal) offer, it will, in part, be based on the organization's determination of what it will take to get you to agree to sign on, and what they are willing to pay for the privilege of having you on staff. Once the offer has been tendered, it is often difficult to negotiate substantial changes. The analogy to a marriage proposal comes to mind: when you reach the point of asking for the hand in marriage, you're pretty sure the answer will be yes. In all of your conversations and meetings, in obvious and subtle ways, the organization is seeing, if it buys what you are selling, what it would take to get you to say yes and asking itself whether it can afford to offer it.

Make a List and Check It Twice
(at Least)

Throughout the many weeks of your job search, you have looked at your job objectives and employer profiles; you have kept an eagle eye on your cashflow; you have spoken to many people in your field (and in others) to get information and referrals; and you have every reason to believe that you are very close to getting an offer.

At this time, you must be certain that you have been sending the correct information to the organization, regarding what you need to see in a job offer from them, and you must also have a clear idea what terms must be present in any offer you may receive from them. Using the Negotiation Worksheet provided in Fig. 12-1, list your first level of priorities—that which must be contained in any job offer. Then, looking at this one organization, what must it offer? Are there any possible tradeoffs? For example: Since you must travel more (or less) than you had originally planned, you can accept a position with a salary level more (or less) than you had at first thought acceptable.

Check off each item, as to whether you feel the organization is aware of this or that requirement of yours. Have you informed them that, because they have an on-site child care center, you would be available to work overtime? Do they know that you are committed to continuing to take evening courses, and therefore wouldn't be available for any late-night meetings on class nights? Have you, in fact, painted an accurate picture of what you would be like as an employee?

Next, based on conversations and information given by the organization, determine which of these items you feel the organization will probably go along with. On the ones that you either don't know or doubt that the organization will offer, you have to make a judgment call. If the item is a deal breaker—for example, you feel they may offer a $55,000 annual salary but, to cover your expenses, you need another $5,000—then you have to remind the people that you're dealing with

NEGOTIATION WORKSHEET

Before you complete all discussions with a would-be employer, determine what areas are still of concern to you and what areas require additional information. This is a prelude to concluding the negotiation stage and obtaining a job offer. The purpose of this exercise is to focus your attention on this specific position at this specific organization in relationship to your stated job objective. All items marked either "No" or "Unknown" are still open for negotiation.

Position:_____ **Organization:**_____

List below all the details of your current job requirements; mark in the right column "Yes" or "No" or "Unknown" as the whether the above position and organization offers it.

MUST HAVES	DETAILS	YES, NO, ?
Salary level:		
Title:		
Position:		
Content of work:		
Pace of work:		
"People" factor:		
Business of organization:		
Location of organization:		
Type of organization:		
Work schedule:		
Benefits offered:		
Other:		

Figure 12-1.

(if you're this close to getting an offer, salary surely is about to be mentioned), in a polite manner, that the salary level you stated is not negotiable. If that's really how you feel, you may lose the offer at that point. But according to your requirements, the offer would have been unacceptable at a lower salary level.

How to Get a Written Job Offer

What are the advantages of a written offer[1]? First it buys you time to think about the offer. Second, it clarifies the issues, both for you and for your would-be employer. It beats taking notes or trying to remember what was said, particularly if you feel that note-taking will make the person you're dealing with uncomfortable.

There are two situations in which an employer might be unwilling to provide a written job offer. First, he or she may have received advice from the organization's legal counsel to put nothing in writing. The organization may have been burned in the past by saying the wrong thing in writing, and it no longer wants to take any chances. This may be the policy. If you request that an offer be put into writing and your request is denied, listen carefully to the explanation for this policy. Wait for the response to your question.

In the second scenario, the problem doesn't stem from the organization but from the person you're dealing with. He/she doesn't want to be pinned down. When asked, this person may just say, "I never give job-offer letters; my word is good enough." As you have already done some research on the organization and this person, their reputations may confirm or deny the "goodness" of that word. Look for other clues: nonverbal messages such as loss of eye contact, or the shuffling of papers, or a quick move to another subject in an attempt to sweep the subject under the rug.

This is another judgment call for you to make. If it's a senior person in the organization you're dealing with, possibly the same one you'll be working closely with, you will have to trust him/her on a great many other matters in the course of your employment. If you feel that you cannot make this leap of faith without a written contract, this may speak volumes for your assessment of the organization as a whole. If it's just a clerk who's giving you the "no writing" line, see if you can subtly check with the department head or with the employee handbook, to determine if this is consistent with the organization's policy.

Do You Want a Contract?

Does it matter whether you get a formal contract, or just a letter? If either is well written, it doesn't. The primary purpose of a written

[1]For additional discussion on the offer, see Week 13.

agreement is to put into writing, in a clear and concise manner, the terms and conditions of your employment as previously discussed. A contract is a more formal agreement. If you're entering into an employment situation calling for step-up levels of benefits, compensation, and specific requirements as to performance, or if the terms of the agreement extend for more than one year, a contract usually is preferable. These contracts also may specify "escape" clauses, such as what you would lose if you quit before one year or what would happen if they fired you under certain circumstances.

Five Reasons It's Always Necessary to Negotiate

You have the offer. Do you accept it as is, or make an additional request (or two, or three)? Actually, it's your call. This is an extremely critical time in the job-search process. The written offer may mean that the organization either chose to ignore the messages you were sending regarding your requirements for acceptance, that they just didn't read you right, or that they love to negotiate. They may make this a test as to who is the better negotiator. The problem may be that you can't figure out why the offer is different from what you had hoped. This is why, at the point when you first thought you and the organization were heading down the same road together, you completed the Negotiation Worksheet (Fig. 12-1). Did you assess the situation accurately? Look back at what items you thought would probably be in the offer. Are the changes from what you had hoped for substantial? Are "deal breakers" involved?

The first point to keep in mind is that any request for different terms may be rebuffed, and the offer withdrawn, if there is any attempt on your part to ask for anything in addition to what has already been given you. It's even more complicated than that. If, as you're going down to the wire and you feel that an offer is about to be made, any subject comes up that has the "seller" (you) saying something that doesn't sound pleasant to the "buyer" (your prospective employer), in all likelihood you will never see an offer.

Let me give you an example. I had the opportunity last year to witness an unusual scenario, one that showed that the world is indeed a small one. I was making a presentation to a group of human resource professionals, gathered at the corporate headquarters of one of the world's leading manufacturers. I was quite impressed when they made a comment to me that showed they truly valued their people throughout the organization. They were about to build a manufacturing facility on the West Coast, and the process had begun with the selection of a person to run the plant. She was already on-site, her mission being to ensure that the facility would be up and running by a date already set. What impressed me so much was that one of her first acts when she arrived was to hire a personnel manager, even though the actual hiring process was still several months away.

I was so impressed (being in the human resources field) by that, that without identifying the client, I took the liberty of telling it to a public gathering of human resource professionals at a hotel on the West Coast. This retelling of the story brought in the "small-world" aspect.

During the break immediately after I had told the story, a fellow approached me and said that he knew the organization in question, and told me its name. I asked him why he had even attempted to guess. He told me he knew a person who had applied for that same human resources position and had been rejected, and that the poor fellow had been talking to himself ever since. When I asked why he had been rejected for the position, I was told he had been taken out of consideration just when he had thought an offer was about to be made (after several meetings). All discussions promptly ended after he was asked to name his price. This fellow who never got the offer was convinced he had been dropped because his price was too high. Wanting to learn more, I asked what salary he had mentioned and I was told $65,000—a figure I felt was entirely reasonable.

Now we get to the small-world part of the story. On this same trip I was visiting my corporate client, and I had the chance to meet the person who had actually won the job. Before I departed, I got to know her qualifications fairly well. Based on her lower level of experience and expertise, I had the opportunity to see the problem. The poor dejected fellow who was sure he had been rebuffed because of his salary demands was correct to an extent, but he didn't see the whole picture. The person who got the job was offered a salary of approximately $35,000. The manager was considering both candidates (at different levels of experience, and trying to determine the most appropriate fit) and realized that even though she had been considering a candidate with more experience and knowhow than the position demanded (seemingly a real advantage), there was a major salary differential here. Therefore, she decided to go with the person whose credentials were not as impressive but who would fit the position. From my knowledge of the organization, the selection was an appropriate one, based on the requirements of the particular job.

Even though that fellow never got the job offer, he did *not* overprice himself. With the level of knowledge and experience I was told he had, I am certain this was not the job for him, because the parameters, demands, and requirements placed on the position would not have utilized his abilities and knowhow to the extent he would have been able to, and wanted to, perform.

The sad thing is, I'm sure he was convinced that the world had changed so much that he never again would be able to command the level of salary he had once earned, and had to that point been seeking to improve upon. I'm sure he's gun-shy now about moving forward, and that's too bad. Had he done some follow-up as to why the job was not offered to him, he might have gotten a better understanding of the situation. Perhaps the grapevine, courtesy of his friend, has already provided him with it. I certainly hope that it has.

Two points that I wish to make here. First, always be on the defensive, because it's a small world out there. Always say and do only those things that you want to get back to someone who means a lot to you—either because you care for them, or because you're dependent on them for your power, security, and/or continued (or future) employment.

Second, don't cite my story as proof that you should never negotiate. Think about what went on here. The recruitment and selection process had gone on for quite a while (too long), before either party was open enough to discuss salary. I think both parties were to a certain extent responsible for waiting too long before addressing the issue, and the candidate should certainly have raised the issue earlier. Nothing heavy, but something simple and direct like "What does the position pay?" would have done just fine. Even if the open answer had been "I'm not sure yet," the conversation could have continued along the lines of "What are your expectations?"

It's even okay to put the candidate on the spot (the salary issue is certainly job-related!) and ask a question like "Knowing that compensation is a subject that will be within your area of responsibility in human resources, what price should we put on this position?" This is a very fair, open-ended question to ask, and the candidate for this position should be readily able to answer it and to thereby provide the interviewer with a lot of insight into the candidate. The second point here, however, is that in the situation described in my story, salary shouldn't have been the basis for negotiation because the dollar parameters should have been discussed earlier. As too much time had passed, both parties were miles apart. Rather than allow things to get confused, think of negotiation as a matter of degrees, of parties not that far apart trying to resolve a matter so that each of them will walk away with the feeling that he/she has won something.[2]

With all those caveats in mind, now consider well the five reasons I believe you still should always negotiate.

1. *You are showing your sophistication.* Negotiation is a form of expertise that few people appreciate or fully comprehend. In order to negotiate, you need to have two types of skills: the skill to separate what is important from what isn't, and the ability to be assertive in the appropriate circumstances. In any negotiation you have the opportunity to ask for something that may or may not be important to you, and to set a "this for that" tone. If the negotiations take place within a "win-win" framework, then everyone will be satisfied with the results. Unfortunately, you may be the only one operating in that framework; others may perceive only a "win or lose" reality. Better to know that from the outset.

2. *You're setting a professional tone from the start.* The world of business is a world of negotiation. Those who ask, get. All business dealings are a matter of self-interest. By demonstrating a willingness to negotiate, and a skill in doing it, you set a tone that shows a level of

---

[2]I know another person who was being considered for a mid-level management position with a Pacific Rim banking facility in the United States. When the $75,000 offer was made, it simply covered base pay and a questionable title. The candidate felt the offer was an opportunity to determine the basis upon which he was going forward in this relationship, so he decided to negotiate. The candidate asked for a meeting to discuss the letter (which in itself is an opportunity to test the relationship—how long does it take to set up the meeting, how do they sound?). At the face-to-face meeting, he started by thanking them for agreeing to the meeting. He then mentioned that the pay offered, while reasonable, was slightly less than he had been willing to consider, and he wondered if they would reconsider. They agreed and asked him what he wanted; he gave them a few options: first, raise the offer by $5000. But if that wasn't possible, consider a low-rate loan or a review date in six months, with a potential increase at that time if his performance warranted it (the normal date for salary changes there is 6 to 18 months).

The last issue was not salary-related, but a concern as well. He was concerned that the title offered placed him below his peers, and he wanted to know if that also was open for discussion. The representatives of the bank thanked him for the meeting, and told him they'd get back to him. They telephoned in a timely manner and said no to all of his requests. They had obviously dug in their heels, and either didn't know how to negotiate (a definite possibility) or had decided he wasn't on a level they wished to negotiate on. It didn't take him long to turn down the offer, because he was concerned not only that they had agreed to nothing but also by the approach they had taken. It seemed to him that once he was in the organization, they might display the same intractable style—not a group of people he was willing to risk his career with.

professionalism that will make you more attractive to your new employer. In fact, refusing to raise issues open to negotiation (if these issues are important to you) may not only be delaying a problem until later but inadvertently be creating an impression that will be difficult to alter once your employment has begun.

3. *It never hurts to ask.* There was a woman who mentioned how embarrassed she used to be as a little girl when she would take trips to the market with her mother, who always would ask for a better price on whatever she was thinking about buying. Now she's grown and she appreciates how effective her mother was, because she constantly practiced a skill and obviously enjoyed it, but, more importantly, more often than not got more than she would have if she hadn't asked in the first place.

4. *You may win.* If you don't attempt to negotiate, you may have a problem that will surface later, and then it will be too late. Let's say you receive a job offer that is close to coinciding with a planned vacation. (The vacation is scheduled to start three months after you start your new job.) When do you raise the issue? If it's important to you and you have done your preparation, consider raising it as part of the job offer. When thinking negotiation, always ask yourself, "What's the biggest risk I face by just placing the issue on the table?" If you really want to have win-win results, use your customer-driven approach in these discussions. Think ahead to all the reasons why the employer will not agree to your request, and of possible ways to "get to yes." On the upcoming vacation issue, if you sense hesitancy about a request for vacation so early in your tenure, on what basis can you compromise? Can you cut the trip shorter this time? Perhaps, instead of paid vacation, you can ask for the time off without pay, if that's doable.

5. *Negotiations with a would-be-employer are a useful barometer that will help you to determine the basis upon which they are considering you.* Earlier I mentioned the Pacific Rim bank that was unwilling to agree to any issues that the mid-level management applicant had suggested. He took the opportunity to assess what the relationship would be after he was hired, because how they dealt with him while courting him for the position would certainly be better than after he had joined the company.

The point to remember is that regardless of whether you are seriously considering the job offer or not, you should *always* consider negotiating.

How to Spot Issues That Should Make or Break the Deal

Read the signs—oral, written, and nonverbal—that were present during the various stages of your interviews with this organization. From the first meeting through the final interviews, size up and continue to question the organization to determine their willingness to negotiate. Test the waters. Start to negotiate before you're actually ready to negotiate—the key is *to understand the relationship.* When setting up meetings, don't be totally open by saying something like, "I'll meet with you anytime." It's better to say "I'll be available [or "in the vicinity"] Friday afternoon. Is that convenient for you? What about the following week? Don't *ever* say (even if it's true), "I don't have any appointments scheduled for all next week, so take you choice." This is especially true the closer you get to the offer. To reveal your utter availability is the same as telling them outright that no one else is looking for you. If they want to see you, they'll make every effort to do so.[3]

Determine What Will and Won't Be Negotiable

As you go through the interview process, look for telltale signs that the organization likes to negotiate, or doesn't. Then, when it comes time to negotiate, you'll be ready to identify what's important to you and what you should and shouldn't negotiate, as well as those areas where they're immovable. Refer to your Meeting and Interview Journals for comments made regarding salary ranges, increases, vacation policies, and other benefits. Were there any red flags hoisted on key areas of your concern? Look back at your Negotiation Worksheet (Fig. 12-1). Now that you're down to the wire, and the next step should be the actual receipt of the offer, are you still in agreement with yourself as to those items marked "must have"? Have you formulated a realistic salary request, both in terms of what you need financially

---

[3]There's an obvious analogy here to dating. "Play hard to get." "Don't seem too anxious." "Don't kiss on the first date!" Also, being an ace poker player could be an advantage. "Wear a poker face." "Don't tip your hand too early." Negotiation is part of our daily life, and not just in the business world. Ask any parent whose kid is trying to wheedle the car for a date on Saturday night!

and what the position is worth?[4] Are there any remaining questions for your prospective employer? If so, resolve them.

Week 12 Checklist

☐ Completed Negotiation Worksheet.

☐ Reviewed Skills Inventory Checklist, Skills Preference Worksheet, and Work Environment Survey.

☐ Reviewed Job Objective and Employer Profile, completed in previous weeks.

---

[4]If you have contacts at organizations similar in size and business to the one where you've been interviewing, check with them to find out what the market pays for that position. Should further conversation be necessary, you will have some facts to back up your contention that the position (and therefore you) are underpriced. A consultant or recruiter familiar with the industry and position should also be able to confirm salary ranges. Look for recent ads for comparable positions, to validate your price.

Week 13
Evaluating the Offer(s)

Day 85

The moment you've been striving toward has at last arrived! All your efforts and hard work have resulted in one or more offers. (To get one is terrific, but to get more than one at the same time is definitely a golden opportunity. Don't blow it by making the wrong choice!) It hasn't been easy but you've stuck with it, and persistence, attention to detail, and maybe a little luck have finally prevailed. Remember, *you* were the one to make it happen! You did it with the help and assistance of a lot of people (several of whom you perhaps don't even remember by name), but you did it in a most difficult job market. So enjoy the moment—you earned it.

But it's all not over yet, so don't let your guard down! Keep the momentum by making sure that you follow up on the items already in motion. The best thing about one job offer is that frequently others are not far behind. Don't stop looking at this point, because things can (and often do) go wrong. The worst story I've heard lately had to do with a career changer from Boston who landed a great job in the financial services industry in New York City. The recruiting and selection process went very smoothly, and he made all his arrangements to relocate (the company was footing the bill), so that all would be done by the time he was ready to start and he therefore could concentrate totally on his new job.

The day he was to start, he purchased *The Wall Street Journal*. A front-page article discussed how the financial services institution he was to join that same day had made a decision to get out of one particular business they had been in. What unit was he about to join? You've already guessed it—the one and the same. Needless to say, his job had already been eliminated, and no one had even bothered to tell him.

This illustration shows that a lot can happen, and frequently does, between the time an offer is made (and accepted) and you are to start work. Therefore you must do your best to ensure that nothing unfavorable happens that could affect the job offer you have received, and that when you report for work there's a real job waiting for you there.

Turning the Offer into a Real Job: Several Items to Look for

Before you even begin to worry about what could happen after you have accepted an offer, let's pause to discuss the offer itself.

Is the Job Offer in Writing?

As mentioned in Week 12, always try to get the offer in writing. This does two things. First and most important, it buys you time to make a decision. Second, it allows you to determine whether the person who made you the offer is speaking with total and complete honesty.

If the person is totally unwilling to compromise on the issue of giving you the offer in writing, you might consider asking if you could take notes, to ensure that you understand all the terms and conditions under which you will work if you accept the job. If you're at a conference table, let the person making the offer look over your notes (if he/she chooses to do so) so that he/she sees that you have nothing to hide and verifies that you are recording accurately what is being said.

Always ensure that you get answers (either verbally or in writing) to all of the following, regardless of the level of the position:

Starting pay, and on what basis you will be paid (weekly, monthly, by check or credit to checking account at bank)

Starting position (title)

Person, title, department, and location that you will be reporting to regularly (if different locations at different times, get specifics; determine the pattern, if one exists)

Start date, start time, and exactly where you should report on your first day

Normally scheduled hours (including arrival and departure times)

Normally scheduled work days (if necessary)

Benefit Details.   What benefits will you be entitled to, and when is the commencement date? Ask for booklets. Consider also the terms and conditions of the health and pension plans. Do you have a choice of health plans to consider? What is the employee contribution for the health plan, and how frequently is the payment deducted? What is the maximum lifetime cap, per individual? What amount (usually a percentage) is the employee expected to pay when submitting a claim? What is the deductible the employee must first pay each year, before any reimbursement considerations commence? What is the out-of-pocket maximum per year? If relevant, in the privacy of your home or some other quiet corner, consider the "preexisting condition" clause of the health plan, to see if that represents a potential problem.

If a preferred provider network of doctors is in the plan, or one of several plans available, see if you can obtain, without causing concern, a current list of doctors, to try to get some indication of what the accessibility and quality of the providers are. A simple way to do this is to see if your own physician is on the list. If he/she isn't, that in itself isn't a cause for worry, unless it will be an issue for you or any other member of your family.

Are there dental or vision plans? Check first-year eligibility and entitlement; it may be to your advantage to halt any dental or vision exams until eligibility has begun.

Don't barrage your contact(s) in the organization with these questions. Make sure you get the books and pamphlets, and scrutinize them in the privacy of your home. You new employer may become concerned, if you show a sophisticated interest and understanding in this area, that you are going to be a heavy user. The Americans with Disabilities Act has gone a long way toward protecting people (employees and their families) with long-standing illnesses and injuries from unscrupulous employers. Still, be circumspect, and don't say or do anything that could jeopardize your chance of getting a job.

What Does the Offer Actually Say?

Through research and preliminary discussions, as well as brochures on benefits, you should have a general idea of what accepting the offer at this organization will involve. All the information will not be spelled out in a written job offer. Consider what the offer that you have received includes and doesn't include. What's missing? Review the details listed next to ensure that you have answers to each item. If you don't, ask. Again, don't expect to get a personalized edition of the employee handbook (although if you can get the published version, it will answer a lot of your questions).

Every offer, oral or written, should always contain the following elements, regardless of level of position, profession/occupation, or industry:

Base salary or wage amount

Title and department

Start date and reporting place

Person, procedure, and date for reporting your decision

These are the bare minimum. Then, depending on position and other factors, the following may also be included:

Employee class or category

Benefits entitlement (including all time off)

Payroll schedule: when you will receive your first payment, and how often you will be paid

The duration of the "probation" period

Plus any other items that are part of the offer. Examples might include a sign-on bonus, relocation expenses, and tuition reimbursements that are beyond the scope of the policy for current employees; and severance arrangements, in the event you and the organization part company during the earliest stage of your relationship. If it hasn't occurred to you yet, please note that the more elements entailed in the job offer—those key points that make the offer competitive or attractive—the greater the reason for getting it all in writing whenever possible.

As for requesting offer details, don't make a request inconsistent with the culture of the organization. You may feel you're a savvy negotiator, but you have to be certain you don't do yourself out of this new job. One candidate for senior management was wanted so badly by an organization that they agreed to a four-day work week, even though no one else at that level in the organization had it. The new senior manager was gone in a year. The sniping from peers, disgruntled over his "special hours," was too strong to ignore.

Also included in the offer may be details about the "probationary" period and projected salary-review date. Finally, the letter also may mention the fact that the offer is conditional upon receipt of satisfactory references, medical exam, or drug testing results. See Figs. 13-1 and 13-2 for examples of offer letters.

When it comes to any arrangements for professional and/or personal item delivery (your boxes of reference books; Rolodex), any special

SAMPLE WRITTEN JOB OFFER

XYZ COMPANY
6484 West Street
New York, New York 10023

Mr. James Fischer   Human Resources Administration
Sr. Vice President   (212)475-5654

June 1, 1994

Ms. June Smith
83762 Ash Drive
Newark, New Jersey

Dear Ms. Smith,

As you and I have discussed, It is with great pleasure that I provide you with additional details regarding our offer of employment to join the Advertising Department of XYZ Company.

To summarize our understanding, discussed below are the details of our arrangements.

You will be joining the Advertising Department as a Vice President - Television Sales. You will receive $6,500 on a monthly basis.

In addition, after completing one year of service with our company, you will be eligible to participate in our bonus program. Although the company does not guarantee that a bonus will be paid, and reserves the right to cancel the bonus program at any time, the company has customarily paid a bonus in December. The bonus is based on individual performance.

On the first business day following the completion of three full months of service, you will be eligible for medical and insurance benefits.

It is important to note that employment at our company is at will, and subject to termination at any time by the company or yourself, with or without cause.

I understand that you will begin work on June 22d. This offer is, of course, contingent upon satisfactory proof of permission to work in this country and the receipt of satisfactory references.

If you begin work on June 22d, you will receive your first salary payment on July 1. You are to report to my office on the 12th floor at 9:15 AM.

We are looking forward to having you join us.

Sincerely,

Figure 13-1.

vacation needs or plans that have already been made, follow this rule of thumb: If you know them, and they are confirmed, raise the issue before you start, regardless of when they are taking place. It's a stronger time to do it. If the organization is fair, it will appreciate your candor. An agreement is being struck, and both parties need to make a decision then and there. If you delay bringing up these issues because you fear the effect they will have on the offer, you're just postponing a potential explosion.

SAMPLE WRITTEN JOB OFFER

Mr. Joseph Medina
President
ProSports Marketing Inc.
5 Wilshire Lane
Stamford, Connecticut 87893

March 15, 1994

Mr. Bill Smith
908 East Park Drive
Kalamazoo, Michigan 34577

Dear Mr. Smith,

The purpose of this letter is to outline the agreement we have reached regarding your employment with ProSports Marketing. We are pleased that you have agreed to accept the position of Sales Representative in our U.S. Sales Department effective April 11, 1994.

Your compensation will be $47,500 annually, paid semi-monthly. Your salary will not be increased through the date of May 1995, but you will go through the annual review process. At your May 1995 review it will be determined if you are to receive an increase.

You will be eligible for the full company benefits that all ProSports employees are entitled to. These benefits are subject to change.

You will be on a three-month probation period, as all our employees in new postions are subject to, beginning on April 11, 1994 and ending on July 11, 1994. ProSports has the right to terminate your employment at any time during this three month probation, or during any other time of your employment. At the end of this three-month probation period, your performance will be evaluated to determine whether or not you have met the requirements for this position.

Please sign this letter where indicated below to acknowledge that you have read, understood and agreed to the terms stated in this letter. Please return a signed copy to my attention at your earliest convenience.

Best wishes,

Signature

Name_____

Date_____

Figure 13-2.

If time sharing is the issue, and it's more than six months away, review privately (without raising the question in any meeting) what the policy is for time off for new hires. If it appears that you will be able to take the time off and it will be on an exception basis (because it's before you're normally entitled to do so), you need to decide how important this issue is at this point. If it's a long-hour, long-day organization, I would advise extreme caution, unless the issue is so important that you're willing to make it an offer breaker.

What is the name, telephone number, and title of the person that you are to call with your decision? If it's the person you have been dealing with throughout the process, ask if there is someone else with whom you may leave your decision if your primary contact isn't around. Sometimes your primary contact will forget to mention that he/she is about to take off for Bora Bora or some other place far removed from the office. In addition to ensuring that you will get an answer, as opposed to having a heart attack when you call in and are told he/she is not there and won't be back for x weeks, if at all, this approach impresses your new employer with your professional manner. The closer they get, the better you look!

What Could Possibly Happen?

After you've worked so hard, I don't want to burst your bubble, but it ain't over yet, even if this job offer looks better than any you ever thought you could get. If there's no such thing as job security, then there *certainly* is no such thing as job-offer security. There are only so many factors that are within your control, and events such as "Acts of God," governmental actions, and the stock market can intervene to prevent this job offer from turning into a job.

The following are examples of things that could (and do) happen to people between the time they get a job offer and the day on which they're scheduled to start.

1. *You could fail the drug test.* You may legitimately "fail" for the obvious reason, but perhaps because a prescription medication you had taken a month ago remained in your system and was reported. If you're honestly surprised that the results are positive, get in touch with your recruiter (the person at the organization that issued the offer) and get some additional details. A mistake may have been made at the testing site or at the laboratory. You may have to get in touch with your physician to determine what the problem is. One woman who was taking medication to treat Lyme disease came up positive; it took a few telephone calls and a letter from her doctor, but it was all resolved in the end.

2. *You could get a lukewarm or negative reference.* Refer back to Week 11 (Reference Check-up) to see what you should have done. You may never know who or why one of your great references bombed out. It may have been something as nonsensical as simply a bad day for

either party when the call was made. Or you misread one of the people you asked to give you a reference, and this is the result.

Offers usually are made conditionally. Don't offer references until requested. Some organizations, afraid of lawsuits as the result of what was said or not said by them in a reference, may require that all requests be in writing and be handled only by the personnel department. The glowing reference you were hoping for may have been reduced to a totally impersonal confirmation of dates of employment, social security number, and position held. In these litigious times, some personnel departments require permission from the employee (or former employee) before they will provide even limited information.

The interpretation of references injurious to former employees is a legal gray area. Everyone has their fans and critics; make certain you only ask *fans* for references. In terms of your most recent employer, if you give someone there as a reference (eyebrows will be raised, if you're not able to find anyone at your former place of employment to give as a reference), be certain that you choose wisely and that he/she knows how seriously you take both references and your reputation. If you left under less than amicable circumstances, make certain your former employer is aware that any problem with references that you might incur from them may lead to a civil lawsuit and a complaint of defamation of character by slander (orally) or libel (in writing).

Of course, if you're asked for references and you have stellar ones to offer, by all means make them as accessible and as appealing as possible. First, before you furnish the names to your would-be employer, call the individuals to share with them the good news and facts of the new position that has opened up for you, and to reconfirm their willingness to give a glowing report. Remember to refer to the key points in your experience that make you an ideal candidate for this job.

3. *A credit report could come in with bad debts, judgments, or personal bankruptcy listed.* This is one area where an employer *can* discriminate, but has to tell you that the decision was based on a credit report. Under the Fair Credit Reporting Act you have a right to know the source of the credit report, and you have an opportunity to verify that the information reported was correct. Check with your local state laws to determine if you have further rights. If the reports *are* correct, you certainly have the right to explain any mitigating circumstances to the prospective employer in hopes of their reconsidering their decision. If the reports are incorrect,[1] and the reporting agency corrects its files,

---

[1] If the report was incorrect and you lost the position solely due to the negative report, you may have recourse to legal action against the reporting agency; again, it depends on the degree of your ire, the damages suffered, and your ability and willingness to sustain the time and costs of a lawsuit.

Figure 13-3.

Job Offer Evaluation Worksheet

Organization Name: _____

Address: _____

Title of Position Offered: _____

Department or Position : _____

Department/Unit Location: _____

Supervisor: _____ Phone # _____

Initial Source of the Opening: _____

Details (for example, base pay, benefits) _____

_____

_____

_____

_____

****

1. What are the major advantages and disadvantages of the offer?

PLUSES   MINUSES

_____   _____

_____   _____

_____   _____

_____   _____

(Continued)

you do have the opportunity to bring this to the attention of the organization that withdrew the offer. How these circumstances are handled will depend on the employer and the specific situation. While you're chasing after the credit bureau, they may have filled the position.

4. *You could fail a medical examination.* It is permissible for an organization to make the passing of a medical examination a requirement of the job offer. You may have cause to sue an employer for a withdrawn offer, but it is an expensive route to pursue (in terms of time and money).

2. What do I think of the job itself? _____

_____

_____

_____

3. What are my initial impressions (positive and negative) about the organization?

POSITIVE IMPRESSIONS   NEGATIVE IMPRESSIONS

_____   _____

_____   _____

_____   _____

_____   _____

_____   _____

_____   _____

4. Are the employees you have been dealing with open and up front or do they seem

to be hiding something (or less than forthright)?

_____

_____

_____

Figure 13-3. (Continued)

5. *The business could merge, or be sold, shut down, consolidated, or in some other way restructured.* You name it (we've all seen the headlines in the business sections) and it certainly has happened. What about all those offers out to candidates, from Eastern Airlines, several years ago when they were shut down? How about those employment offers from Manufacturer's Hanover Trust Company, the week before it was merged into Chemical Bank?

6. *A major organization officer could leave or be indicted.* When John Akers left IBM, what hires were left dangling? Apple Computer and John Sculley and Steve Jobs have had their ups and downs; imagine the trauma to those who were in their final stages of interviews, or

5. What about the industry and the product/service of the organizational unit you will be joining: are they growing, declining or dying?

_____

_____

_____

_____

_____

6. What about your direct supervisor? Describe your initial impressions of his/her strengths and weaknesses (include comments on leadership style).

_____

_____

_____

_____

7. If I accept the job and things really work out, what is the best I can expect from accepting this offer?

_____

_____

_____

_____

_____

Figure 13-3. (Continued)

who may already have given notice to their employer when the news of executive changes broke in the paper.

7. *A financial report could be published that provides a major negative shock to the investment community.* A corporation's bonds are down-rated, or an earnings report comes out that shows substantial loan write-offs or losses due to R&D cost overruns. An organization (particularly if the department you were slated for was kept in the dark about the financial situation) could suddenly be forced to slash budgets or institute a hiring freeze.

8. What would be the worst that could happen if I accept this offer?

_____

_____

_____

_____

_____

9. What are my risks/options if I choose to decline the offer?

_____

_____

_____

_____

_____

10. Whom could I contact for assistance in making my decision (anyone who knows

me and the organization)? _____

_____

_____

Offer accepted/rejected on_____ because_____

_____

_____

_____

Figure 13-3. (Continued)

8. *A technological change could occur that makes your product (or service) obsolete.* Are you an expert in eight-track tape recordings? A black-and-white-TV repair person?

9. *The person you were to report to could die, or suffer some other tragic loss.* The daily obituaries include many active business people who passed away—and out of the department where you might have gone to work. If he/she was the one who made the hiring decision, that decision could be put on hold indefinitely.

10. *The person that you were to report to could quit.* If the person you were to directly report to is suddenly awarded an exciting assignment in Paris, where does that leave you? Holding a job offer that may not be viable. If you were hired to work on a particular project or a new product, and the brains behind that idea has suddenly accepted a better offer somewhere else, where does that leave you? Quite possibly, it leaves you with a meaningless job offer.

11. *The plant where you were to report for work could be burned down in a fire.* Industrial fires are everyday occurrences, and jobs are disrupted and lost.

12. *A natural disaster could occur.* What happened to all the people scheduled to report to their new jobs the week after Hurricane Andrew hit Florida?

13. *A negative report could be issued on the product that you manufacture.* All those products lines that relied on Red Dye #2 were temporarily out of business. You might be a red M & M specialist....

14. *The law or regulations could change.* The government contract that your new employer used to hire you fell through.

The Job Offer: Do You Have All the Facts?

As stated earlier, the actual job offer (whether in writing or given verbally) will be predicated on a series of discussions and interviews. In the course of this mutual "discovery period," both you and the prospective employer have been learning about each other. If it's a case of the more you know, the more you like, then you will have received a job offer. Even if you've received all the information that should normally be included in every job offer, that information must not be taken at face value. Consider carefully the following issues.

1. *Is the start date appropriate for the situation they are portraying?* If they're saying that they need you right away but the start date is one month hence, what's the reason for the discrepancy? If they know that you must relocate yourself and your family, and that your spouse must also give notice and relocate, is a two-weeks-hence start date feasible? How can you expect to devote 100 percent of your energy and attention to your new position, when you're living out of a suitcase and apartment-hunting every evening? Still, when it's a great offer, you do what you have to do.

The issue on starting dates is usually at the other extreme. There may be pressure on you not only to start immediately but to come to an immediate decision on the offer as well. Unless your instincts (or any other source of advice that you trust) tell you to, *never* accept an offer immediately. Always respond that you are "delighted with the offer...thank you so much. Let me consider it, together with all the elements and details, and give you an answer on [ask for two or three days (if the offer is given on a Friday, ask if Monday will be okay)]." If you want to delay longer, perhaps because another offer is expected or you want an attorney or friend in the human resource field to look over the offer, give a later date. Under no circumstances mention that you're waiting to review the offer with anyone, including an attorney, your spouse or significant other, or worse, one or both of your parents. You need to show that you're decisive but wish to reflect on this important decision rather than come to a hasty decision. In most situations, the request will be accepted and respected, that respect itself constituting a good reason to ask for time to consider the offer.

As for a start date, that can be delayed and finalized until you've come to a decision (another reason to ask for extra time). Don't let your guard down here. If you're currently working, don't burn your bridges behind you. You should have a sense from the way others have been treated as to the length of time you will be asked to stay to ensure a "smooth transition." Your new employer will be interested in knowing what happens here. If your current employer lets you go as soon as you announce your decision, or for any other reason you are immediately available, be careful before you commit to start uncharacteristically soon. Once the report date has been finalized, avoid changing it. You look much more professional if the first start date is the only start date.

2. *Have your resources been specified?* Do you know where you will be sitting/located? What's the appearance of your desk or office? Regardless of level, if it's appropriate, ask to see your work environment and the specific location where you'll be stationed. Sometimes applicants are never shown the work area. If it wasn't done before, ask for a tour now. If there *is* any reluctance, watch out. Try to find out why. They may not yet have told the person you're replacing that he/she has been fired. Under similar circumstances, the same thing could happen to you.

3. *Are you welcomed in advance?* Are you included in communications and events before you actually commence work? Does your new boss return any calls you make in a timely manner? Is he/she on time for any meetings prior to your arrival? Do you feel wanted, or an inconvenience?

4. *Is the organization efficient?* Is it getting things to you when promised? Did you get the offer letter on time, as promised? There's a

woman who went to work for a major Japanese facility located here in the United States, as a member of the management team. Although it had been promised for several days, the offer letter never arrived. The scenario, fortunately, was not a reneging on the intent to issue the offer, but a clear indication of the problems the organization was having in communication, and a lack of ability to get even the most basic things done.

How to Ask When Something Is Missing

Once an offer has been made, what should you do if you don't like what you've received, either because of an omission or because an item (such as pay) is at a level different from what you had been led to believe? *Watch out*, even in the unlikely circumstance that you are faced with a higher offer than what you had been led to believe. You need, even here, to learn the reason for the difference, or whether you had misunderstood the terms.

The first piece of advice, then, is to be careful. The second is to move ahead, and pursue. The reason to pursue is to evaluate the organization and its people one more time before you become an employee. If there are to be any mishaps, better to deal with them now, even if the offer goes out the window, than sweep it under the carpet only to discover after your arrival that more problems are surfacing and they all seem to stem from misunderstandings.

Whether the offer is given to you in writing or not, the agreement may not include all the details you had thought would be included. So what to do when something has been left out? The answer, not meant to be cute but simply on-target, is that it all depends on whether it is a "form" or "content" issue. Form issues are superficial or minor issues. For instance, the start date for insurance coverage would generally be considered a form issue.

Content issues, on the other hand, are so important that if not agreed to they may be considered potential deal breakers. A substantial change in salary level, span of responsibility, or reporting relationships may be grounds for seriously considering walking away from the offer.

An Unwritten Offer

If the offer isn't yet in writing, you may have an advantage. You'll be able to ask for the written offer and use the delay to postpone any decision. If you do want a written offer, ask for it directly. It's not an unusual request. As mentioned previously, there are at least two possible reasons why the offer wasn't put in writing. After you make the request be quiet and listen carefully, so that you'll be able to determine the intent and reasons for the unwillingness. To get a written offer is to your advantage, but to theirs as well, because by putting the agreement down in writing there is less likelihood of any misunderstanding. On the other hand, once the offer is in writing it may be considered too late to ask for anything more—particularly if it was your language they used in the first place.

How Not to Blow the Offer

Don't forget that the offer you have received isn't etched in stone. In fact, it could still be withdrawn. Keep your defenses up, and avoid losing it. Here are some suggestions that don't constitute 100 percent protection but will increase the likelihood that the offer will remain intact and you will start your new job as arranged.

1. *Keep a low profile.* Don't hang around your new employer's facilities. Don't call unless you have something of importance to ask. If you do have a question, take it up only with the person you feel won't be bothered by your query and have second or third or even fourth thoughts about the new hire and the decision made.

2. *Submit paperwork and other administrative details requested on time.* Not early, certainly not late, but on time. If a medical examination is to be arranged by you directly with the doctor or facility, do so as soon as you are asked to, but ask if you may take the examination when it is most convenient for you to do so. Try to be ready for the examination by being as fit as you can be. If you can, avoid going to the exam with a cold or the flu. Make sure you get a good night's sleep the night before, follow the instructions, are prepared with any specimens, and have eaten nothing since the night before if requested.

3. *Be sure that you follow up on any requests made by your new organization.* Take advantage of any communication they request to show that you are professional in every way, and that their hiring decision was a sound one. You may be asked to give them a call when you have made your decision to take the job. Be sure you call within the prescribed time period (for example, "by April 18th," or "next Friday," or "tomorrow"). When calling, be sure you speak to the appropriate person. Be very wary of leaving a message with the person who just happened to be there and took the call. Always get the name of the message-taker, if you really must leave a message, and call back at a later time to be certain the message was delivered.

4. *Don't try to reopen negotiations.* If you forgot to ask or mention or raise a question about something, and the offer was made in writing and signed by both parties, or just by you if that was the procedure, leave it alone. To reopen the agreement at this point would be dangerous, and indicate a lack of preparedness on your part. Even if the matter is a major one for you, all the more reason not to show a lack of preparation and structure on your part by admitting that something slipped past you. What's the worst possible thing that could happen if you raised the issue? The offer could be withdrawn! Think about it. Throughout this book you've been encouraged to be *outward* in your thinking. Your presentation always was done with the recipient (the buyer) in mind. In this instance, take a moment to consider what the situation would be like if *you* were discussing a job offer with an applicant, and he/she raised new issues that required renegotiation of the agreement. What would *you* think about your new hire?

Is It as Good (or Bad) as It Sounds?

How can you tell if the offer is a good one? You were asked earlier to always attempt to get any employer you're meeting with to make you an offer, and then determine whether you were interested in accepting it. If that was the approach you took as your own, then once any offer has been obtained, it's all the more important to carefully assess it, even if it comes from an organization you weren't interested in joining—for whatever reason—in the first place. Keep in mind that your requirements and preferences may have changed.

Go back to the exercises you performed in Week 12 of your search, and in earlier chapters when you were trying to decide what your job and organizational preferences were at that time. Don't forget to link what your concerns are here with the major "must-haves" you checked off in your analysis when you started this search. Then you're ready to perform this analysis for each offer.

Use the Job Offer Evaluation Worksheet (Fig. 13-3) to record all the good and the bad points of the offer. Also look at your prediction and must-have analysis on the Negotiation Worksheet (Fig. 12-1). After you've looked at the offer, the organization, and your potential new supervisor, you should be able to come to a decision. It's important that you record what your decision is and why you came to it. If you take the job, you can use this evaluation to remind you, on those "bad" days, exactly why you took this job! If you don't accept the offer, it will prevent you from having selective memory ("I should have taken that job; it wasn't so bad.").

If you have any choice in the matter, set a start date as soon as possible. The longer the time frame between acceptance and start, the greater the likelihood that events will intervene to change the situation entirely. Don't postpone your start date for a lengthy (but admittedly well-deserved) vacation. Opt for a short, battery-recharging get-away now, while planning a longer trip later on that will fall within the position's parameters.

If You Turn Down the Offer

Despite your high hopes, negotiations, and efforts, the job offer simply doesn't satisfy your requirements. As requested of you in the offer, you telephone the person indicated and express your thanks, but no thanks. Put as positive a spin on it as possible—you never know whether, after looking around some more, your requests for higher salary or other accommodations won't come to seem eminently more reasonable. Never definitively turn down an offer that you might want to renegotiate on, unless you truly have nothing to lose and don't mind losing.

As in all your other dealings in your job search, follow up with a thank-you note to those persons at the organization responsible for the offer. Don't neglect to telephone or write the person(s) responsible for the referral, to thank them and let them know of your decision. Be as positive as you can; leave fans in your wake.

Next, continue on with your search. As you have still been investigating prospects and other job leads even while negotiations for this position were ongoing, you haven't lost any momentum. Indeed, the fact that you've come this close should inspire rather than depress you.

Go through all the items pending; send out letters and make those telephone calls.

Yes, You Have Found Your New Job!

Thanks to a little luck, lots of friends and contacts, and a lot of focused effort on your part, you and a position are a true "fit." You have contacted the individual cited in the offer to formally accept. Any last questions and details have been arranged.

If the new employer is astute and you are currently employed, they may request a telephone call from you after you have announced your departure. The thinking here is that it's easy to say yes, you will accept a job. On the other hand, it can be difficult to tell your current employer that you're leaving. In these situations, anything is possible, from the employer telling you to clear out your desk immediately to giving a counter-offer that matches or even surpasses the offer you have just received. Your soon-to-be new employer doesn't want to get involved in a bidding war.

Don't broadcast your good fortune. By all means share your news with close family and friends, particularly those who were instrumental in helping you to obtain the position, but after that, until you're sitting in your new position, keep a low profile. There are a lot of strange people in our small business world, and their motivations can be as unfathomable as they are diverse. It only takes one such "loose cannon" to take some action that will undermine your job offer.

For example, a person applied through a *New York Times* business section advertisement for a mid-level position in a high-tech organization out of state, requiring relocation. Everything in the application and interview process went by the book, with speed and efficiency. A visit was made to the small town where the company was located, and the applicant got a complete tour and met with several of the people he would be working with. An oral offer was made. In his enthusiasm and naiveté, he called a former colleague who didn't even know he was applying for the position. Within 24 hours of that conversation (the only one he had outside of his immediate family), the entire deal had unraveled. To this day, he feels that the falling apart of the offer can be traced to the telephone call he made to his former friend.

Follow-up

Send a letter to thank those in whose name the offer was sent, and to reconfirm your start date and time. A sample of an acceptance and appreciation letter may be seen in Fig. 13-4. In the absence of any further information (which could only be bad news about references, drug tests, economic fallout), your letter will finalize your acceptance of the offer.

Of course, if you've been offered a contract, sign the contract (retain a confirmation copy for yourself) and return it with a cover letter expressing appreciation.

Lastly, after you've started the new job, mail thank-you letters to those whose direct assistance or referrals led you to it. You can write and post-date the letters now if you wish, but don't mail them until the offer is hard reality. Don't get so caught up in your new job that you neglect to recognize all of those friends whose efforts supported your search. Keep (don't throw away) all of your logs, index cards,

THANK YOU
AND ACCEPTANCE OF JOB OFFER

[ON YOUR LETTERHEAD]

June 12,1994

Mr. Robert S. Sutton
Senior Vice President
Human Resources
The Denver Venture Association
8570 Skyway
Denver, Colorado

Dear Mr. Sutton,

Thank you for offering me the position of Senior Accountant. The Denver Venture Association was revealed to me to be an dynamic and aggressive organization and I highly value your confidence in offering me the position. I look forward to making a contribution immediately to the association's mission.

You were most informative and gracious. It is with sincere appreciation that I accept your challenging and attractive offer. As requested, I will report to work on August 1 at 9:00 directly to the Personnel Department.

Looking forward to working on your team,

Signature

Figure 13-4.

and journals; this is your network. Make a firm resolution to maintain relationships built up or initiated during your job search, and to be of assistance when and if others now approach you for helping in *their* search for a new job.

Once you're in place in your new position, send a letter announcing your new organization and position to all your friends, everyone you contacted for help and referrals (even those who didn't lead you to this job), and all the members of your network. Thank them again for all their help, and stand ready to reciprocate should you ever be asked.

Thanks, but No Thanks

If you decline the job offer, do so in the manner requested in the job offer itself. That usually means a telephone call, but you still should send a written letter of appreciation, highlighting the major reason why you couldn't accept the offer. You may still be continuing your job search, or you may be accepting another offer; in any case, leave behind you both goodwill and future contacts.

As there are people you contacted and who led you to this job offer, even though you didn't accept it, you owe it to those supporters to inform them of the offer, your decision, and the reason(s) for your declination. Figure 13-5 is an example of a declination letter.

THANK YOU
AND DECLINATION OF JOB OFFER

[ON YOUR LETTERHEAD]

June 12,1994

Mr. Robert S. Sutton
Senior Vice President
Human Resources
The Denver Venture Association
8570 Skyway
Denver, Colorado

Dear Mr. Sutton,

Thank you for offering me the position of Senior Accountant. The Denver Venture Association was revealed to me to be an dynamic and aggressive organization, and I highly value your confidence in offering me the position.

However, as I stated on the telephone, I am not able to commit to the amount of overtime you might require without an on-site child care facility. I applaud your efforts to establish a facility within the next ten to twelve months, and I fully recognize the commitment you are personally making to the families of your employees. At this time, to be able to support your needs, I would need appropriate child care arrangements immediately.

You were most informative and gracious. It is with sincere regret that I must respectfully decline your most attractive offer. I hope that should either of our circumstances change in the future you would consider me for another position.

Appreciatively,

Signature

Figure 13-5.

Week 13 Checklist

☐ Received one or more job offers, in writing or verbally.

☐ Completed Job Offer Evaluation Worksheet.

☐ Made a decision on job offer.

☐ Telephoned and mailed letter of acceptance and thanks.

☐ Telephoned and mailed letters of declination and thanks.

After You Start Your New Job

☐ Thank-you letters to every person who provided direct assistance leading to this job opening.

☐ Announcement letter to all your friends, business contacts, and network associates, informing each of your new position and thanking them for their support and assistance during your recent job search.

☐ Keeping all records, files, and lists accumulated during your search, for future reference and to maintain networking relationships.

Week 14

Summary and Conclusion

Day 92: Getting Ready for the New Job

This is the chapter you've earned. You did all the work, got some breaks, and successfully landed an offer that you accepted. Not one to drop the ball after the offer was made, you also were able to successfully avoid any postoffer traumas or events as discussed in Week 12 (your employer was there, alive and well on your start date, and your references were stellar). In this concluding chapter I will discuss issues for you to consider, not only so you'll be ready for your new job but also to provide you with the opportunity to avoid ever going through this process again—to the extent that it is within your power.

Preparation for the new job is essential. First you must get mentally prepared and then physically prepared.

Mental Preparation

You need to switch gears and think in terms of characteristics that will make you an effective person from the outset. Shed whatever baggage that makes you feel defensive and/or grateful about the position you are about to assume. Whether the organization is the most prestigious or the least, establish a mental attitude that says you are important and you have earned a place in the organization. You were hired not because they were desperate or charitable but because you are perceived as someone who will add value and make them more effective. Remember to realize that the price you are being paid—in direct pay as well as benefits—for your services is the amount that you and they agreed to. If you start or continue to feel it is unreasonable, you need to deal with that and get it resolved before you start.

Become enthusiastic about the job and the organization. After you start, practice telling others about your new job in face-to-face meetings as well as over the telephone. Listen to what they say, and how they respond. The more of this informal research you conduct, the more you are performing market analysis, gathering insight from a variety of sources. Take notes and keep a journal. Do more formal research to find out as much as you can about the organization—current as well as past. Most large organizations have orientation meetings for new employees. Unless you were invited to a session during your early days on the job, inquire about the procedure for sitting in on the next session.

Find out who founded the organization, and what he/she was like. Determine how old it is, and where it started. Learn what business it was in when it started. Trace the expansions and contractions. What is its history regarding its employees? Was there ever a union involved? If so, which and what type? What segment of the employee population is organized? What kind of press do they get? What has given them notoriety? Who are the representatives that get visibility?

With electronic databases and the more sophisticated newspapers such as *The Wall Street Journal*, which has an index of organizational names every day in section B that lists every organization named that day, for whatever reason, anywhere in the newspaper, you can be brought up to date on any and all issues that impact on your employer. Read/watch your new organization's advertisements, annual reports, proxy statements, and any other form of corporate organizational communication you can get your hands on without being perceived as annoying and nettlesome. Get additional insight into the industry—where they're coming from and where they're going. What environmental demands must they address? What kind of culture do they have? Visit any retail stores or other locations they may have, to get a feeling for the organization. Look at the artworks displayed (or not), and the building styles. Consider any plaques and other items on display; what kinds of messages do they send?

While waiting to get started, get current. Improve your professional skills. Practice communication skills. Improve organizational skills—take courses in negotiations, selling, time management, and so forth to develop skills to be more effective professionally. What worked yesterday isn't good enough for today. Don't *forget* what worked yesterday or the day before; just make sure you sharpen skills that will combine yesterday's experience with today's and tomorrow's demands. If you're going to have to use a rusty second language in your new job, brush up on it immediately. All of these suggestions shouldn't require you to spend one cent of money you may not have; investigate public libraries and videotapes. If the tape turns out to be terrible, practice your time management skills and stop watching it! There's no scorekeeper out there, decreeing that everything you see or read—including this book, for that matter!—must be finished.

Regardless of your occupation, read the papers. Peter Drucker and others talk about "the knowledge worker." Reading the papers not only helps you to stay current but exercises your mind as well. Catch the news on TV if you want to, but what you see there will to a great extent be a limited restatement of items that have already appeared in the papers. Use the TV and its plethora of news programs to supplement your reading, not the other way around.

Practice the lost art of conversation. Take the data gleaned from your reading of current periodicals, and pepper your comments with references to what you just read (and saw). In addition to practicing your communication skills (including your active listening skills—don't talk too much), you will be using this technique as an opportunity to practice retention and recall skills as well as to think on your feet. Something else will happen, and that will be the sharpening of your self-confidence—a skill that can never be too well honed in any workplace, not to mention your new one.

Plan to start with a run out of the gate. Rehearse your first days in the organization and how you plan to spend them. Try to identify what priorities you will be expected to address, and prepare for them as much as you can. Practice your routes and alternative methods of transportation, and make a practice run to determine the best route to travel and how long the trip will take. Simulate the trip under the proper conditions, by going on a workday and planning to arrive at the same time you will be hoping to arrive when you begin your workday. If accessible and appropriate, meet with friends, neighbors, and/or relatives, as well as newly found colleagues from the organization, to gain additional insights and enthusiasms. Determine how best to complete the forms required, so that on the first day you don't spend all day whiling away the time in personnel, unless it can't be avoided.[1] Get to your department as soon as possible. They should be

---

[1] Some organizations require a structured orientation session that commences immediately upon employment and may last a day or more before you're allowed to work at your assignment. The Disney Corporation, for example, has an orientation lasting several days that even includes an exercise to make sure everyone knows the names of all seven dwarfs. If you're required by the organization to attend an orientation session, then you must, but avoid if at all possible languishing in Human Resources by getting whatever forms must be completed *before* you begin work, if it is even remotely possible to do so.

delighted to see you, and will be impressed that you want to roll up your sleeves and get at it.

Get Physically Prepared. Build up your stamina. Get fit. Work out on a daily basis. Get quality sleep, eat the right foods, drop bad eating habits. A fit first-day appearance will add to the positive first impressions of those around you. No partying till you start—and definitely not the night before.

Avoiding Mistakes You Made in Your Old Job (and Some Completely New Ones)

In Week 1, you were asked to consider what had happened that put you in the position of needing to find another job. You were to look at all the aspects that impacted on your position and to consider your areas of effectiveness and ineffectiveness. Throughout your job campaign, I have tried to focus your attention on self-evaluation skills, and you have repeatedly looked at what you were doing (making telephone calls, writing letters) and attempted to measure your effectiveness against your stated objectives. It was not enough to be doing things right—you had to know why it was working just as much as why it was not.

Conscious competence was your goal, almost as much as a new job. This journey to a new job involved too much hard work and determination for you to not recognize the skills that you had developed along the way. In some ways, perhaps in many, you are not the same person who left your last employer. You may have been humbled along the way by rejection letters, or have discovered skills and a focus level you had no idea you possessed. My hope is that you have been on a journey of self-discovery, with the reward of the right job at journey's end.

Look back for a moment to the reasons you gave for being in a job search in the first place. Do you still agree with your evaluation? _____ If not, what is your current understanding of why you needed a new job? _____

_____

_____

_____

Name at least five things you have learned about yourself, or skills that you have discovered during the job search:

1. _____

2. _____

3. _____

4. _____

5. _____

How do you see using these skills to your advantage in your new job, and in the future? _____

_____

_____

Set the correct tone in your new position right from the start. But what is the "correct tone"? If you've gotten this far in the job search, you've had it all along! Establish a positive, confident image that says, "I am able to do this job, and I am willing to learn to do it better. I can express myself, and I can listen. I know when to talk and when to be silent."

Promise yourself that you'll never say anything even closely resembling: "When I was at [one of your past jobs] we always did it this way." Use your active listening skills at every opportunity, particularly in the early days on the job.

I hate hackneyed expressions, but this is the best way to say it. To be sure you're setting the right tone and creating the most positive image, always be "on your game." I won't talk about "keeping your defenses up," but as I mentioned earlier, psychologists say that first impressions are lasting. You absolutely *must* project the right image from the start. If there's anything you can do to enhance that image, *do it*. Avoid at all costs anything that detracts from that image.

Watch Your Wardrobe. Pay attention to the clothes you plan to wear, not just on the first day but on each day of the entire first week. Any weak areas? Go shopping.[2] Consider in your selection those items of clothing and footwear that seem to be appropriate for the organization you're about to join. Unorthodox outfits, hairstyles, and jewelry may be on target (or even required) for the creative areas of a major entertain-

---

[2]Don't assume in advance what your wardrobe needs may be. Better to be understated for the first few days than to acquire a closetful of clothes that just won't do. Particularly if your first day on the job is spent filling out forms in personnel, getting your ID card, and sitting through an orientation presentation, you may not get a true feeling of what the standard of dress is in your department until you have actually arrived there. I hope you were able to "get a tour," and have a good memory for details when it comes to who wore what.

ment company, but the business side is considered to be the place where the "suits" reside. So even within an organization, the appearance that you project must be relevant and appropriate for the segment in which you will be located.

One last comment here: the goal of your appearance should be to "blend in." Your clothes and overall presentation should make a statement to that effect. Use your good judgment to select the right clothes, and if you're able to make your appearance distinctive within the framework of your blended-in appearance, then you're truly on your way. Allow yourself the distinctive tie or special earrings, if appropriate. But if you'll be the only one with such accouterments, watch out. Rule of thumb: If you're going to err, err on the side of the conservative.

If you're in doubt, *always* get out and visit the building that your employer is in. Look around at what others are wearing, what they're carrying (briefcases or knapsacks?). Keep an eye on footwear in the lobby. In many American cities people going to work (both male and female) will frequently wear jogging or other athletic footgear to work. Those working in offices, performing white- or pink-collar jobs, have either buried on their person or stashed away in their desks business shoes that they switch into.

Remember also that some people can be deadly. Recently a woman began a new job for a major financial services institution, located in the Wall Street area of New York City. On her first day of work she wore what she considered to be a snappy outfit, and her most expensive one: a tailored suit. But instead of a skirt, it had as its bottom piece a pair of shorts that most people would take to be the bottom part of a dress. She lost her job two weeks later; the reason: the "no shorts" rule was in effect. It didn't matter that no one gave her a chance to stop wearing them by simply telling her that she shouldn't wear them. No, she was suddenly just "short" one new job! Sad, but true. Be watchful of what's going on around you, and avoid looking different, or you could pay a high price. The fashion police are watching you!

Be Circumspect in Word and Deed. Be careful about initiating any communication with anyone in your new organization before you start. If you've established a rapport with someone in the organization—perhaps your new boss—and he/she wants a meeting, that's fine, as long as you're careful about what you say. Listen more than you speak, and consider carefully what you're going to say before you say it.

Get Organized. Take time out to find what material will help you in your new organization. Go through your job-search material and throw away all the valueless paperwork. Keep the index card, Rolodex, and other pertinent information.

Determine the best method for staying on top of situations in your new organization. Think about what has worked for you in the past. Determine the applicability of any past system you have used to keep straight your priorities, projects, appointments, and meetings on the most hectic of days. If you want to try a new system, put it together in ample time before you start to determine what works and what doesn't. Don't be afraid to make a clean break with any past system, when you choose a new one.

If you've been letting things slide in your personal life, get a handle on them before you start your new job, so that your focus will remain on what is of prime importance: your work. Make any looming doctor, dental, podiatrist appointments *before* the start date. Likewise any plumber or painter home visits; schedule them for before you will be at work.

Don't Move In.   Don't bring all your family photos, knickknacks, plants, personal items with you in a box on the first day. It doesn't matter that they were a part of your old office. Bring only the "tools of your trade." If, after some time on the job, you see that other respected employees have personal items in view, then you may follow suit. I, myself, however, subscribe to the "less is more" theory; keep your work area entirely businesslike.

Keep it Simple.   These first days at work are not the time to bring in a new software package and install it on your PC, because you think it's better than the one they're using. Don't plan outside lunches or right-after-work appointments. Don't start (unless you have absolutely no choice, or it's tied in to your employment) any new endeavors at this time (house hunting, redecorating, getting married, returning to school at night). Let your focus during business hours be on business; all those other projects involve telephone calls, discussions, and time. Allow yourself the luxury of taking one thing at a time.

Go on Instincts.   No matter how much you plan ahead or how well you polish your skills, you will run into situations (during your first days, and throughout your professional and personal life) that you couldn't have planned for. You have to rely solely on whatever feels right.

Look for Opportunities to Shine.   Through your words and deeds, make use of some of those skills you've been using for these past 90 days, and before that. After you've sized up a problem, if you feel you have a solution, offer it. If you have nothing to say, don't. As the Serb proverb has it, "Better to keep quiet and let people think you are a fool, than to open your mouth and prove it."

Tread Carefully in your New Environment. People's agendas may be complicated, but you have an advantage at the start that others will envy: you have just arrived, and therefore aren't expected to know what's going on internally. Be friendly to everyone, and don't align yourself with any issues or individuals (or allow others to feel that you are on one side or the other) until you know the lay of the land. You have seen enough soap operas and movies to know the treachery of office politics; don't get drawn in by other people's hidden (or frank) agendas.

Your Next Job Search

It's already started! Here are six reasons to start looking for your next job as soon as you start your new one.

1. *The honeymoon period will end sooner or later.* The analogy is an apt one. Everyone allows for mistakes at the beginning of a marriage. Management wants to feel they've made a great hire, so you always look great to them in the beginning. You, of course, are looking to reaffirm your decision to take the job, and feel good about it. The rose-colored glasses may stay on for a while, but eventually reality sinks in. Everyone is human after all. There are pluses and minuses to every situation.

2. *Organizations change.* New products and new markets come, old ones go. Management strategies may force new directions, new challenges. Or they may not, and problems ensue. If you loved the position that you came into, there's no assurance that the status quo will be maintained. Something as simple as changing departmental reporting arrangements may have a radical effect on the organization and your position.

3. *People change.* There's no marriage clause between employer and employee that includes the words "for better or worse." Employees and managers come and go; some departures barely cause a ripple, while others cause storms to rage.

4. *The best time to look is when you don't need a job.* There's no pressure. You're confident, because you have a job. And, because you have a job and are active in the market, you have access to many other positions and organizations to network with. Last, because you are perceived to be a winner (a job-holder), you are now a prime target for headhunters.

5. *The grass is always greener (well, almost always).* All those other organizations, all your peers—they never seem to have your problems. To paraphrase, "Take a realistic look at the situation of others." If you have developed your self-evaluation skills and are focusing a trained

eye and ear on other situations, you should be able to tell the real green grass from the Astroturf.

6. *It keeps you sharp.* Complacency is one of life's danger signs. Someone may be targeting your position. Somewhere, in the back of your mind, there should be contingency plans. Be up to date with what's going on throughout the organization; don't be the last one to know. Be the one who's indispensable, because you have all the information on market and industry trends.

How to Avoid Having to Job-Search Again

There are some tactics you should use, starting today, to keep the situation you have just experienced from ever happening again.

After you've started, announce to the world that you have gotten a job. Make sure that on that list is each and every name who helped you in any way at all during the search. Be sure to include others as well. That is your new network.

Build your new network. Find reasons to keep in touch. Send articles, telephone, meet for coffee or lunch. Seek others to add to the network. Introduce some friends to others, to intertwine and strengthen relationships. When you're in a position to do so, mentor someone else, or help another to make contacts or find leads. Be active in professional organizations. Read.

Continue to grow; take continuing-ed or related courses. Keep in touch personally (not only in search of business-related topics). If your new company conducts meetings, conferences, or workshops, volunteer to attend. Improve your computer literacy.

Get a life! You need to eat breakfast, go to lunch, enjoy dinners. Don't burn out by giving 150 percent all the time. There's a real danger in always giving "extra" as a matter of course. If you are doing "extra," before you realize it your staff and supervisors will consider this work mode "the norm." Naturally, you will want to put extra effort into the beginning of your new job, but don't cross the line and lead others to expect you to work *every* Saturday morning.

You need to be fit. Looking good makes you feel good. Feeling good breeds confidence, and confidence leads to success in many different areas. Be kind to yourself. If your employer offers you use of a fitness center, avail yourself of it. Walk a bit every day, a lot on some.

Enjoy yourself. In the urgency of the job search, you may have been unable to enjoy some of the pleasures of life that you had known before. Go back to old pleasures. Find new ones. Share some with others. Do you only live to work, or do you work to live (or somewhere in between)?

Farewell, and Good Luck!

Books abound about how to find a job. The best ones talk about the need to determine one's value and consider oneself a free agent who offers his/her services to the highest bidder. The days of lifetime employment seem to have gone forever. Whether, in the long run, that is going to benefit each of us, and society too, doesn't matter, because there seems to be no alternative—and no organization is immune, regardless of sector. Even the not-for-profit sector and educational institutions realize that survival is the prime directive. Every organization needs to be financially healthy if it is to survive over the short term as well as the long. Trite as it is to say so, any staff adjustments (up or down) in an organization are just an organization's attempts to do what it perceives to be its duty at that moment. Those who get swept away in the staffing adjustments that occur due to changing markets, obsolescing technology, or a merger or acquisition just happened to be at the wrong place at the wrong time. The myth of the employer as good citizen is meaningless if the company can't meet its payroll on any and every occasion.

We all become effective personally if we accept the fact that we may be affected by a change tomorrow (or later today) that will alter our economic health and well-being. We should realize that we are fortunate to have a job, and yet always be on the lookout for a better one. If we no longer feel challenged and wish to seek a new opportunity, we are free to look. Either way we will all be better off and less dependent on one employer who is perceived as our protector. When we have come to see the world as a vast and welcoming market, rather than as a single employer on whom we will be forever dependent, we have found at last the best of both worlds: financial security and personal growth.

Index

About the Author

Matthew J. DeLuca is president of the Management Resource Group, Inc. a New York–based recruitment and management consulting firm that specializes in professional placement, training, and other human resource activities, including career development and outplacement. Before starting his own firm eight years ago he was responsible for managing the human resources function for the New York facilities of two major global banks.

Matt has written four other books on a variety of human resource topics. For several years he has taught career management workshops at New York University and other major institutions throughout the New York metropolitan area. He is frequently invited to make presentations on a variety of workplace issues throughout the United States.